Reginald Blomfield

A History of Renaissance Architecture in England, 1500-1800

Vol. 1

Reginald Blomfield

A History of Renaissance Architecture in England, 1500-1800
Vol. 1

ISBN/EAN: 9783337321970

Printed in Europe, USA, Canada, Australia, Japan

Cover: Foto ©ninafisch / pixelio.de

More available books at **www.hansebooks.com**

A HISTORY OF
RENAISSANCE ARCHITECTURE
IN ENGLAND, 1500–1800

BY REGINALD BLOMFIELD, M.A.
EXETER COLLEGE, OXFORD, ARCHITECT.
AUTHOR OF "THE FORMAL GARDEN IN
ENGLAND." WITH DRAWINGS BY THE
AUTHOR AND OTHER ILLUSTRATIONS

VOL. I

LONDON
GEORGE BELL AND SONS
1897

CHISWICK PRESS:—CHARLES WHITTINGHAM AND CO.
TOOKS COURT, CHANCERY LANE, LONDON.

PREFACE.

IN the following pages I have attempted to give a consecutive account of Renaissance architecture in England from its first experimental efforts, through its mature expression, to its ultimate decay. So far as my opportunities have allowed, I have endeavoured to make this survey complete; but my object has been, not to present a catalogue raisonné of English architecture during these three hundred years, but to classify the immense amount of material included in this period, to show how one phase of its development followed inevitably from another, and to trace the intimate relation which from first to last binds together a series of historical facts which have been generally regarded as out of relation to each other. It has not been possible in such an endeavour to obtain absolute verification in every detail. Where I have been able to do so, I have verified by comparison with the actual building, but there still exists a great amount of documentary evidence in regard to private buildings which is not yet accessible, and which may possibly modify some of the statements as to details advanced in these pages. Neither, again, would it be possible within the limits of this book to mention every interesting building, domestic or otherwise, erected during the period. England is exceedingly rich in examples of Renaissance architecture, and I have confined my selection to those buildings which are of historical importance, or, in my opinion, best illustrate the main lines of development of English architecture from the sixteenth to the eighteenth century.

A word of explanation may be necessary in regard to the title "Renaissance Architecture." By the Renaissance is generally understood the Humanist Revival of the fifteenth and sixteenth centuries, and the term has not been extended to its subsequent phases. Yet no other term exactly covers the ground in regard to architecture. The

PREFACE

term Classical is too wide in its application, for it would include Greek architecture and such modern architecture as has attempted to imitate it in this century. The term, moreover, might with equal propriety be applied to the monumental architecture of the Assyrians and Egyptians, and Classical is a term of wider significance, in so far as it expresses the fundamental distinction which underlies all art, as between Classical and Romantic. By Renaissance architecture is to be understood the art that derived its first impulse from the revived interest in scholarship at the end of the fifteenth century,—particularly in the remains of Roman architecture in Italy,—and which ran its course through successive and clearly traceable stages until the original inspiration was superseded by other motives. It is for this reason that I have begun my account with the first attempts by Italian workmen in England, and closed it at the end of the eighteenth century, when architects abandoned the models of Roman and Italian architecture, and applied themselves to the more or less literal revivalism of various other styles.

I have, so far as possible, avoided controversial questions in the following pages. They are out of place in a history, which is less concerned with theories than with facts. Moreover, the point of view of students of architecture has changed. Forty years ago, architects, whose training should have given them a wider outlook, accepted with enthusiasm Mr. Ruskin's passionate advocacy of Gothic art, and his no less passionate condemnation of the art of the Renaissance. This attitude of mind has yielded to a more critical and intimate study of architecture. The dispute, as between Gothic and Classical architecture, is about as much out of date as the controversies of the schoolmen, and we have learnt to look upon both forms of architecture as expressions of the human intelligence, without regard to the ethical valuations introduced by the most intolerant and uncritical of amateurs. Both Gothic and Renaissance architecture—I should say both Romantic and Classical art—are admirable, but each within its own limits and in regard to its ultimate intention ; and it is unphilosophical to argue from one to the other, or, because one's personal predilection inclines to the one, to contend that the other is wholly damnable. There are certain considerations of fact which tend to show that the peculiar qualities of Gothic art are no longer attainable, the conditions from which they sprang no longer exist, but though it has been necessary to point this out, I share to the full the admiration which every intelligent artist must entertain for mediæval architecture. The amateur and archæological Gothic of this century is, of course, another affair.

I must express my obligations to the Warden and Fellows of All Souls' College, and the Provost and Fellows of Worcester College, Oxford, and to the Trustees of the Soane Museum, for permission to reproduce drawings by Wren, Inigo Jones, and others in their collections, also to Mr. Birch, the Curator of the Soane Museum, Mr. Oman and Mr. Pottinger, Librarians of All Souls' and Worcester Colleges, for their courteous assistance. I have also to thank Mr. Gotch and Mr. Batsford for permission to reproduce four plates published in Mr. Gotch's "Architecture of the Renaissance in England," and Messrs. Belcher and Macartney and Mr. Batsford for the opportunity of seeing the photographs now being published by them in their "Later Renaissance Architecture in England," 1897, and for permission to reproduce the view of Somerset House. The plates issued in both these publications are invaluable in illustration of the entire period covered in this history; and I would particularly call the attention of the reader to Messrs. Belcher and Macartney's series as illustrating a period of English architecture little understood and imperfectly appreciated, as yet, by the general public. I have also to thank Mr. Batsford for permission to reproduce the view of St. Paul's from Mr. Birch's "City Churches," and Messrs. Varney and Son of Buckingham, Mr. Ault of Aldbourne, Wilts, and other photographers for permission to make use of their work. The plans, of Christ Church, Spitalfields, and the Club House at Eltham, Kent, have been prepared from measurements taken by Mr. P. Bauhof, and that of Groombridge from measurements by Mr. G. Streatfield. A list of the principal works consulted will be found at the beginning of the book.

NEW COURT,
TEMPLE.

CONTENTS OF VOL. I.

CHAPTER		PAGE
I.	THE ITALIANS IN ENGLAND. HENRY VIII.—EDWARD VI.	1
II.	THE GERMANS IN ENGLAND. ELIZABETH. JAMES I.	25
III.	THE ENGLISH BUILDERS	42
IV.	SIXTEENTH CENTURY HOUSE PLANNING AND ARCHITECTURAL TREATISES	67
V.	INIGO JONES	97
VI.	JOHN WEBB, MARSH, AND GERBIER: THE LAST SURVIVALS OF GOTHIC . . .	123
VII.	SIR CHRISTOPHER WREN	149

LIST OF ILLUSTRATIONS.

	PAGE
WOOD PANEL IN UPPER GALLERY. THE VYNE	1
HEAD FROM FRIEZE. EAST BARSHAM	4
TERRA-COTTA PLAQUE. WOLSEY'S ARMS, HAMPTON COURT	6
PANEL, CHRISTCHURCH, HANTS. WOLSEY, CAMPEGGIO, AND CATHERINE OF ARRAGON	11
SCREEN TO GARDINER'S CHANTRY, WINCHESTER	20
CHESTS ON SCREEN TO CHOIR, WINCHESTER	22
PANEL OVER DOOR IN BURGATE STREET, CANTERBURY	25
CHIMNEY-PIECE, SOUTH WRAXHALL	37
A GABLE AT KNOLE	44
THE TRIANGULAR LODGE AT RUSHTON	46
DETAIL OF DOORWAY TO TRIANGULAR LODGE, RUSHTON	47
THE TOWER OF THE SCHOOLS, OXFORD	55
GATEWAY AT COBHAM COLLEGE	59
PORCH AT WEOBLEY IN HEREFORDSHIRE	61
CARVING IN BUTCHER'S ROW, HEREFORD	62
THE GRANGE, LEOMINSTER	63
THE SCHOOL AND ALMSHOUSE, CORSHAM	65
PLAN OF BUCKHURST HOUSE IN SUSSEX. (SOANE COLLECTION)	68
AUDLEY END IN ESSEX. (SOANE COLLECTION)	71
PLAN OF HOLLAND HOUSE. (SOANE COLLECTION)	73
PLAN OF THE FISHING HOUSE AT MEARE	75
GARDEN HOUSE AT AMESBURY	77
PLAN OF GARDEN HOUSE AT AMESBURY	78
UNNAMED PLAN IN SOANE COLLECTION	79
THORNTON COLLEGE, SIR VINCENT SKYNNER'S. SECOND STOREY, SHOWING THE GALLERY. (SOANE COLLECTION)	81
WYMBLEDON (SOANE COLLECTION)	83
WOLLATON HALL. (SOANE COLLECTION)	85
PLAN AND ELEVATION FROM SOANE COLLECTION	87
STAIRS, WYE COLLEGE, KENT	89
STAIRCASE TO HOUSE IN WHITECROSS STREET AS EXISTING IN 1888	91
STAIRCASE AT HAWKHURST, KENT	93
STAIRS, CHRIST'S COLLEGE, CAMBRIDGE	95
A DESIGN, BY INIGO JONES, FOR THE SCENERY OF A MASQUE	101
CEILING, WILTON	105
DOOR, WHITEHALL	107

LIST OF ILLUSTRATIONS

GREENWICH HOSPITAL	111
EAVES, CORNICE, AND QUOINS, CRANBORNE	113
PORCH, WEST WOODHAY	114
CAPITAL TO PORCH, WEST WOODHAY	115
PANELLING IN DOUBLE CUBE ROOM, WILTON	117
ENTRANCE FRONT, RAYNHAM PARK, NORFOLK	119
SKETCH FOR CHIMNEY PIECE, BY INIGO JONES	121
ENTRANCE PIER, AMESBURY	124
DOORWAY AT THE VYNE, NEAR BASINGSTOKE, BY JOHN WEBB	125
STONE MANTELPIECE. THE VYNE, NEAR BASINGSTOKE	126
ENTRANCE PORCH, THORPE HALL	127
THE STABLES, THORPE HALL	129
PART OF A DESIGN FOR A CEILING AT GREENWICH, BY JOHN WEBB	131
DESIGN FOR A MANTELPIECE AT GREENWICH, BY JOHN WEBB	133
SOUTH PORCH OF GROOMBRIDGE CHURCH, KENT, BUILT 1625 BY WILLIAM CAMFIELD. "OB FŒLICISSIMUM CAROLI PRINCIPIS EX HISPANIS REDDITUM"	135
NICHE AT WEST END OF PETERHOUSE CHAPEL, CAMBRIDGE	139
THE CHAPEL, LYTES-CARY	141
THE CHAPEL, BURFORD PRIORY, OXFORDSHIRE	143
THE CHAPEL, BRAZENOSE, OXFORD	145
THE ASHMOLEAN MUSEUM, OXFORD	151
FONT, CHRISTCHURCH, NEWGATE STREET	157
INTERIOR OF ST. STEPHEN'S, WALBROOK	159
ST. BRIDE'S	163
ST. BENET'S, UPPER THAMES STREET	165
FONT, ST. STEPHEN'S, WALBROOK	171
CHAPEL TO BISHOP'S PALACE, WOLVESEY, WINCHESTER	174
HAMPTON COURT, NORTH-EAST CORNER	175
DETAIL OF GATES, EAST FRONT OF HAMPTON COURT	177
THE ENTRANCE, KENSINGTON PALACE	179
GROOMBRIDGE PLACE IN KENT	183
PLAN OF GROOMBRIDGE PLACE	184

LIST OF SEPARATE PLATES.

TERRA-COTTA ROUNDEL, HAMPTON COURT . . . *To face page*	2
THE PALACE OF NONESUCH . . . . "	16
COUNTESS OF SALISBURY'S CHANTRY, CHRISTCHURCH, HANTS . . . . "	18
COUNTESS OF SALISBURY'S CHANTRY, CHRISTCHURCH. DETAILS	20

LIST OF ILLUSTRATIONS

Ceiling of Bishop West's Chapel, Ely	*To face page* 20
Gateway, Montacute House, Somerset . . .	,, 22
The Royal Exchange, as built by Sir T. Gresham .	,, 34
Doorway at Tenterden, Kent	,, 34
From a Plate in Vriese's "Architectura" . . .	,, 36
The Hertford Monument, Salisbury Cathedral	,, 38
St. John's College, Oxford, Gate of Gardens . .	,, 38
Sir T. Bodley's. Monument, Merton College, Oxford	,, 38
Chimney Piece, Cobham, Kent	,, 38
Barrington Court	,, 40
Knole, Sevenoaks	,, 44
Kirby, Northants	,, 46
Audley End	,, 50
Bolsover Castle, the Terrace	,, 52
Oriel College, Oxford	,, 56
Screen, Abbey Dore Church, Herefordshire . .	,, 60
St. John's College, Cambridge	,, 60
Newel, Hatfield House	,, 82
Whitehall. Part Elevation	,, 106
,, ,, ,, ...	,, 106
,, The Banqueting House	,, 108
,, Details	,, 108
,, Ground Plan	,, 108
,, Plan of First Floor	,, 110
,, ,, Second Floor . . .	,, 110
Design for a Church (probably sketch for St. Paul's, Covent Garden)	,, 112
St. Mary's Church, Oxford	,, 112
Somerset House. "Upright of Yᴇ Palace" . .	,, 114
Old Somerset House. Details	,, 116
Design for a Ceiling (Countess of Carnarvon's Bedchamber	,, 116
Chimney Piece, Wilton	,, 116
Wilton, Centre Bay of South Front	,, 118
Stoke Park	,, 120
Kirby, Northants, Doorway and Balcony . . .	,, 120
Ashdown House, Berkshire	,, 130
St. John's Church, Leeds	,, 136
Trinity College Chapel, Oxford	,, 152
Emmanuel College, Cambridge	,, 154
Wren's Plan for Re-building London (*Double plate*) .	,, 154-5
St. Paul's Cathedral. West Elevation . . .	,, 166
,, ,, Interior	,, 168
,, ,, ,, (Wren's Drawing) (*Double plate*)	,, 168-170

LIST OF ILLUSTRATIONS

St. Paul's Cathedral. Plan (nearly as executed).	*To face page*	168
St. Paul's Cathedral. Wren's rejected Design, Section and Elevation	,,	170
St. Paul's Cathedral. Rejected Plan and Warrant Design	,,	170
Trinity College, Cambridge. Neville's Court.	,,	174
,, ,, ,, The Library: Plan and Elevation by Wren	,,	176
Trinity College, Cambridge. Details of Library.	,,	176
Greenwich Hospital. Plan laid before the House of Commons	,,	180
Greenwich Hospital. Elevation.	,,	182
,, ,, ,,	,,	182
Hampton Court.	,,	184
Plan and Elevation in Wren's Drawings.	,,	186
Design for a Monument.	,,	186

AUTHORITIES CONSULTED.

ADAM, ROBERT and JAMES, Works of. London, 1778.
ADAM, ROBERT. Ruins of the Palace of the Emperor Diocletian at Spalatro. London, 1764.
ADAMS, M. B. Examples of Old English Houses. London, 1888.
ALDRICH, HENRY. Elementa Architecturæ Civilis. Oxford, 1789.

BELCHER, JOHN. Later Renaissance Architecture in England. By John Belcher and Mervyn Macartney. Part I. Batsford, 1897.
BIRCH, G. H. London Churches of the 17th and 18th Centuries. Batsford, 1896.
BLOOME, HANS. Five Orders. Zurich, 1550. London, 1608.
BONNEY. Cathedrals, Abbeys and Churches of England and Wales. 2 vols. London, 1888-91.
BOORD, ANDREW. A boke for to cause a man to be wyse in buildynge of his house, etc. 1549.
BRAYLEY and HERBERT. Lambeth Palace. London, 1806.
BRETTINGHAM, MATTHEW. Plans, Elevations, and Sections of Holkham. London, 1773.
BRITTON and PUGIN. Illustrations of the Public Buildings of London. London, 1825.
BUILDER, THE. Vols. xiii. 2, xxxvii. 20, and *passim*.
BULMER, G. B. Architectural Studies in Yorkshire. London, 1887.

CAMPBELL, COLIN, Architect. Vitruvius Britannicus. Vols. i., ii., 1715; vol. iii., 1725; vols. iv. and v. continued by Wolfe and Gandon. London, 1767-71.— Vols. vi. and vii., continued by Richardson, 1802-8.
CALENDARS OF STATE PAPERS (Domestic series) and Venetian State Papers, *passim*.
CARTER, JOHN. Gentleman's Magazine. *See* The Gentleman's Magazine Library: Architectural Antiquities, part ii., edited by G. L. Gomme. London, 1891.
CHAMBERS, SIR WILLIAM. A Treatise on the Decorative Part of Civil Architecture. London, 1791.
CASTELL, ROBERT. Villas of the Ancients. Illustrated. London, 1728.
CUNNINGHAM, ALLAN. Lives of the most eminent British Painters, Sculptors, and Architects. London, 1829-33.
CUNNINGHAM, PETER. Inigo Jones. London, 1848.

xvi   AUTHORITIES CONSULTED

DICTIONARIUM POLYGRAPHICUM ; or, The Whole Body of Arts Regularly Digested. 2 vols. London, 1758.
DICTIONARY OF ARCHITECTURE. Architectural Publication Society, 1852-87, *passim*.
DICTIONARY OF NATIONAL BIOGRAPHY, 1885-97, *passim*.
DIETTERLIN, WENDEL. De quinque columnarum, etc. 1593.—Architectura. 1594.
DRAKE, FRANCIS. Eboracum. London, 1736.

ELMES, JAMES. Memoirs of the Life and Works of Sir Christopher Wren. London, 1823.—Sir Christopher Wren and his Times. London, 1852.
ENGLISH ARCHITECTURE ; or, The Public Buildings of London and Westminster, with plans of the streets and squares, with a succinct review of their history, and a candid examination of their perfections and defects. London, for T. Osborne in Gray's Inn. 123 folio plates. Date about 1755.
EVELYN, JOHN. The Whole Body of Ancient and Modern Architecture, with L. B. Alberti's Treatise of the Statues. London, 1680. (This is the title to Evelyn's translation of A Parallel of Architecture, both Ancient and Modern, by Roland Fréart, Sr. de Chambray.

FERGUSSON, JAMES. History of the Modern Styles of Architecture. Third edition, 2 vols. John Murray, London, 1891.

GERBIER, BALTHAZAR. Counsel and Advice to all Builders. London, 1663.— Brief Discourse Concerning Three Chief Principles of Magnificent Building. London, 1662.
GIBBS, JAMES. Bibliotheca Radcliviana. London, 1747.—Rules for Drawing the Several Parts of Architecture. London, 1733.—A Book of Architecture. London, 1728.
GIDDE, WALTER. Booke of Sundry Draughts. 1615. Republished by Henry Shaw, F.S.A.
GODWIN, GEORGE. The Churches of London. 2 vols. London, 1838.
GOTCH, J. ALFRED. Complete Account of Buildings erected by Sir T. Tresham. Northampton, 1883.—Architecture of the Renaissance in England, 1560-1635. 2 vols. Batsford, London, 1894.
GWILT, JOSEPH. An Encyclopædia of Architecture. 1st edition, 1842. New edition, revised by W. Papworth, London, 1876.

HAKEWELL, A. W. Plan and External Details, etc., of Thorpe Hall, Peterboro'. London, 1852.—Architecture of the Seventeenth Century. London, 1856.
HANDMAID TO THE ARTS, THE. 2 vols. London, 1764.
HARRISON, FREDERICK. Annals of an Old Manor House. Macmillan, 1893.
HAYDOCKE, RICHARD. Tract Containing the Arts of Curious Painting, etc. 1598.

INDERWICK, F. A. Calendar of Inner Temple Records. London, 1896.

AUTHORITIES CONSULTED xvii

INIGO JONES. Architecture of: by W. Kent. 1727. (*See also* VARDY and WARE.)

JACKSON, T. G. A History of Wadham College, Oxford. Oxford : Clarendon Press, 1893.
JAMES, JOHN. Theory and Practice of Gardening. London, 1712.—Translation of Pozzo's Rules and Examples of Perspective. 1707.—Translation of Perrault's Treatise of the Five Orders of Columns in Architecture. 1708.
JEWETT, ORLANDO. On the late Gothic Buildings of Oxford. London, 1850.

KIP and KNYFF. Noblemen's Seats. London, 1709.

LABORATORY, or School of Arts. London, 1738.
LANGLEY, BATTY. A Sure Guide to Builders. London, 1729.—The Builder's Complete Assistant. London, 1738.—The City and Country Builders' and Workmen's Treasury of Designs. London, 1740.—The Builders' Director or Benchmate ; being a Pocket Treasury of the Grecian, Roman, and Gothic Orders of Architecture. London, 1767.—Ancient Architect, e. London, 1742.—Gothic Architecture. London, 1747.
LAUD. Autobiography of. Oxford, 1839. Articles exhibited in Parliament against William, Archbishop of Canterbury, 1640-43. (*See also* Harleian Miscellany, vol. iv., 1744.)
LAW, ERNEST. A History of Hampton Court Palace. London, 1885-91.
LE MUET. The First Book of Architecture: by Andrea Palladio, with an appendix containing doors and windows. 1668.—The Art of Fair Building, etc. Published by R. Pricke. London, 1675.
LEONI, GIACOMO. Alberti, etc. 1726. (*See also* Palladio, below, editions 1715, 1725, and 1742.)
LETHABY, W. R. Leadwork. Macmillan. 1893.
LEYBURN, WM. The Mirror of Architecture : from Scamozzi. London, 1700. —The City and Country Purchaser : enlarged from Primatt. London, 1680.
LOFTIE, W. J. Inigo Jones and Wren. Rivington, Perceval and Co. 1893.
LONGMAN, W. A History of the Three Cathedrals dedicated to St. Paul. Longmans, Green and Co. 1873.
LYSONS, DANIEL. Environs of London. 4 vols. London, 1792-96.—Magna Britannia. Vols. i.-vi. London, 1806-22.

MACARTNEY, MERVYN. Later Renaissance Architecture in England. (*See* BELCHER, above.)
MACKERELL, B. History, etc., of King's Lynn. London, 1738.
MAUCLERC, JULIEN. Le Premier Livre d'Architecture. La Rochelle, 1600.
MILLAR, W. Plastering, Plain and Decorative. Batsford. 1897.
MORRIS, ROBERT. Architectural Remembrancer. London, 1751.—Rural Architecture. London, 1750.—An Essay in Defence of Ancient Architecture. London, 1728.—Lectures on Architecture. London, 1734.
MULVANEY, THOMAS. Life of J. Gandon. 1846.

xviii   AUTHORITIES CONSULTED

NASH, JOSEPH. Mansions of England in the Olden Time. Folio, 1839.
NICHOLS, JOHN. History and Antiquities of Lambeth Palace. London, 1782.

PAIN, WILLIAM. The Practical House Carpenter. London, 1794.—The Practical Builder. 1774.
PAINE, JAMES. Plans, Elevations, etc., of Noblemen's and Gentlemen's Houses, etc. 2 vols., 2nd edition. London, 1783.
PALLADIO, ANDREA. Four books translated by I. Ware. (*See* WARE.)—The First Book of Architecture: by A. Palladio, after Le Muet, by Richards. London, 1668.—Architecture of: by Leoni. London, 1715. 2nd edition, 1725. 3rd edition, 1742.—Fabbriche antiche designate da A. Palladio, etc. London, 1730.
PAPWORTH, WYATT. A List of Dated Examples of the Renaissance and Italian Styles of Architecture in Great Britain. Batsford. 1883.
PEACH, R. E. M. Bath, Old and New. London, 1888.—Historic Houses in Bath. London, 1883.
PHILLIMORE, LUCY. Sir Christopher Wren, his Family and his Times. London, 1881.
PRIMATT, STEPHEN. City and Country Purchaser. 1667. (*See* LEYBURN.)

RICHARDSON, GEORGE. Treatise on the Five Orders. London, 1787.—A Book of Ceilings. London, 1776.—The New Vitruvius Britannicus. London, 1802-8.
RICHARDSON, C. J. Architectural Remains of the Reigns of Elizabeth and James. Vol. I. London, 1840.—Observations on the Architecture of England, etc. London, 1837.
RYE, WM. BRENCHLEY. England as Seen by Foreigners in the Days of Elizabeth and James I. London, 1865.

SERLIO. Five Books on Architecture: translated by Robert Peake. 1611.
SHAW, HENRY, F.S.A. Details of Elizabethan Architecture. London, 1839.
SHUTE, JOHN. First and Chief Grounds of Architecture. 1563.
STEVENSON, J. J. House Architecture. Macmillan, 1880.
STOW, JOHN. A Survey of London, etc. 1st edition. London, 1598. And A Survey of the Cities of London and Westminster, brought down from the year 1633 to the present time by J. Strype. London, 1720.

TAYLOR, WM. Antiquities of King's Lynn. Lynn, 1844.
TAYLOR. Old Halls in Cheshire. Manchester, 1884.
TIJOU, JOHN. A New Booke of Drawings Invented and Desined by John Tijou. 1693. Reproduced by B. T. Batsford, 1896.
TRANSACTIONS of the Royal Institute of British Architects. *Passim*.

VARDY, JOHN. Some Designs of Inigo Jones. Published by J. Vardy, 1744.
VETUSTA MONUMENTA. London, 1747.
VRIESE. Perspective. 1559.—Fountains. 1568.—Architectura. 1577.

AUTHORITIES CONSULTED

WALPOLE, HORACE. Anecdotes of Painting, etc. Ed. Wornum.
WARE, ISAAC. A Complete Body of Architecture. London, 1756.—The Four Books of Palladio's Architecture. 1738.—Plans and Elevations of Houghton in Norfolk. London, 1735.—Designs of Inigo Jones: by I. W. 1757.
WILLIS, R., and CLARK, J. W. The Architectural History of the University of Cambridge. Cambridge, 1886.
WOOD, ANTHONY. Athenæ Oxoniensis. 2nd edition, 1721. (1st edition, 1691.)
WOTTON, SIR HENRY. Elements of Architecture. 1624.
WREN, CHRISTOPHER (SON OF SIR C.). Parentalia. London, 1750.

ERRATA.

Vol. I., p. 166, line 12, *for* "the South Kensington Museum" *read* "St. Paul's Cathedral."

Vol. II., p. 228, line 24, *after* 1862, *insert* "and since rebuilt."

WOOD PANEL IN UPPER GALLERY, THE VYNE.

A HISTORY OF RENAISSANCE ARCHITECTURE IN ENGLAND
1500—1800.

CHAPTER I.
THE ITALIANS IN ENGLAND. HENRY VIII.—EDWARD VI.

FOR the purposes of this history the Renaissance in England will be taken to mean that fresh departure in architecture which began with the tentative efforts of imported workmen in the reign of Henry VIII., which reached its highest development in the hands of Inigo Jones and Wren, and eventually ran itself out in the uncertainties induced by the literary eclecticism of the end of the eighteenth century. The remarkable expansion of the English people in the sixteenth and seventeenth centuries, and the strong conservative instinct of the race, constitute the two contending influences which struggled for the mastery in this new movement, and finally united to give it a distinctly national character. The two factors to be considered are, on the one hand, the constant importation of foreign ideas, and, on the other, the tenacious tradition of a people with a great historic past in architecture. From first to last the process of fusion and adjustment between these two elements occupied rather over 100 years, and it was the work of the greatest architect this country has possessed, perhaps our one architect of quite commanding genius, to gather up the broken threads and weave them together into one splendid and harmonious architecture.

For various reasons the Renaissance was slow to gain a permanent footing in England. Brunelleschi died in 1444, Alberti in 1472, forty years before the first Italian artist of importance had set foot in England, and both of these men had done work such as could not even have been conceived of in England till at least 150 years later. Of all the Northern peoples the English were the most tenacious of the past, the slowest to accept these foreign ways. Though commercial relations with the Italian States had existed since the thirteenth century, the influence of Italian intelligence was confined to the population of London and the principal seaport towns; moreover, in the reign of Henry VIII., the people, as opposed to the nobility, were poor, and evidently hampered by a certain old world inaccessibility to ideas. The consequence was that the first efforts of the Renaissance in England were abortive, they merely glanced off the strong habit of tradition without affecting the organic structure, and in fact several false starts were made before native builders took up the running, and though they blundered egregiously, cleared the way for the abler men of the seventeenth century.

Broadly speaking, there are four main divisions, four groups of facts to be considered in dealing with the development of architecture in England since the days of the Renaissance: (1) the various isolated attempts of foreign workmen, in nearly every case Italians, to introduce their own methods of workmanship; (2) the efforts of half-instructed native builders, and of Flemish and German workmen; (3) the mature Palladianism introduced by Inigo Jones, a method so modified and adapted by his genius as to be the foundation of all subsequent architecture in England for the next 200 years. These three types are so distinct that there is, as a rule, little difficulty in distinguishing instances. The third type is so clearly marked off from its predecessors, and so much more permanent in its results, that the first two can only be regarded as byways of history, interesting indeed, and pathetic as the efforts of men groping in the dark, but off the main

TERRA-COTTA ROUNDEL, HAMPTON COURT.

track of the Renaissance movement, and least of all to be taken as typical models of its methods. All three, however, bear on the history of the Renaissance in England, but besides, and outside these three groups, there are buildings which there is no reason to identify with Renaissance rather than with Gothic architecture, buildings which fairly represent the continuous building tradition of the country. This fourth group is illustrated by such houses as Lake House near Salisbury, and on a smaller scale by cottages in every part of the country, and ranging down to the beginning of the present century. Farm buildings, erected since 1800, may yet be found in remote country districts, which show distinct traces of the mediæval tradition.

The first memorable introduction of foreign workmen into England was due to Henry VIII. and Wolsey. By an indenture dated Jan. 11, 1515, Wolsey leased Hampton Court for ninety-nine years, and he at once set to work to transform it into a palace of unexampled magnificence. His architect is unknown. Mr. Law (to whose excellent history of Hampton Court I must refer the reader for a complete account of the buildings) inclines to think it might have been "Mr. Williams, a priest surveyor of the works." There were also on the works James Bettes, "master of the workes," and Nicholas Towneley, "clerk comptroller of workes." But it is probable that, as was the common custom, the general design was directed by Wolsey himself, and the work was carried out by workmen who contracted for each trade, and designed and executed their own details. Wolsey's work, probably the west front and the outer court, was more or less completed by 1520. The fabric was built by Englishmen, but Italians were employed for some, at least, of the ornament. The terra-cotta busts of emperors over the entrance are now known to have been made by Giovanni de Majano, whose name appears in the state papers in all sorts of distorted forms, and to whom we shall have to return later. In the state papers of Henry VIII.[1] is a letter from Joannes de Majano to Wolsey, dated June 18, 1521, requesting payment of balance (£21 13s. 4d.) for the ten medallions of terra-cotta ("rotundæ imagines ex terra depictæ") which he had supplied for the palace at "anton cort." The price was £2 6s. 8d. a-piece, and three "histories" of Hercules at £4 each. In January, 1511, the king had paid £10 for "an image of Hercules made of earth," and while the Italian influence lasted in England terra-cotta busts and figures seem to have been in demand

---

[1] Brewer, Calendar of State Papers, Henry VIII., 3. 1. 1355.

4 RENAISSANCE ARCHITECTURE IN ENGLAND

for the outside of buildings, the niches and hollow circles which are now empty having probably been designed to receive these decorations. There is one instance of this on the entrance front of Cranborne in Dorsetshire, and a complete example of a bust surrounded by a double wreath of foliage at St. Donat's Castle in Glamorganshire; but the most perfect instance is undoubtedly the terra-cotta plaque of Wolsey's arms supported by two amorini under a cardinal's hat, which is set on the wall above the gateway of the clock tower at Hampton Court.

HEAD FROM FRIEZE. EAST BARSHAM.

This is dated 1525. The most famous example of the use of terra-cotta for large figure work in England is the tomb of John Young, Master of the Rolls, in the Rolls Chapel. This was executed by Torrigiano in 1516, and consists of a recumbent figure on a sarcophagus under an arch, with a figure of Christ and two angels at the back. Though the modelling of the Christ is rather coarse, and the colour truculent, the design as a whole is very fine.

Under the stimulus thus given, ornamental terra-cotta came into use in England for about forty years, 1500 to 1540. Terra-cotta as a building material is only a species of brickwork burnt extremely hard and moulded, and in this form, as Digby Wyatt points out, it had been in use in England before the Italians came, particularly along the east coast. It is by no means clear, however, that it was used except in a very rudimentary way. At East Barsham, where terra-cotta is used with great freedom and complete mastery of the material, there is distinct evidence in the detail that the artist had some acquaintance with Italian art. The greater part of the detail is ordinary Perpendicular, but interspersed with it are little plaques cast from a mould, with heads of a man and woman alternately. They measure about 10 in. by 8 in., and are unmistakably Italian. This influence is even more marked in Great Snoring Rectory about three miles distant. Here the upper frieze is formed by a series of heads divided by balusters, which are ornamented with acanthus leaves and surmounted by small heads. Both East Barsham Manor House and Great Snoring Rectory date from the end of the fifteenth or very early part of the sixteenth century, and it seems probable that the English workmen were very much helped by the Italians in their manipulation of terra-cotta, or that the work was actually cast by Italians to English directions. The Italians who were familiar with the work of the Della Robbias introduced "terra-cotta invetriata, that is terra-cotta covered with a stanniferous glaze, and susceptible of receiving colour at will," though here again they found in the rough green[1] encaustic tiles of the country a crude anticipation of their own glazed and coloured terra-cotta. The ruined house of Layer Marney in Essex, begun in 1500 and left unfinished in 1525, is a well-known example of the use of terra-cotta detail. Other instances are Sutton Place in Surrey, built between 1521-1527, the tomb of Lord Henry Marney at Layer Marney, 1525, and the tomb of one of the Earls of Arundel in the Fitz-Alan Chapel at Arundel. After the Italians left England the use of terra-cotta ornamentation died out almost entirely. It was still used in the seventeenth century for copings, as at Abbot's Hospital, Guildford, and for pierced balustrades and similar details, as at Hatfield, but I do not think any instances exist of its use in the elaborate manner practised by the Italians after the end of the sixteenth century. With good reason, the sound taste of the English rejected it as harsh and discordant with the beautiful texture of their brickwork. The charm of the work at East Barsham is due to its disintegration;—where it remains in its original state and unimpaired

[1] Green glazed earthenware pots were in use in the Inns of Court in the sixteenth century, the clay from which they were made being dug in Farnham Park. *See* Mr. Inderwick's introduction to the "Collection of Inner Temple Records," pp. lxxxvi-lxxxvii.

6   RENAISSANCE ARCHITECTURE IN ENGLAND

by the weather, it is quite as unpleasantly hard as modern work. Moreover, as its manufacture must always be mechanical, no alteration could

TERRA-COTTA PLAQUE.   WOLSEY'S ARMS, HAMPTON COURT.

be made in it, no slip of the chisel could be converted into some happy fancy. Nothing more was heard of terra-cotta in this country as a

THE ITALIANS IN ENGLAND   7

building material until it was revived as a commercial speculation in the latter half of this century.

There is no record of the names of other Italians employed by Wolsey at Hampton Court, but there is further evidence of their handiwork in the ceiling of Cardinal Wolsey's closet, and Mr. Law suggests that the paintings in this room below the frieze may have been by Luca Penni or Toto del Nunziata, Italians subsequently in the service of Henry VIII. Wolsey was a munificent patron of art, and had all that keen enjoyment of beauty characteristic of the most gifted minds of the Renaissance, for the great statesmen and scholars of the Renaissance were men of all-round attainment—their whole life was in scale, at every point it was touched by some ray of genius, and Wolsey, magnificent in his statesmanship, loved to surround himself with beautiful works of art, carpets from the East, and sumptuous hangings, and was by no means scrupulous as to the steps he took to gratify this desire. He did not hesitate to use his position as a means of extracting from the Venetian senate sixty fine Damascene carpets for his palace in 1521,[1] and Sir Richard Gresham in 1522 bought for him twenty-one complete sets of tapestry in a hundred and thirty-two pieces, with various scriptural subjects, and classical and other pieces, such as Hercules and Jason, Dame Pleasaunce, the "Storye of L'Amante or the Romaunte of the Rose"; many of these tapestries had borders specially designed for the Cardinal.[2] Their titles alone suggest the strange mixture of ideas, characteristic of Tudor England, its curious interest in the New Learning, side by side with its invincible affection for the fancies of mediævalism. Again and again the spirit of the old world and the new assert themselves side by side, in the work of this time, at first without conflict and yet without fusion, much in the manner of two different types of beauty, each setting off the other, unlike but yet in harmony. Wolsey's subtle and highly-cultivated intelligence was quick to assimilate this feeling, and his enormous wealth and commanding position enabled him to realize his dreams in the magnificent patronage of the best artificers of his time.

In this, however, he was far outdone by the king. Henry VIII. inherited a vast accumulation of money from his parsimonious father,[3]

---

[1] Law, i. 71.
[2] Wolsey's wealth was enormous. In 1527 the Venetian ambassador estimated his plate to be worth 300,000 gold ducats, which Mr. Law puts at one and a half million sterling.
[3] Sebastian Giustiniani, in a report to the Venetian senate, dated September 10th, 1519, gives the following particulars of Henry's resources. His father left him ten millions

8 RENAISSANCE ARCHITECTURE IN ENGLAND

and nothing less than these resources could have met his prodigal expenditure on dress, uniforms, and goldsmiths' work, and the large staff of foreign artists more or less permanently in his pay. In the king's book of payments there are constant entries of payments to Italians and others for costly stuffs. Thus, in 1513, Amadas and Mortimer, "the brawderer," were paid £887 8s. 6d. for gold and silver stuff, and £2,000 for horse harness and trappings of goldsmith's work. In 1514 Amadas is paid £1,906 8s. 4d. for goldsmith's work. These instances are sufficient to show the scale of Henry's expenses in simple ornament, and besides these there are constant entries of pensions to artists and musicians, and of payments for work done. The most famous of these artists was Torrigiano, or Peter Torrysany as the English used to call him. His career in England was as chequered as all the other episodes in the life of this furious artist. He came to England in the company of some Florentine merchants before 1512. The tomb to John Young, 1516, in the Rolls Chapel (now destroyed), was his first completed work in England,[1] but while making this he must also have been employed on the tomb of Henry VII. in Westminster Abbey, the indenture for which is dated October 26th, 1512. The indenture bound Torrigiano to

---

of ready money in gold, of which he spent half on his three armies when at war with France. His revenues amounted to about 350,000 ducats per annum, derived from the following sources: estates, forests and meres, customs, hereditary and confiscated properties, the duchies of Lancaster, York, Cornwall, and Suffolk, the county palatine of Chester, the principality of Wales, export duties, the wool staple, the great seal, annats of Church benefices, court of wards, and new year's gifts, from which the king received much more than he gave. To this must be added the farming out of exchanges and the like. Thus, in 1508, Peter Corsey, of Florence, was appointed warden of exchange in England on paying to the king £240 a year. Giustiniani reckoned his annual expenses at 100,000 ducats. Wolsey's income he put at 42,000 ducats, the Duke of Buckingham's at 30,000, the Dukes of Norfolk and Suffolk at 12,000 each. Henry was a large creditor with the Florentine merchants, who sometimes owed him as much as 300,000 ducats. This explains his payment of Torrigiano and others by bonds and drafts on Italian merchants. The value of the ducat between 1442 and 1512 is put by Mr. Rawdon Browne as varying between 39¾d. and 56½d. Daniel Barbaro, in his report to the Venetian senate in 1550, says that Henry VIII. was master of all the gold and silver of his realm, which was the cause of its ruin, and he calculates that he amassed 20,340,000 ducats, of which 5,000,000 ducats of gold came from the plunder of Church plate alone between 1537-1547.

[1] Mr. Alfred Higgins, however, considers that the monument to the Countess of Richmond was Torrigiano's earliest work in England, and that this led to the monument to Henry VII. *See* Mr. Higgins's paper on the work of Florentine sculptors in England in the early part of the sixteenth century, "Archæological Journal," September, 1894, for a very complete account of these monuments.

complete the tomb[1] by 1519, for £1,500, but it appears to have been completed by 1518, as it is referred to in the indenture for the making of Henry VIII.'s tomb. The tomb of Henry VII. consists of a sarcophagus of black marble divided by gilded bronze pilasters, on which rest the effigies of the king and Elizabeth of York, his queen, in bronze. In the panels are bas-reliefs in bronze of the Virgin and Child, the Archangel Michael, the two St. Johns, SS. George of England, Anthony of Padua, Christopher and Vincent, the Magdalene, and SS. Barbara and Anne. These bas-reliefs are set in wreaths carved out of the black marble. At the ends of the tomb are the armorial bearings of England, France, Wales, and Mortimer. All the details of this beautiful work, executed in bronze, are unmistakably Italian, and probably executed by Torrigiano himself; but it is almost certain that, in carrying out the accessories, Torrigiano employed English workmen. Their names are not known, but it is probable that some of the men who gave estimates for "Master Pageny's" rejected design were employed on Torrigiano's tomb, namely: Laurence Ymber, carver; Humphrey Walker, founder; Nicholas Ewer, coppersmith and gilder; John Bell and John Maynard, painters; Robert Vertue,[2] Robert Jennings, and John Lebuis, master masons. The grille is probably English both in design and workmanship. Mr. Higgins has pointed out that Henry VII. had begun a monument at Windsor in 1501, in which year a payment of £10 was made to "Master Esterfelde for the Kinge's tombe," and in 1502-3 £10 more was paid him for moving the tomb to Westminster, and further payments were made him, amounting to £68 3s. 2d. By his will, dated 1509, Henry VII. directed that "the grate in manner of a closure" already begun was to be completed. Mr. Higgins thinks that the grille which surrounds the tomb is the actual "grate" begun by Master Esterfelde, which was intended to inclose Master Pageny's monument—the monument[3] for which Ymber and others gave estimates. Torrigiano also made some images, "a garnishment and an awlter," for Henry VII.'s Chapel. The contract for this high altar was made March 11th, 1516-17, but Torrigiano did not actually begin work till 1520, on his return to England from Florence,

[1] "A tombe or sepulture of whit marbill and of black touch stone wt ymags, figures, beasts and other things of coppure gilt." *See* "Archæologia," vol. xvi., p. 84, quoted by Mr. Higgins.
[2] Vertue was the king's master mason.
[3] Mr. Micklethwaite has identified "Master Pageny" with Guido Mazzoni of Modena, sometimes called Paganino, who made the tomb of Charles VIII. in the choir of St. Denis.

10 RENAISSANCE ARCHITECTURE IN ENGLAND

and appears to have completed it by about 1522. It consisted of an altar with a reredos and a flat baldachino of white marble over it, carried by four detached columns of gilt bronze on pedestals of black and white marble. Above the baldachino were set the royal arms, with four terra-cotta figures of angels at each of the angles, holding emblems of the Passion. The reredos was flanked by two pilasters, all in bronze-gilt, and the altar consisted of a black marble slab, supported by square white marble piers at the angles, with gilt bronze balusters between, and within was "a bakyn image of erthe coloured of Christ dede." This altar was destroyed in 1643 by the notorious Sir Robert Harlow, who also broke up the fittings of Hampton Court Chapel in 1645. Vasari, in his free manner, states that Torrigiano executed "infinite works in marble, bronze, and wood" in England. In the south aisle of Henry VII.'s Chapel is his monument to Margaret, Countess of Richmond, who died in 1509. Burges supposed that this was the earlier work of the two; the figure is possibly even finer than those on Henry VII.'s tomb, and the conspicuous ability displayed in both these works led to the next contract which Torrigiano undertook—that for the tomb of Henry VIII. In the Calendar of State Papers (Brewer, 3. 1. 7.) the abstract of the contract is given as follows: " Form of indenture 5 Jan. 1518. between A. B. and C. D. on behalf of the King, and Peter Torrysany of Florence, graver, now resident in the precinct of St. Peter's, Westminster, for the making of a tomb in white marble and black touchstone for Henry VIII. and Queen Catherine, one fourth larger than that which he has already made for Henry VII in pursuance of his indenture with the late King's executors, dated 26. Oct. 1512. This tomb is not to cost more than 2,000 £, and to be completed in 4 years under the direction of Wolsey, a model to be sent in . . . .[1] months. On notifying the completion of the work, Torrigiano will be informed where it is to be placed, and shall then set it up. On fulfilling the contract, he shall receive back the following obligations, viz. 2 of John Frauncels and Reyner de Baud, amounting to 600 £, 3 of John Cavalcanti and other merchants of Florence for 400 £, and another of the same for 1,000 £."[2] The history of this tomb is obscure. It is doubtful if it was ever begun at all, as soon afterwards Wolsey ordered his own monument, and after Wolsey's fall this monument was appropriated by the king for his own use. The history

[1] Blank in MS.
[2] Another draft of this indenture is given in "Archæologia," vol. xvi., p. 84, and is quoted in Mr. Perkins's "Italian Sculptors."

of the Wolsey monument will be described later. After signing his contract, Torrigiano returned to Italy to engage workmen, and tried to induce Cellini to come, but Cellini could not forgive Torrigiano's attack on Michael Angelo, and declined to go anywhere near "those beasts the English." In September, 1519, Torrigiano entered into agreements with Antonio di Piergiovanni di Lorenzo, sculptor of Settignano, and Toto del Nunziata, painter, and in October, 1519, with Jacopo da Verona, binding these artists to work with him for four and a half years, in France, Italy, Flanders, England, Germany, or any other part of the world, for three gold florins a month for the first year, and forty ducats a year for the remainder, with cost of living and horse hire.[1] Torrigiano seems to have returned with his three men in 1519-20, and to have at once begun the work for the high altar, which he appears to have completed by 1522. Vasari says that he went to Spain, and died in the

PANEL, CHRISTCHURCH, HANTS. WOLSEY, CAMPEGGIO, AND CATHERINE OF ARRAGON.

dungeons of Seville in 1522, but Milanesi has pointed out that he actually died in 1528.

Vasari says that Baccio Bandinelli "prepared a very beautiful model in wood, with the figures in wax, for the sepulchral monument of the King of England. The work was, nevertheless, not executed by Bandinelli, but was given to Benedette da Rovezzano, who cast it in metal." This, however, is inexact; for it was on Wolsey's monument that Rovezzano was first employed, and the immediate successors of Torrigiano in England were Rovezzano and Giovanni da Majano. The latter has already appeared as the modeller of Wolsey's terra-cotta medallions at Hampton Court. He came of a well-known Florentine family of artists,[2] and was, perhaps, the nephew of Girolamo (died 1490),

[1] Authorities quoted in Mr. Higgins's paper.
[2] Mr. Higgins considers this very doubtful.

and Benedetto di Nardo da Majano, the famous intarsiatore, who died in 1497, and of whom Vasari says that he carved a likeness of Henry VII. from a drawing supplied him by certain Florentine merchants. Rovezzano appears to have come to England about 1520. In the Calendar of State Papers (Brewer, 4. 3. 5743.) is a letter dated June 30th, 1529, from "Benedictus Sculptor Florentinus" to Wolsey, in Latin. The writer says that at command of Thomas Cromwell, he will narrate the history and sums received for an altar (erected soon after at Christ Church, Oxford), and a tomb for the cardinal on which he is at work. He had agreed with one Antonio Cavallari, that the tomb should not be less magnificent than that of Henry VII. The price was to be equivalent, paid by instalments on outlay, the balance due to be valued by experts; the gilding to be extra. From June 1st, 1524, to May, 1529, he received from Cavallari and Antonio Bonvisi about 4,250 ducats. Besides this he had advanced money himself, and borrowed of friends in London and Florence. Meanwhile Cavallari had died, and the debts were outstanding. He points out that he had been so successful in transport of marble, bronze, founding, and obtaining of good workmen, that the cost would be much less than was to be expected *pro tam operosâ mole*. The gilding was very expensive. For Henry VII.'s tomb £200 had been enough: for this, close on £800 was wanted, thus showing its greater importance, *testorque in simplicitate mea, id tuum sepulchrum in duplo regium superare, aut plus eo, sumptu arte, decore*. Knowing this, Cavallari had promised that he should soon go to Oxford to make the altar, and on behalf of Wolsey that he should have the king's monument. He is anxious to serve his grace in everything; but not having seen his wife or children for ten years, he is compelled to go and see them, and maybe bring them over to England. He therefore begs Wolsey to instruct Cromwell to take the matter up and settle his accounts. This letter was accompanied by one written before his death by Cavallari to Wolsey, stating that he had paid out £380 13s.[1] for gilding, and praying that if the tomb was not to be finished the gilder might return to Antwerp, and Benedict, the carver, to Italy. Wolsey, whose fortunes were now shattered, was near his end, and probably powerless to do anything; and Rovezzano must have referred the matter to the king who, with indecent haste, had already seized the cardinal's monument for himself. Rovezzano obtained his leave of absence, and before leaving drew up a list of what he had done for Wolsey's tomb.

[1] About £4,000 of our money.

"FOR THE KING'S HIGHNESS.
" 4 graven copper pillars, 9 feet long.
" 4 angels to kneel at the head and foot of the tomb ready gilt and burnished.
" 4 angels with candlesticks to stand on the said pillars.
" 4 naked children to stand at the head and foot of the tomb with the arms.
" 2 pieces of copper with epitaphs.
" a tomb of black touchstone 7 ft. by 4 ft. and 2½ ft. high.
" 4 copper leaves for the corners of the tomb.
" 12 pieces of black touch, and 8 of white marble for the base of the tomb.
" a step of black touch.
" 7 pieces of copper wrought like cloth of gold.
" 4 small pillars for the corners of an altar.
" Things to be ordered at the King's pleasure.
" The image of the Cardinal gilt and burnished. 2 griphins to be at his feet. The Cardinal's hat with 12 buttons and strings, 2 scutcheons with his arms and 14 small scutcheons of his Churches, 12 images of saints, a cross, 2 pillars." In another list is added a white marble "chaminaye, and 6 clay figures, 7 feet high, which should have served for Oxford." For the above work he had received 4,250 ducats, at 4s. 6d. a ducat. "And moreover for to leave an inventory of all that doth appertain to the King's most noble grace, or ever I go to Florence, it rests in the house 4 pillars which was left of the altar of K. Henry VII. which were not sufficient to stand to the weight of the said altar which Master Peter Torrygan had made of the said pillars, which appertaineth to the King's most noble grace." After Rovezzano's return from Florence, he resumed his work on the tomb, and John da Majano was associated with him. Entries of receipts for payments by Cromwell on the king's account, for labour on the king's tomb, occur in 1531-32-33; Rovezzano being variously described as "Rovessanne" and "Rovesham," and Majano as "John de Manns," "John Demans," and "John Demyans." The entries continue in 1536 "to Benedict and John, gravers working upon the King's tomb at Westminster in May, June, July and August, £38. 3¹/1. 2040 lbs of copper for the tomb, £22. 17/4." I have not been able to discover any entries relating to the tomb, or any mention of Rovezzano or Majano after 1536. The history of this monument is a strange one. As already stated, it was originally begun for Wolsey; and Rovezzano appears to have more or less completed it as first designed, at

the time of Wolsey's fall. At this date, it seems to have consisted of a recumbent figure of the cardinal in gilt bronze, resting on a sarcophagus of black touchstone with gilt bronze enrichments at the angles. The sarcophagus stood on a rectangular base of black and white marble, and at each angle were tall square pillars of gilt bronze 9 ft. high, supporting angels 3 ft. 4 in. high with candlesticks. At the ends of the tomb were figures of boys supporting the cardinal's arms, and at the sides were scutcheons for the inscriptions fixed to the base, with kneeling figures of angels at either end. Twelve small images of saints, 1 ft. high, were ranged along the top of the base to the sarcophagus. When Henry annexed this monument, he determined that it should be a much more magnificent affair. The sarcophagus and base of Wolsey's tomb were taken, but Wolsey's effigy was replaced by one of the king, and the tomb placed on a second base which, in its turn, stood upon a podium 14 ft. 6 in. by 10 ft. 6 in. by 5 ft. high, of black marble ornamented with bronze.[1] Round this podium were placed ten square pillars of bronze, 12 in. by 12 in. and 10 ft. high, supporting figures of apostles 4 ft. 6 in. high, with three smaller figures, 2 ft. 1 in. high, set round the base of each pillar. Between the pillars were ranged eight great candlesticks 9 ft. high. The whole was surrounded by an inclosure of bronze, 4 ft. 6 in. high, set in a framing of black and white marble, of a total height of 5 ft. The latter end of this splendid monument was as melancholy as the beginning. It was left unfinished in the Lady Chapel of Henry VII. at Windsor, when Henry VIII. died, and never completed, though a survey was made for the purpose in the reign of Elizabeth. Charles I. intended to be buried in it; but after his execution Parliament ordered the sale of all the bronze work to the monument, and it was sold in 1646 for something over £400, four of the candlesticks finding their way to the Church of St. Bavon at Ghent. Between 1806-1810 the marble sarcophagus and upper base were removed to form Nelson's tomb in the crypt of St. Paul's; and about 1811 the whole floor of the Chapel at Windsor was taken up to form the royal vault for George III., and with this disappeared the last trace of this monument, which had occupied some of the best years of Rovezzano's life.

Vasari says that Rovezzano returned to Italy about 1540, his sight having failed through his standing too near the furnaces while founding

---

[1] The reader will find full particulars and a conjectural restoration of this monument in Mr. Higgins's paper. Mr. Higgins also gives a restoration of the chantry altar, which stood to the east of the tomb.

THE ITALIANS IN ENGLAND 15

metal. He died about 1550. Vasari particularly praises the lightness of his sculpture, the skill with which he detached his figures and foliage so that they seemed to flutter in the air. Da Majano probably left England at about the same time. His name also appears in the accounts for building a banqueting house at Greenwich on May 7th, 1527,[1] evidently a temporary pavilion. "To John Demyans, for 6 antique heads, gilt silvered and painted at 26/ each," and on November 19th, 1527, for preparing two of the arches "For John Demanyanns Italian graver and his company 56/8." For 1528, £5 paid to "John Demayns graver." In the same account for work at Greenwich[2] occur items for various paints and oils spent by "Mr. Hans and his company and of payments to Italian painters and gilders, "Nicholas Florentine at 23^d, and Domyngo at 16^d, day and night; to Vincent Vulp and Ellys Carmyan (also Italian painters) at 20/ the week." Holbein's work was a temporary arch for the pageant of "the Father of Hevin." Vincent Vulp painted the banners for the great Harry in 1514, "a streamer with a dragon 45 yards long." The names of other Italians and foreigners in the employment of the king are given in a paper by Digby Wyatt.[3] The most important were Luca Penni, Gerome da Trevigi, and Toto del Nunziata, all men of independent reputations, apart from their employment in England. On June 26th, 1537, letters of denization were granted to Anthony Toto, painter of Florence, and he was made sergeant painter to the king, but his name occurs seven years earlier, in 1530. In the privy purse accounts[4] is an entry of £18 15s. paid as wages to Anthony Toto and Bartholmewe Penni, painters of Florence at the rate of £25 a year apiece. Their names occur in November, 1531; after this, Toto is mentioned alone.[5] He was employed by Henry in continuing the works at Hampton Court. In 1530 he received for five "tables" (pictures) for the king's

[1] Brewer, 4. 2. 3107.
[2] *Ibid.*, 3104.
[3] Transactions of R.I.B.A., May 18th, 1867. This paper, however, is not quite accurate in one or two points, such, for instance, as the reference to Cavallari's letter, described in the text. Wyatt, following Walpole, identifies Cavallari with the Flemish gilder. Cavallari appears to have been an Italian merchant who acted as middleman. Walpole's account, based on the notes left by Vertue, is, I need hardly say, readable, but untrustworthy. Wyatt also gives Anthony Toto, and Toto del Nunziata, as names of two separate artists. There is no doubt, however, that they are only different versions of the name "Antonio, called Toto del Nunziata."
[4] Brewer, Calendar of State Papers, vol. v., p. 319.
[5] His name occurs in the Losely MSS. as "drawing patrons for the masks."

library " by a bargain in gret, £6 13/4,[1] and for 4 others for the king's closet, £20." Gerome da Trevigi, or Girolamo Penacchi, of Treviso, was employed by Henry chiefly as a military engineer. Vasari says that he was a poor designer but a pleasant colourist in the manner of Raphael. He left Bologna in anger at the unfairness of a competition for the decoration of the Spedale del Monte, and came over to England, where he was employed by Henry at a salary of 400 crowns a year and a house. In 1544 he was cut in half by a cannon ball while directing the formation of some batteries round Boulogne. Anthony Toto or Toto del Nunziata is said by Vasari to have built for Henry VIII. his principal palace. This palace was probably Nonesuch. In point of fact it is most unlikely that Toto del Nunziata designed this building, but he may very well have been employed on its decoration with many other foreigners.

Nonesuch seems to have been the most important building erected in England in the reign of Henry VIII. It was built on a manor bought by Henry from Richard de Codington in 1537. After Henry's death it passed into the hands of Lord Arundel, " who, for the love and honour he bare to his old master," bought it from Mary, and completed the works " for the honour of this realme as a pearle thereof." In 1591 Elizabeth bought it back from Lord Lumley, Arundel's son-in-law. In 1670 Charles II. gave it to Barbara, Lady Castlemaine, and this attractive but unprincipled person had the manor disparked, and ordered the building to be pulled down and sold as old materials. In 1650 a commission had been appointed by Parliament to survey the buildings, and their report (given in full " Archæologia," vol. v.) gives a vivid idea of what Henry and his men understood by a royal palace. The palace consisted of two courts; an outer court paved with stone 150 ft. long by 132 ft. broad, inside, surrounded by a two-storey building of freestone roofed with slates. This was entered through a gatehouse three stories high, with turrets at the four angles. Opposite this gatehouse was a second gatehouse similar to the first, except that it was surmounted by an elaborate clock turret. Through this gatehouse a flight of steps led to an inner court, which measured 116 ft. long by

---

[1] The extract from the Chapter House accounts given by Law, " History of Hampton Court," i. 129, contains the following list : " Firste, one table of Joachyn and Saint Anne.
"Then another table how Adam dylffed in the grounde.
"Then the third table how Adam was driven ought of Paradise.
"Then the fourth table of the buryinge of Our Lord.
"Then the fifth table, being the last table, of the buryinge of Our blessed Ladye."

THE PALACE OF NONESUCH.

(By Hoefnagle, from Braun's "Urbium praecipuarum Mundi Theatrum quintum.")

137 ft. broad. The level of this court was 8 ft. higher than that of the outer court. The lower storey of the inner court was of stone, but the upper of half timber work, "richly adorned and set forth and garnished with a variety of pictures and other antick forms of excellent art and workmanship, and of no small cost." This ornament was executed on plaster by Italians. Evelyn, who saw the place January 3rd, 1666, was astonished at the perfect state of preservation of the "plaster statues," and he noted " some mezzo relievos as big as life. The storie is the heathen gods, emblems, compartments, etc." The puncheons, or wooden uprights, were, he says, covered with scales of slate; but Pepys, a not less accurate observer, says (September 21st, 1668), " one great thing is that most of the house is covered, I mean the posts and quarters on the walls, with lead, and gilded." At the east and west outer angles of the inner court were two great towers, facing the Privy Garden, five storeys high. These were covered with lead, and " battled round with frames of wood covered with lead." In the middle of the inner court stood a fountain of white marble and bronze on a flight of three steps. In front of the house was a balustrade of freestone, inclosing the forecourt, and round the three outer sides of the inner court was the Privy Garden, surrounded by a wall 14 ft. high, and divided into several "allyes, quarters, and rounds, set about with thorne hedge," and adorned with a fountain of a pelican, and "two other marble pinnacles or pyramids, called the Faulcon perches, betwixt which is placed a fountaine of white marble with a lead cisterne, which fountaine is set round with 6 trees called lilack trees, which trees bear no fruit but only a very pleasant flower." The banqueting house, a square half timber building, three storeys high, containing a hall and eight rooms, with windows on every side, stood on the highest part of the park. Above the third storey was a lantern covered with lead, and at each corner a balcony for the view. The Commissioners of 1650 estimated the gross value of the materials only, after allowing for cost of taking down, at £7,020, and they reported that the building was in very good repair. There is a view of the house in Speed's map of England, but the best print of it is Hoefnagle's large folio made in 1582, for George Braun's " Urbium Præcipuarum Mundi Theatrum quintum." This print tallies pretty closely with the report of the Commissioners, though the bulbous cupolas on the towers are probably a fancy of the German draughtsman. The description in the text says: " Diversarum nationum præstantes opifices architectos sculptores et statuarios, Italos, Gallos, Hollandos, et patriotas sumptu regio eo invitavit, qui mirabile

artis suæ experimentum, in hac arce ornanda ediderunt, statuis eam intus et foris condecorarunt magnificis, quæ Romanas antiquitates partim apprime referunt partim superant." It will be noticed that this description expressly limits the work of the foreigners to decoration (" in hac arce ornanda "), they did not design the architecture as a whole. The mention of Frenchmen is also remarkable. The names of French artists or workmen scarcely ever occur in the State Papers, and there are few instances of Renaissance work in England which can be attributed to them. The capitals to the arch between the More chantry and the chancel of old Chelsea Church are an unusual instance. They closely resemble French work of the early sixteenth century, such as is found along the banks of the Seine, between Paris and Rouen. The monument in the Oxenbrigge chapel in Brede Church, Sussex, dated 1537, is another rare example. It is of Caen stone, admirably carved, and was probably made in France and shipped to the port of Rye, some nine miles distant from Brede.

Besides the Italians already mentioned, a certain John of Padua has obtained a position of undue prominence from the fact that his name occurs in a grant from the king, dated June 30th, 1544, of 2s. a day for his services in architecture and music, which grant was renewed by Edward VI. on December 13th, 1547, and June 5th, 1548. No building can be attributed to him with any certainty. He is said to have designed Protector Somerset's palace in the Strand in 1549 (old Somerset House, destroyed 1776-1784), and Longleat in Wiltshire, begun by Sir John Thynne in 1567, but there is no evidence whatever to prove this tradition. With the exception of the additions made by Inigo Jones in the following century, the architecture of old Somerset House appears to have followed the methods habitual in England in the middle of the sixteenth century. The stonework of Longleat shows knowledge of Italian detail, but it has none of the distinctive character which marks the work of the Italians imported by Henry VIII., and, to hazard a guess, it is more probable that it was the work of an Englishman who had travelled in Italy, such, for instance, as John Shute. Holbein, who designed architecture and everything else, must be reckoned with the Italians. Besides his innumerable designs for plate and jewellery, he is said to have designed two gatehouses at Whitehall, pulled down in 1770. These resembled Wolsey's gateway at Hampton Court, and are said to have had terra-cotta busts in niches, and other ornaments in terra-cotta. There is a small building in the garden at Wilton, which is called a gateway, but is much more probably a garden house. It is

Face p. 18.

COUNTESS OF SALISBURY'S CHANTRY, CHRISTCHURCH, HANTS.

in two storeys, with a room above a small open loggia. The Tudor rose appears in the pedestals to the lower order. Between the columns are heads, rather German in feeling, in roundels. Except for tradition, and certain peculiarities of the design, such as a distinct suggestion of goldsmith's work, there is no evidence for assigning this to Holbein. As Holbein died in 1543, and the abbey lands of Wilton were not conferred on Sir William Herbert till 1544, the porch, if it was designed by Holbein, must have been a posthumous work, or brought from some other place. In the Cathedral of Chichester there are some pictures of the kings of England and of the bishops of the see, supposed to have been painted for Bishop Shurburne about 1519 by an Italian named Bernardi. Shurburne died in 1536, but he had his monument put up for him in Chichester Cathedral during his lifetime. It consists of a recumbent effigy on an altar tomb, with a small figure of an angel by the head and two angels holding a mitre. The architectural details are English, but the treatment of the figures, which closely resembles similar work at Hampton Court, make it almost certain that all the figures were carved by Italians, and it is probable that Shurburne employed the Bernardis for the work. The Bernardis settled in Chichester, and Dallaway thought it probable that they executed the curious paintings in Cowdray House, destroyed by fire in 1793.

That the Italians were present in England in considerable numbers in the early part of the sixteenth century is evident, but in spite of Henry's lavish employment of Italian artists, we cannot point to a single instance of a building of the sixteenth century designed and carried through by any one Italian in England. The evidence on every hand points to the conclusion that they were employed as workmen, and in no sense as architects. At Hampton Court the fabric of the building is purely English in design and execution, and the names of the English workmen are known. So too with Holbein's gateways at Whitehall. Terra-cotta plaques and medallions were merely inserted into the brick walls of an ordinary English building, which indeed architecturally might have been very much better without them. When the English masons had built the screen or the chantry after their own fashion, the Italian carver was called in, and he set to work in his way and incontinently covered the surface with arabesques and cherubs' heads and other fancies brought from his home in the south. Thus in the Chapel built for Margaret, Countess of Salisbury, at Christchurch in Hampshire, probably about 1520, the fan vaulting, mouldings, tracery, cusping, and crockets, are ordinary late Perpendicular,

20 RENAISSANCE ARCHITECTURE IN ENGLAND

of a rather feeble sort, whereas the sides of the engaged shafts, the spandrels and other details, are distinctly Italian not only in design, but in the extreme finish and delicacy of their execution. The screen in the south chapel of the choir is another instance. So too in the chantry and tomb of Stephen Gardiner, Bishop of Winchester (died 1535), there is a similar mixture of English Perpendicular masonry and Italian surface sculpture. The vaulting of the chantry is Perpendicular, but at the east end is a little reredos of three niches with Ionic pilasters.

SCREEN TO GARDINER'S CHANTRY, WINCHESTER.

This instance is even more remarkable than that at Christchurch. Above the four light windows with Perpendicular tracery in the heads, runs an entablature of the Doric order, with triglyphs, discs, and oxens' heads in the frieze. All the work is clearly of one date, but two sets of men must have been employed on it, with the result of a curious uncertainty as to which set of details was to be followed. The ceiling and details of Bishop West's chapel at Ely (about 1533) illustrate clearly this struggle between the old tradition and the new detail, and I think it is evident that Henry and other princely patrons of art

Face p. 20.

FROM THE SALISBURY CHANTRY, CHRISTCHURCH, HANTS.

treated the Italian as a very humble person, not to be intrusted with large designs, but as fit only to take his place with other workmen in the execution of one particular piece of ornament. Torrigiano, Rovezzano, or Holbein, might be allowed more freedom, or the whole contract for a magnificent piece of work, such as the screen at King's, Cambridge, might be given to an Italian carver of admitted reputation; but the panels at St. Cross, near Winchester, and those round the choir at Christchurch, represent the ordinary employment of the Italian under Henry. In the latter instance the Italian carver appears to have competed with Flemish, and possibly French, workmen, probably all three coming out from Southampton to pick up any work they could in the neighbourhood.

Another noticeable point about this early work of the Italians in England is its local character. With exceptions in the east of England, it was pretty well confined to the districts that lay between London and the south coast ports, particularly Hampshire, and the prevalence of Italian work in this part of England is no doubt to be attributed to the settlement of the Italian merchants[1] at Winchester, and the constant passage of foreigners between that town and the port of Southampton. Italian merchants had resided and traded in Winchester since the middle of the fifteenth century, whereas the Londoners never liked them, and on "the evil Mayday" of 1517, rose upon the foreigners. The rising was summarily suppressed by the king, but the jealousy of the foreigner which it revealed was likely to deter the Italians from going far out of Hampshire, and this part of England is richest in specimens of their work. The models for the terra-cotta detail at Sutton Place were probably supplied by Italian workmen. Italian carvers were employed by Lord Sandys for his new buildings at the Vyne,[2] near Basingstoke. Round the canopy above the stalls in the chapel there is a running band of foliage on which are amorini blowing horns, shooting at stags, hunting goats, and owls playing flutes and drums in and out of a branch of pomegranate. This, though on a very small scale, is a charming example of the mixture of Italian motives with the traditional Gothic feeling. The so-called mortuary chests placed on the top of the north and south screens to the choir at Winchester are clearly Italian, with the exception of the two at the west end, which are copies made in 1661 to replace those destroyed by the Puritans in 1649. These chests

[1] I am indebted to Mr. Herbert Horne, who has made a special study of the Italians in England under Henry VIII., for this reference to the Winchester merchants.
[2] Lord Sandys married the niece and heiress of Sir Reginald Bray, and died in 1540.

22 RENAISSANCE ARCHITECTURE IN ENGLAND

are oblong boxes about 5 feet long, 2 wide, and 2 feet 6 inches deep. The front is panelled with a cartouche containing the inscription, supported by cherubs and griffins. Above this is a frieze of arabesque, or to use the language of the Hampton Court accounts, " a frieze of antick work." The details are in low relief, either in gesso or lead, and are painted in green, red, white, and gold. The original chests probably date from the end of the fifteenth and early part of the six-

CHESTS ON SCREEN TO CHOIR, WINCHESTER.

teenth centuries. Mr. Rawdon Browne[1] suggests that some of the painted Italian chests at South Kensington may have been the cases in which presents of confections and the like were sent over by the Venetian Republic to the kings of England. Thus in 1458 the seigneury sent to Henry VI. four butts of malmsey and two painted chests containing liqueurs. Similar presents were made him annually from 1459 to 1468, the total number of these painted chests amounting

[1] Introduction to vol. vi., Part I., "Calendar of Venetian State Papers."

GATEWAY, MONTACUTE HOUSE, SOMERSET.

to twenty-two, and the specimens of old glass and majolica to several thousands. It is quite possible that the Winchester chests may have had a similar origin, and, apart from their intrinsic beauty, their interest lies in the indication of one possible means by which the English may have gained some knowledge of the details of the Italian Renaissance.

The conclusion to which a survey of existing evidence leads, is that the direct influence of this first advance of the Italian Renaissance on the development of architecture in England was not considerable. Its area did not extend far beyond the southern counties, and it was an affair of detail of all sorts, of ornamentation of surfaces, of delicate arabesque and dainty plaster modelling, of terra-cotta medallions, and beautiful carving in low relief and absolute drawing, rather than of architecture in a large and comprehensive sense. Possibly the Italians were not given the chance, but it is hardly a matter for regret that the solid tradition of English building was not abandoned as yet for an architecture which in its pure Italian form was unsuited to the conditions of our climate. At the same time the indirect influence of the Italians must not be underrated. The mere fact that men of the ability of Torrigiano, Rovezzano, and Majano, were working in England for several years, must have had its effect on the native workmen among whom they worked, and families of Italian artists, such as the Bernardis at Chichester, must have done something to familiarize these workmen with Italian detail and its very high standard of workmanship. The plaster work on ceilings and friezes which became so common towards the end of the sixteenth century is usually assigned by local tradition to travelling companies of Italians. The inferiority of workmanship and the character of the design show clearly that it was executed by Englishmen long after most of the Italians had left this country. But that it was inspired by the specimens of plaster work executed by the Italians in the time of Henry VIII. is very probable, and some of the Englishmen very early picked up the new manner. For instance, when Henry VIII. built the hall of Hampton Court, Richard Ridge of London carved the great pendants under the hammerbeams of the roof, and, though the roof is of ordinary late Gothic construction, the details of these pendants are of comparatively pure Renaissance character, and here, as in the carving at the Vyne, we see how the influence of the humanist was winning its way over the harsher fancy of the later Gothic tradition. This influence was as yet solvent rather than synthetic.

24 RENAISSANCE ARCHITECTURE IN ENGLAND

It broke up the ground for new ideas; at its higher level it prepared the way for the maturer architecture of Inigo Jones, at its lower, for all that charming play of simple fancy which marks the best English craftsmanship of the sixteenth century, for the new half pagan delight in all rare and beautiful things which gives to the Renaissance its undying interest as one of the recurring outbreaks of humanity against the tyranny of another world.

PANEL OVER DOOR IN BURGATE STREET, CANTERBURY.

CHAPTER II.

THE GERMANS IN ENGLAND. ELIZABETH. JAMES I.

THE death of Henry VIII. marks a turning point in English history. The end of his despotism was as the end of a long nightmare; and when, after the brief reigns of Edward VI. and Mary, Elizabeth ascended the throne, the long repressed energy of the English began to realize itself with all the delight of recovered liberty, with something of the joyous carelessness of children turned out to play. Henceforward the English instinct asserts itself with increasing strength, not so much in the details as in the substantial forms of architecture.

For various reasons the Italians gradually retired from this country after the death of Henry VIII. The change of religion in 1536 does not appear to have immediately affected the commercial relations of Venice with England. In 1548 Daniel Barbaro, who subsequently translated "Vitruvius,"[1] was appointed Venetian ambassador in England,

[1] Printed at Venice, 1567.

but he only stayed in England eighteen months, and was ordered to return to Venice towards the end of 1550. It is probable that Barbaro who was in touch with the court, and a distinguished amateur, helped to stimulate the interest of the nobility in Italian architecture, and perhaps induced them to send over students to Italy, partly as agents and partly to educate themselves. From the date of Elizabeth's accession to 1570, the Venetian traders in London were represented by a vice-consul. Between 1570 and 1575 there were no regular diplomatic relations with Venice, and though the Venetians in London offered to defray the cost of an embassy, the proposal was defeated in the senate, and in 1578 the Papal Nuncio extracted from the Doge a public declaration that the idea of such an embassy had never been entertained, and regular diplomatic relations with Venice were not resumed till the accession of James I. Pius V. in fact made every effort to induce all Roman Catholic powers to break off relations with England, and in spite of Elizabeth's caution, her sympathy with the Protestants on the continent was an open secret. Cavalli (the Venetian Ambassador in France) wrote, in 1573, that the heretics of La Rochelle, of Germany, and of England, were solid, and thus, owing to the drift of political affairs, the Venetian trade with England gradually disappeared. The patronage of the Bardis and Cavalcantis passed into the hands of Flemish merchants, and after Edward VI. we find little trace of Italian artists. The numerous foreigners who came to England during the reigns of Elizabeth and James I. were nearly all natives of Germany and the Low Countries.

Another reason for the disappearance of the Italians was the poverty of Edward VI. Whereas Henry VIII. had begun Nonesuch, and the palaces of St. James's and Whitehall, and had spent vast sums in completing Hampton Court, neither Edward VI. nor Mary ordered any new building of importance. The utmost that Edward was allowed to do, was to maintain his father's pensions and keep his palaces in repair. His father had left him burdened with debts, and a coinage so debased that plated copper was circulated as silver. Instead of prodigal orders for goldsmiths' work, the State Papers record warrants of discharge by the king and council for the melting down of royal plate.[1] There was therefore little likelihood of employment for the Italians, and the small outlay made to rehabilitate the old religion

[1] In 1550 warrants of discharge were signed by the king and council to Sir Edmund Pecham and Sir Anthony Auger, of the value of gold, parcel gilt and silver plate, melted down and delivered by them to the Lord High Treasurer.

THE GERMANS IN ENGLAND

under Mary was hardly a sufficient inducement to them to stay. We have now to turn our attention to the invasion of German and Flemish workmen who succeeded the Italians in England, and to the native builders who at first worked side by side with the foreigners, and eventually superseded them.

When Elizabeth began to reign, the architect, as we now understand him, had not yet detached himself in England as an independent designer from the general body of craftsmen. He was still in the position of the master mason or carpenter who contracted for his own particular trade, and in this capacity provided his own details, either designing them himself, or using stock patterns, such as " the broadleaf and the rose, the rose and the garnet, the leaf, the double ring, the double flower, the great pillar, the little flower, the two dolphins and the little pillar."[1] The building owner, the "client," to use the modern term, gave general directions as to what he wanted, probably including a rough ground plan, though many of these were made on the spot by the foreman, as in the old accounts occur "skins for making platts" (plans). The work was carried out partly by contracts with separate trades, partly by day work, the owner usually providing all materials,[2] and the workmen being employed by agents, who are called variously "surveyor of the works," "comptroller of the works," clerk overseer of works," "clerk of accounts," and "clerk of the check," who appear to have divided among themselves the work now done by the builder's clerk, the builder's foreman, and the clerk of the works.[3] The one person who is never mentioned at all is "the architect," for Sir Reginald Bray, sometimes referred to as architect of Henry VII.'s chapel and other buildings, though a person of much consideration, was not an architect at all, but a fighting man and an agent of the king. To modern notions the business of building operations in the sixteenth century seems to have been conducted somewhat loosely. Rough contracts were made with the different trades, and after that, the trades were left to themselves to supply the designs and to execute the work, though there was often a foreman designer, such as Arnold at Wadham, or Cecil's man at

[1] Accounts for the banqueting house at Greenwich. Calendar of State Papers, Brewer, 4. 2. 3104.
[2] For instance, in the accounts for building the hall at Hampton Court, 1530-1532. " Pencelling (pointing) the two gabul ends of the Haull, with 3 vyces (turrets) adjoining to the same, the Kynge fyndyng all manner of stuff and scaffolding, 14£." Similar entries occur for " Empcion of painter's stuff."
[3] The question is discussed exhaustively by Mr. Wyatt Papworth in a paper contained in the Transactions of the Institute of British Architects for 1887.

Burghley, and each trade was directly responsible to the employer. No drawings, except the roughest possible sketches, were prepared, and the specifications, beyond giving general dimensions and naming materials, tended to leave the rest to that convenient clause of the modern specification, "everything to be the best of its kind." In regard to materials, the practice varied : sometimes these were found by the trades, sometimes by the employer. At Clare, Cambridge, for instance, in 1635, the Bursar bought brick earth and had bricks made for the college, at a price of sixpence per M for the brick earth, though later on he bought the bricks at five shillings per M. Wainscot, deal, and fir were bought from King's Lynn, stone from Ketton and Welldon, slates from Collyweston, and lead from Derbyshire. All these were supplied by the college, and the "work was carried on either by day work, or by small bargains for particular jobs" (Willis and Clarke). John Westley was the principal workman, and the works included the inner quadrangle, when they were interrupted by the Civil War. The history of Clare shows how tenaciously the system was adhered to. The buildings were resumed in 1669, after the Restoration, and the beautiful river front of Clare and the bridge were completed under Robert Grumbold, Freemason, who, it appears, not only made the designs, but was employed on the works as a working mason. In 1685 he was receiving twenty shillings a week for designs and for his work as mason, the college still finding all materials. The pay certainly seems small, for it is the exact amount that was paid to William Arnold for similar work at Wadham, 1610-11.

Where the trades found their own materials some form of contract was always made. In Messrs. Willis and Clarke's History[1] there is given in full the contract between the Master and Fellows of St. Catherine's Hall, Cambridge, and John Atkinson, dated April 18th, 1611, to erect a good and substantial range of buildings as below specified : the house to be two storeys high, each 9 feet from floor to ceiling, the studs to be 12 inches apart, and the width " 18 feet from the inside of the brickwork unto the outside of the groundsill ; " the case of stairs to be large enough to contain " a fair paire of staires up to every of the 6 roomes," each room to have a fair bay on the college side, with one at the end, and convenient lights on the other side, " the windows to have fourteen iron casements placed in the most convenient places, and all to be coloured with white lead and oil ;" each room to be divided

[1] "Architectural History of the University of Cambridge," vol. ii., p. 90.

into a study and bed-chamber, "with sufficient doares, locks, hingells and stapells;" the floors to be of good oak or deal, the rooms to be ceiled with lime and hair. Jo. Atkinson is to make two chimney-stacks with three fires in each stack, and to remove the old buildings, the whole to be completed within twenty days after next Michaelmas, and the builder to be paid £60 at the time of sealing, and a hundred marks on October 22nd, or £126 13s. 4d. in all, and to have the old materials, and "the said Jo. Atkinson covenanteth that all and every the timber wh. shall be used in the said buyldynge shall be sound, firm, stronge and of a good scantlinge, and all the stone tyle glasse iron morter brick and whatsoever thing else is necessary shall be of the best for continuance, and to make it a strong seemly buyldynge and habitable." No drawings were given, and no other specification than what is contained in the above, and the building lasted till 1673, when it was rebuilt by Grumbold. The contract made between the Master and Fellows of St. John's and Ralph Symmons and Gilbert Wigge, August 7th, 1598, for the second court, is more formal. The indenture refers to the "platts and uprights drawn by the said Symmons or Wigg or their assignes," and specifies the bricks and stones, the accommodation, length, height of floors, thickness of walls, size and height of lights, water tables, cornices, crests, and gables, floors, roofs, and stairs; the old details of the upper court to be followed in all respects—the work to be completed in four years, each part having its time limit, and the sides are not to be carried up simultaneously. Payment is to be made by instalments for work done and materials delivered, but the college to be free to repay either in money or in materials on three months' notice on either side. In case of disagreement, the matter was to be referred to the Archbishop of Canterbury and the Bishop of London, whose decision was to be final and binding;[1] and the builders to give two bonds of £500 each. The "platts" referred to in this indenture consisted of three plans of the three floors drawn to one-sixteenth scale, and three "uprights" or elevations. The latter are little more than rough geometrical sketches, not to scale, with washes of colour sufficient to indicate the materials, and it is probable that no other drawings were used in carrying out these buildings. When Dr. Nevile began his important additions to Trinity, Cambridge, early in the seventeenth century, rather more care was taken. Ralph Symmons made a model of the Great Hall, but before proceeding to carry it out, the Bursar, accompanied by John Symmes, Freemason, went to London

[1] As usual, this clause was disregarded, for the business ended in a law-suit.

30 RENAISSANCE ARCHITECTURE IN ENGLAND

to examine and measure various halls,[1] and the work was ultimately carried out by Symmes.

It is evident that as yet no necessity was felt for a trained designer in building, and this method of designing and executing buildings continued in common use till the end of the sixteenth century, and was not abandoned generally till the middle of the eighteenth. So long as son succeeded father with an uninterrupted tradition of methods of workmanship the system answered admirably, but when, as was the case in the latter part of the sixteenth century, all kinds of new motives were introduced, there was clearly need of some person of wider knowledge and more discerning taste to control the aberrations of the workmen. No such person had yet emerged, and the consequence was that though the work of this period is nearly always picturesque, it is marked by extreme ignorance of the scholarship of architecture, the orders are grouped and separated and inverted with a singular disregard of the recognized canons, and the proportions followed no rule but that of the builder's inner consciousness. Where the builders dispensed with ornamentation they were still capable of doing excellent plain work, such as parts of Knole, some of the colleges at Oxford and Cambridge, and many a quiet manor house. Occasionally one comes across instances which display greater learning but less originality, such as Longleat, but most of the important buildings carried out in the reign of Elizabeth are wanting in distinction. Though picturesque in outline—the legacy of the Gothic tradition—they are overcrowded with abominable ornament, they bear evident marks of having been designed by men without any great knowledge of architecture, men who were destitute of a taste sufficiently mature to save them from the silly extravagance of the Germans. The result would probably have been even worse, except that the nobleman of that time had actually some knowledge of architecture, and there did exist a genuine liking for art, and a general level of taste which was certainly higher than it is at the present day.

The building schemes of Protector Somerset were cut short by his execution in 1552. His palace, afterwards Somerset House, was begun about 1547-48, and it appears that between April, 1548, and October, 1550, £10,091 9s. 2d. had been expended on the building, and it was charged against Somerset as early as October, 1549; that he was heaping

---

[1] The Bursar measured the halls of Westminster, Guildhall, Hampton Court, Lambeth, Lincoln's Inn, Crosby Hall, and Christ Church, Oxford. The hall actually selected as a model was the Middle Temple Hall, built 1562-72, measuring 100 × 40 × 50.

up money and building himself great houses, and "leaving the King's poore souldiers unpaid of their wages."

Little was done in the reigns of Edward VI. and Mary, though perhaps the faith of the latter may have arrested for a time the slow decay of Gothic architecture. Charlecote in Warwickshire, begun in 1558, the year of Elizabeth's accession, is the earliest of the famous Elizabethan manor houses. The first record,[1] however, of any considerable undertaking, after Edward's death, is the letter from Roger Warde, mason at Burghley, to Sir William Cecil, desiring instructions as to the building of three "lucan" windows for the inner court, and for the stairs from the base-court to the terrace, and for the gate at the end of the terrace. In 1561-62, Peter Kemp sends Cecil a plan of the brewhouse, and various building accounts to be settled. In August, 1561, John Shers writes to Sir William Cecil that he has purchased for him at Venice the statues of twelve of the emperors. Under date February 19th, 1567 (State Papers, Domestic, Elizabeth), there is a note of certain "works of art, of marble jasper," brought into England for Sir William Cecil and the Earl of Pembroke by Dominique Troisrieux, a Frenchman, those unsold to be returned duty free. In 1570 Sir T. Gresham is writing to Cecil that his pillars of marble have arrived in good order from Hamburg, and on April 5th, 1571, Casper Vosbergh reports the progress of the works at Stamford. These entries enable one to form some idea of the manner in which such a house as Burghley was built in the time of Elizabeth. There is no mention of any architect or general contractor. The work began with the English mason who applied directly to Cecil for instructions. Meanwhile Cecil had his agents abroad, on the look-out for choice marbles and statuary, and finally, after fifteen years of building, the German appears on the scene, probably for carving and ornamental detail, and perhaps accompanied by a staff of German workmen, for in 1572 Vosberg petitioned Cecil (now Lord Burghley) for privileges for a German Church to be founded at Stamford.[2] The noticeable points are: (1) the absence of any trained designer to control the whole; (2) the leisurely manner of building: these men thought nothing of spending fifteen to twenty years over a house—Longleat, for instance, begun in 1567, was not finished in 1580;

[1] Calendar of State Papers, Mary, vol. ix., June, 1556.
[2] The design of Burghley has been attributed to John Thorpe, some account of whom is given below. The only evidence bearing on the point are the two plans in the Soane Museum; as the plans are not signed, and Thorpe's name appears nowhere else in connection with the house, this evidence is not conclusive.

32 RENAISSANCE ARCHITECTURE IN ENGLAND

(3) the introduction of German workmen to ornament the building, where Wolsey would have employed Italian workmen, Burghley employed German.

About this period the Germans and Flemings came over to England in considerable numbers. The powerful corporation known as the Steelyard had been in existence since 1296, and, in spite of the protest by the English merchants in 1552, these merchants of the Steelyard continued to flourish till the end of the century, and it was not till 1601 that Elizabeth finally ordered their expulsion. Various settlements of Flemish weavers were started about the middle of the sixteenth century with special privileges. There was one at Glastonbury, under special articles entered into with Protector Somerset; another at Barcheston in Warwickshire; and at Colchester and other places along the east coast of England there were colonies of Dutch and Flemish artisans. In 1580 the town of Halsted and eight adjoining towns sent a petition to the Council praying that twenty families of Dutchmen who had moved to Colchester might be made to return to continue their trade of bay-making, as heretofore. There were similar settlements in the Isle of Thanet and in the Weald of Kent. In 1561 a warrant was issued to Sir Nicholas Bacon for a grant to the Mayor of Sandwich, allowing the settlement of a limited number of foreigners in Sandwich. The wording of this warrant is significant. The settlement was permitted "as well for the helpe, repaire, and amendment of our said town and porte of Sandwich by plantynge in the same men of knowledge in sundry handycrafts, as also for the relief of certaine strangers now resyding in our said citie of London being verye skilful therein." The number was limited to twenty-five households of from ten to twelve each,[1]

---

[1] Boys, "History of Sandwich," p. 747, gives the following list of foreign traders settled in Sandwich in 1582:

Apothecaries	2	Cardmakers	2	Grogram weavers	4	Packmaker	1
Aqua vitæ seller	1	Carpenters	3	Hatcheler	1	Painter	1
Bay makers	86	Coblers	3	Joiners	5	Potter	1
Bayweavers	74	Coopers	2	L. (linsey) weavers	24	Post into Flanders	1
Baybroker	1	Cowkeepers	4	Linen weavers	1	Sawyers	3
Bakers	4	Crier of the lieu		Linsey-wolsey		Schoolmasters	3
Basket maker	1	cope*	1	weavers	2	Sealer of bayes	1
Beater of millstones	1	Denizen	1	Laborers	6	Shipwright	1
		Dier	1	Loder to mill	1	Smiths	5
Bookbinder	1	Fullers	17	Merchants	7	Spinners	3
Bounes Clark	1	Gardners	13	Millers	4	Spoler for bays	1
Brewers	3	Goldsmith	1	Millwright	1	Spoller of yarn	2

* Auctioneer; the word "liscoup" was in use in Sandhurst when Boys wrote.

THE GERMANS IN ENGLAND

and all the names given are Dutch. All these men were industrious artisans, and undoubtedly had some influence on the vernacular architecture of the districts in which they settled, as is evident from the resemblance of the brick buildings of the Isle of Thanet and the eastern counties to Dutch architecture of a rather earlier date. This, moreover, was no new thing. It seems certain that the extreme richness and delicacy of detail found in many of the mediæval churches of the eastern counties, had its origin in the constant intercourse between the traders of King's Lynn and the east coast seaports, and the great cities of the Netherlands.

In spite of their skill in painting and carving, the influence of the Italian workmen was confined to a somewhat narrow field, and they had left the technical industries of England pretty much where they found them. When Elizabeth wished to develop the mineral resources of the country she had to import German miners and metal workers for the purpose. In 1564 Daniel Hechstetten made an indenture for mining with the queen. In 1565 a grant was made to Humfrey, paymaster of the mint, and to Christopher Shutz, "an Almain born," authorizing them to search for mines, and smelt minerals in England and Ireland. These Germans seem to have had a monopoly of the art of "battery and batten work," and showed no inclination to part with their secrets, as Humfrey complained to Cecil in 1565,[1] in spite of the fact that Christopher Shutz "was bound in £10,000 to communicate his art in working metals." So again in glass work, after the gradual withdrawal of the Italians,[2] glass and pottery work had to be renewed under the guidance of Flemings. In 1565 Armigall Waade, in a report to Cecil on the progress of the glass works under Cornelius de Lannoy, dwells on the clumsiness of the English glassworkers. Thomas Larke and Galyon Hoone and the glaziers of Southwark, who designed and executed the windows of King's, Cambridge, seem to have carried

Strykers of bays . . 2	Maker of teazle handles 1	Upholsterer 1	Woolbeater 1
Surgeon and woolcomber 1	Tiler 1	Wagoner 1	Woolcombers . . 24
Tailors 6	Turners 3	Wood carrier . . . 1	Occupations not
		Wheelwright . . . 1	mentioned . . . 6

[1] Domestic State Papers, vol. xxxvii.
[2] In 1550 Edward VI. contracted with certain Venetian glass makers that they should start glassworks in London, and leave was given them to extend their stay from six to eighteen months. Mr. Rawdon Browne (Cal. Ven. State Papers, vol. v. 669) thinks that this establishment was the one at Belsize, from which Waade wrote to Cecil in 1565. Stow says the first making of Venice glasses in England was begun at the Crutched Friars, " by one Jacob Venalinni, an Italian."

34 RENAISSANCE ARCHITECTURE IN ENGLAND.

away their secret with them. There were, indeed, some rare survivals here and there. When the chapel of Trinity, Cambridge, was built in 1556-1560, the white glass and heraldic and other devices for the windows were supplied by William Blithe, of Thacksted in Essex, and Miles Jugg;[1] but it is to the Flemings that we must attribute most of the characteristic glass of the early part of the seventeenth century. Bernard and Abraham Van Ling carried out windows for St. Paul's, London, Christ Church, Oxford (the well-known window with Jonah sitting under a gourd), and for Lincoln, Balliol, and University Chapels, between 1620 and 1640. Native artists were also to be found, such as Robert Rudland of Oxford, who made some of the windows in Wadham Chapel. But for more important work recourse was had to the Flemings, and Bernard Van Ling was employed to execute the great east window of the chapel at Wadham. Mr. Jackson, in his history of Wadham, gives a full account of the agreement made between the college and Bernard Van Ling of Emden, July 6th, 1621.

This large importation of foreign craftsmen had its effect on the details of Elizabethan work. Not only were designs obtained from abroad, or from foreign pattern books, but Flemish or German workmen were often brought over for important buildings, as at Burghley and Sir Thomas Gresham's Exchange. Sir Thomas Gresham, who was a general merchant in a large way of business, imported not only the design, but the stone paving from Flanders.[2] The design is said to have been supplied by Henry de Pas, who subsequently designed the Hôtel des Villes Hanséatiques at Antwerp. Gresham's building was begun on June 7th, 1566, and was not completed in 1570.[3] There are two views of it by Hollar. It consisted of a square quadrangular court of two storeys and an attic, with a colonnade of semicircular arches on the inner side, and was paved throughout with

[1] Willis and Clark. These windows were broken up on the accession of Elizabeth, November 17th, 1565-66: "Item for repairinge of the places which wer broken forth in all the windoes whearin dyd appeare superstition, 16d."

[2] Harrison, after referring to the abundance of building stones in England, says: "Howbeit for all this, we must fetch them still from far, as did the Hull men their stones out of Iceland, wherewith they paved their town, for want of the like in England; or as Sir Thomas Gresham did, when he bought the stones in Flanders wherewith he paved the Burse. But as he will answer (peradventure), that he bargained for the whole mould and. substance of his workmanship in Flanders."

[3] Cal. Domestic State Papers, Eliz., vol. lxxiv., on October 26th, 1570, Gresham requested leave for "a special license for a ship to go to Flanders with alabaster, as he had a special license for transportation of his stones from Antwerp for his Burse." Gresham probably exchanged English alabaster for the stone and marble he imported from Antwerp.

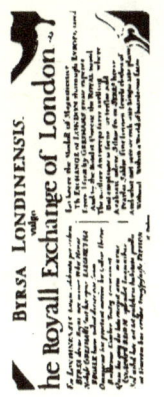

DOORWAY AT TENTERDEN, KENT.

black and white marble. Over each arch was a niche, with a life-size statue of a king or emperor. To the right of the entrance was a lofty clock tower, with two projecting galleries and an open cupola, surmounted by a gigantic grasshopper. Grasshoppers, probably in lead or copper gilt, and suggested, no doubt, by the magnificent vanes of Holland, were placed as finials at the ends of the roof ridges. The building was of brick, with stone dressings, and, on the whole, of a reasonable and unpretentious character, rather Dutch than German in feeling. The lofty clock tower closely resembled the towers of many a Dutch town-hall of about the same period. The building was consumed in the fire of London, and was replaced by a sumptuous building of Portland stone, which was also burnt in 1838. Had all the buildings in England which were built under German influence been equally sane there would be less reason for regretting this element in the development of English art; as it is we have to attribute to the Germans the invention of the meaningless ornament and ugly proportion which usually disfigured the work of the Elizabethan builders.

But throughout the reign of Elizabeth the German influence was in the air and predominant. The screens and mantelpieces of old Charterhouse, of Longleat, and of Hatfield, the ponderous entrance porch of Audley End, the strapwork gables to the towers of Wollaton, the barbarous notion of using Tuscan and other columns as chimneys, the shapes of men and women ending in balusters, all show the heavy hand, the merely mechanical instinct, of the German workman; and architectural design being at a low ebb at this period, or being rather, one should say, in an undeveloped state, people who built houses had recourse to that last refuge of the destitute, the pattern book, that is, folio pages of design done into space, designs not made in relation to specific conditions, but made as merely academical or commercial exercises by some facile designer of tailpieces and title-pages. Such was the "architectura" of that exuberant draughtsman, J. V. Frisius, or Vrese, of Antwerp, published in 1563, a book which was used with disastrous readiness by the English builders of this period. It was unfortunate that the treatises most in use in England at this time were German rather than Italian. Such obscure persons as Cammermayer and Wendel Dietterlin were preferred to Alberti and Palladio; and the various superb Italian editions of "Vitruvius" seem hardly to have been known in England till the end of the sixteenth century. It is evident, in fact, that the English builder-architect of the time of Elizabeth was a somewhat ignorant and ill-educated person, and did not follow better models for the simple reason that he was unconscious of their existence.

The "porta honoris" at Caius, Cambridge, is a good instance of the confusion in which this practice resulted. In itself it is not a bad design, but in the position in which it stands, it is mean and disappointing, being totally out of scale with the surrounding architecture. It has even been suggested that the builder mistook the scale. The design of this was long attributed to Theodore Haveus of Cleves, "artifex egregius et insignis architecturæ professor," as he is called in the college books, acting under the direction of Dr. Caius. But Messrs. Willis and Clark say that there is no foundation for this, and that the only work which can certainly be assigned to Haveus was a curious stone column having sixty facets to act as sundials, and adorned with the names of all the gentlemen then in residence at Caius, and a figure of Pegasus as a weather-cock at the top. This column has been destroyed. There is a similar monument on a smaller scale in the quadrangle of Corpus College, Oxford. In 1573-75, "Theodore" and others were paid £33 16s. 8d. for carving to Dr. Caius' tomb. Mr. Lionel Cust has discovered the name of Theodore Haveus as a settler with his family at King's Lynn, and he was probably summoned to Cambridge by Caius while residing there.

Another instance of German influence is Longford Castle in Wilts, now so much enlarged and modernized that it is difficult to disentangle the original design. The centre façade of the entrance front is a regular German composition, and a very bad one. It bears no relation at all to the angle towers which flank it. The latter, as will be pointed out later, are probably part of the original building by John Thorpe, and this centre façade is most likely from a design bought by Sir Thomas Gorges either in Germany or from a German in England, and carried out wholesale, without any regard to the architectural features of the older building.

The Germans continued to find employment in England till they were routed by Inigo Jones, but towards the end of Elizabeth's reign their principal work consisted in the making of monuments and chimney-pieces. Instances of the latter are to be found in nearly every Elizabethan house of any importance. There are elaborate examples at Hatfield, South Wraxhall, Loseley, Cobham, Blickling, the Charterhouse, and elsewhere. The finest series in any house in England is probably to be found at Knole. Several of these chimney-pieces show undeniable vigour and originality in design, and a sense of scale and

FROM A PLATE IN VRIESE'S "ARCHITECTURA."

Face p. 36.

proportion not common in German work. The marbles are well combined, and the general effect is sumptuous and magnificent, if lacking in the well-ordered simplicity of fine Italian work. The Knole series, however, is exceptionally fine, and by no means represents the average

CHIMNEY-PIECE, SOUTH WRAXHALL.

In this example the architrave of the entablature is put above the frieze instead of below it ; the architrave is also turned upside down.

level of the Elizabethan mantelpiece. The details of the latter are frequently coarse, and even ridiculous, and the incessant repetition of the same trick of design suggest the hand of the tradesman rather than of the artist, the German pattern book, rather than the fresh spontaneous fancy of the English designer of the sixteenth century. The

38 RENAISSANCE ARCHITECTURE IN ENGLAND

chimney-pieces usually consist of marble columns of various orders superimposed, and separated by bold projecting mouldings, with rich carvings of arabesques and armorial bearings on the panels and entablatures. The tombs have also a strong family resemblance. When detached, they begin with a marble pedestal tomb on which the effigy rests surrounded by marble columns, usually of the Corinthian order, carrying a rich entablature with an open arcade in the centre. Where the monument was fixed against a wall, the back of the arched canopy was filled with a cartouche containing the inscription, and fruit, flowers, ribbons, and other conventional ornaments. The chief difficulty with the designer seems to have been where to stay his hand, for he continued above the cornice with shields, and cartouches, heraldic beasts and obelisks in unrestrained prodigality. The figures and the armorial bearings were usually gilt and coloured. In spite of the narrow range of their design, these monuments are certainly fine pieces of workmanship. The marbles and alabasters are skilfully managed, the details of the carving and the low relief of the arabesques are often executed with admirable delicacy, and in some instances, such as the monument to Lord and Lady Dacre (died 1595), in Chelsea Parish Church, the figures are carved with restraint and genuine feeling. The most important instances are: the monument to Elizabeth in Westminster Abbey, erected in 1604 by Maximilian Powtram, or Colte, with the help of Patrick the blacksmith, and John de Critz, painter; the monuments to Mary, Queen of Scots, Westminster, and to Radcliffe, Earl of Sussex at Boreham Church in Essex, executed by Richard Stevens, a Dutchman;[1] that of Carey, Lord Hunsdon, at Westminster, the Hertford monument in the Lady Chapel at Salisbury, and the tomb of Sir Laurence Tanfelde (1625) in Burford Church. In fact, most of our English cathedrals possess sumptuous monuments of marble, black touchstone and alabaster, designed in this manner which continued in use down to the Restoration. The small seventeenth century mural monuments of alabaster and other marbles, to be found in most parish churches, are in some ways the most admirable examples left in England of this particular branch of design. The very beautiful monument to George Broke, Lord Cobham, in the church of Cobham in Kent, is in a different manner. It consists of an oblong pedestal tomb, 7 ft. 6 in. by 4 ft. 6 in., divided into five bays at the sides, and

---

[1] This monument was erected after 1583, when the Earl of Sussex died, leaving £1,500 for the tomb and effigies of himself, his father and grandfather.

F. G. O. Stuart, Photo.

THE HERTFORD MONUMENT, SALISBURY CATHEDRAL.

DOORWAY TO GARDENS, ST. JOHN'S, OXFORD.

Face p. 38.
MONUMENT OF SIR THOMAS BODLEY, MERTON COLLEGE CHAPEL, OXFORD.
BY NICHOLAS STONE.

CHIMNEY-PIECE, COBHAM, KENT.

three at the ends, by small detached Ionic columns, supporting a slab of black marble, on which lie the figures of Lord Cobham and his wife. Smaller figures of their ten sons and four daughters occupy the bays at the sides and ends. The peculiarity of this monument is its lavish use of niello. The whole of it, except the black marble slab, is of alabaster, and the armour of the figures and all the armorial bearings, have their surfaces graved out and filled in flush with a composition of wax and mastic, coloured red, black, yellow and other colours. This was rubbed down smooth to the adjacent surfaces, and though it has blistered here and there, the face is still very hard and firm, and the colour permanent. Lord Cobham died in 1561. In the Groote Kirk of Nymegen there is a splendid monument to Catherine of Bourbon (died 1469), executed in a similar method, and the Cobham tomb was no doubt made by a Fleming. Towards the end of the sixteenth century, a certain Giles de Whitt[1] was employed by Henry, Lord Cobham, on chimney-pieces in the Hall, and on a tomb to Lord Cobham's father. It is possible that we have in De Whitt the artist who made this admirable monument.

Bernard Jansen, a Fleming, is said to have been employed at Audley End and at Northumberland House. He certainly worked with Nicholas Stone on Sutton's monument in the old Charterhouse Chapel, probably supplying the architectural details while Stone did the figures. The last of these foreign designers, whose work was based on German models, was probably De Caux, a Gascon, and drawing-master to Prince Henry. De Caux did a good deal of work till superseded by Inigo Jones. He built a picture gallery for Prince Henry at Richmond, and laid out the gardens at Wilton as appears from his book of folio designs, published in 1615, and certainly had something to do with the buildings, but what he actually did is obscure. Aubrey, who is not always to be trusted, states that De Caux designed the south front of the house "al Italiano" about 1635, "with the advice and approbation of Mr. Jones." This front was burnt down soon afterwards and rebuilt from Inigo Jones's designs under the superintendence of John Webb. Of De Caux's work at Wilton all that remains are the niches on either side of the archway on the east side[2] which used to form the main entrance, and possibly a clumsy garden-house of stone. The niches are meanly designed, and instead of being "al

---

[1] State Papers, Elizabeth, Dom., vol. cclxxvi., No. 37, quoted by Mr. Gotch.
[2] That is, on the side facing towards Salisbury.

40 RENAISSANCE ARCHITECTURE IN ENGLAND

Italiano" are very clearly in the German manner. De Caux was also employed at Heidelberg. Aubrey says he died about 1656.

The influence of German art in England had run itself out nearly twenty years before. The effect on English architecture was greater for the time than that of the Italians, but it was less permanent in its results. German motives were freely adopted by English builders in regard to the elevations and architectural details of important buildings. Their crudeness and the mechanical method of their ornamentation made these motives peculiarly easy to reproduce in large quantity at an inconsiderable cost. They were accordingly taken up for much the same reasons as those which have led to their repetition in the last few years. In consequence of this, for one piece of ornament that can be traced to an Italian motive, there are twenty that are clearly due to German influence, in Elizabethan and early Jacobean buildings. That this influence, however, had not sunk very deeply into the minds of the English is evident from the ease with which Inigo Jones threw it overboard, and it did not reappear again in England so long as the development of architecture was spontaneous, and traditional, and though not unconscious, was not the result of deliberate eclecticism. Moreover, the earlier Italian influence was not wasted. Houses were built in England by gentlemen of less degree, but superior taste, which in the main adhered to the traditions of English house building, and in their ornamentation deliberately followed Italian models. The beautiful panel above the entrance porch to Montacute House (1580-1600), Sir Thomas Tresham's buildings in Northamptonshire (1575-80), the details of the entrance garden door to Shaw House near Newbury (1571), show no trace of the Germans at all; and indeed, the refinement of details, the all-pervading simplicity and reserve of such a design as the entrance front of Montacute, or Barrington in Somersetshire, are plain evidence that the saner traditions of English building were not materially affected by the eccentric German. The elevations of Littlecote (about 1580), with its sober brick front running up uninterrupted to the great eaves course, and its multitudinous gables on the garden side are absolutely and solely English. They might, indeed, have been built a hundred years earlier, and, as will be pointed out, the essential parts of the English house, its plan, and the blocking out of the building, were as yet not modified at all by either Italians or Germans. The traditional English house plan, attained by slow development through successive phases of civilization, held its own alike in the palace and the manor house, in spite of the fantastic foreign

Face p. 40.

dress, with which the builder's ambition clothed it. The real and essential change in English architecture, the change which altered not merely its detail, but its whole intention in building, is not to be found in these experiments of the sixteenth century, but in the far-reaching revolution introduced by Inigo Jones, the first Englishman to grasp in its full significance the art of the Italian Renaissance.

CHAPTER III.

THE ENGLISH BUILDERS.

OF the English master builders themselves, of the men, that is, who were not quite what we now understand by builders, and still less, what we understand by architects, very little is known. The name most frequently referred to is that of John Thorpe, yet, for any certain knowledge about him, John Thorpe is not very far removed from that other *ignis fatuus* of archæology, John of Padua. The history of his life is almost entirely conjectural, and is based on the miscellaneous collection of drawings now in the Soane Museum, and if, as was at one time asserted, John Thorpe was really the architect of all the buildings included in that collection, it is almost incredible that a man who must in that case have been widely known at the time should, so far as is known, be referred to only once in contemporary literature. The collection comprises some two hundred and eighty sheets, consisting mainly of plans of various houses, a few full-sized sections of stonework, a few elevations, a sheet of the five orders, and a diagram of perspective, with MS. directions for making perspective drawings. As these drawings contain the whole of the material available for any account of John Thorpe, it is necessary to consider them in some detail. The plans include several of the most notable houses built in Elizabeth's reign. Somerset House, Buckhurst in Sussex, Copthall, Wollaton Notts, Burghley juxta Stamford, and Burghley-on-the-Hill, Sir Walter Cope's house at Kensington [that is Holland House], a great house at Wimbledon for Sir T. Cecil, Longford Castle, Holdenby, Audley End, "Ampthill old house enlardged by J. Thorpe," "Kerby whereof I laid the first stone 1570," Loseley in Surrey, Aston Hall Birmingham, and other less famous houses. There are various reasons which make it improbable that Thorpe had anything to do with any but a few of these houses. In the first place, as already mentioned, if Thorpe really designed all these buildings, he must have been better known, whereas his name was first mentioned by Horace Walpole, who saw this collection of drawings when it belonged to the

THE ENGLISH BUILDERS 43

Earl of Warwick, and without further inquiry, jumped to the conclusion that he had found in Thorpe the architect of all the great Elizabethan houses. In the second place, so far as has at present been ascertained, in no case where documentary evidence, apart from drawings, exists in regard to the building of the house, does Thorpe's name occur. Thirdly, very few of the drawings are signed, and there are wide differences of writing and draughtsmanship in the various drawings of the collection. Lastly, there is the internal evidence of Thorpe's own manner, in so far as it can be gathered from the few drawings in the collection which can be assigned to him with any certainty. If, for instance, Thorpe designed Kirby in Northamptonshire, it is most improbable that he also designed a house of such a very different kind as Wollaton—for though it is easy nowadays for a designer to imitate any quantity of styles, at the end of the seventeenth century neither the necessary knowledge nor the inclination existed for such extreme versatility of design.

Buckhurst in Sussex, an immense house which was finished in 1568, and is now entirely destroyed, may or may not have been designed by Thorpe. Buckhurst was built by Sir Richard Sackville, who afterwards, as Earl of Dorset, carried out extensive alterations and additions at Knole between 1603 and 1605, the dates on the rainwater heads. The gables and treatment of the south side of the inner court at Knole rather resemble an undoubted design of Thorpe's, and it is possible that he may have had something to do with both these buildings. Mr. Gotch[1] has, I think, established the probability that Thorpe designed the plan of the original house at Kirby in Northamptonshire (not Kirby House, London, as stated by Dallaway). This house was built between 1570 and 1575 for Sir Humphrey Stafford, and on his death it was sold to Sir Christopher Hatton. The plan in the Soane Museum varies considerably in detail from the plan as actually executed; for instance, a spacious loggia with a colonnade in nineteen bays is shown in Thorpe's plan running along the west side. This was never built. A somewhat similar loggia on a very much smaller scale was afterwards carried out at Holland House. Then, again, Thorpe's plan is rectangular, whereas the actual plan is irregular, but the general resemblance between the two is unmistakable, and so far is valuable as enabling us to form some sort of conjecture as to the kind of work which Thorpe actually did.

Holdenby in Northamptonshire, built for Sir Christopher Hatton

---

[1] "Architecture of the Renaissance in England," an invaluable series of views of buildings erected between 1560 and 1630.

44 RENAISSANCE ARCHITECTURE IN ENGLAND

before 1580, is, with the exception of part of the front, destroyed. The only reason for assigning it to Thorpe is that there is a plan and elevation of it in the Soane Museum, but the research of the late Mr. Wyatt Papworth has proved that Thorpe only surveyed this building after it was built. Mr. Papworth found an entry in the State Papers,

A GABLE AT KNOLE.

June 4, 1606, of payment to John Thorpe " for his charges in taking the survey of the house and land by plots (? plans) at Holdenby, with the several rates and values of both, particularly with his own pains, and three others a long time employed in drawing down and writing fair the plots of that and of Ampthill House and the Earl of Salisbury's . . . £70 8s. 8d." Devon Issues, " Pell Records," James I., 1836, p. 37.

KNOLE, SEVENOAKS.

The words "enlardged by J. Thorpe," on the plan in the Soane Collection, therefore probably mean, drawn to a larger scale by J. Thorpe. Confining ourselves to work which has been assigned to him on some reasonable authority, we are reduced to the Lyveden new building, erected before the end of the sixteenth century on a very curious plan, Longford Castle, some unknown work at Paris, the earlier part of Holland House, and another freak of design, the monogram house made on the plan ⊢T and explained by a rhyme,

> "Thes 2 letters I & T
> Joyned together as you see,
> is meant for a dwelling house for me."

This plan is accompanied by a perspective elevation of the house, which is of an unpretentious character, three storeys and an attic, with octagon buttresses at the angles, such as are common in the plainer sixteenth century houses, and simple gables not unlike those at Knole. The whole rather resembles a brick house at Wrotham, in Kent, and many of the smaller brick houses of about this date. This design, the plan of Kirby, the drawings for Sir Walter Cope's house, the house for the Queen Mother at Paris, and the plan of Ampthill, are the only drawings in the whole collection which can be assigned to Thorpe with any degree of certainty, and as such, throw some light on the authenticity of other buildings which have been attributed to him—assuming, that is, that Thorpe was an architect—for the weight of such little evidence as there is, points to the conclusion that he was not a designer, but a surveyor and a draughtsman, a man whose profession it was to measure up and place on record plans of buildings after they had been completely finished by other men.

Lyveden new building is still standing, though dismantled. It is a two-storey building, at the level of the first floor runs an entablature, in the frieze of which are triglyphs with emblematic symbols carved in the metopes, and round the frieze of the upper entablature runs an inscription. The profile of the mouldings and all the details are executed with much refinement. Now a plan very similar to the plan of this house exists in the Soane collection, and Mr. Gotch thence infers that Thorpe was the architect of this house, and that Sir Thomas Tresham, who built it, also employed Thorpe for the Rothwell market house, now dismantled, for the triangular lodge at Rushton, and for Rushton Manor. The first two of these are almost certainly by the same hand, but whether that hand was Thorpe's is by no means certain. The delicacy and reserve

46 RENAISSANCE ARCHITECTURE IN ENGLAND

of the designs of the Lyveden and Rothwell buildings are entirely wanting in the picturesque and exuberant but rather ignorant work of

THE TRIANGULAR LODGE AT RUSHTON.

the architect who designed Kirby. An artist of any attainment usually has his earlier and later manner, but unless he is a simple copyist, one distinct individuality underlies them both. Now the work assigned to Thorpe at Kirby shows a good deal of invention, but a somewhat florid

Face p. 46.

DETAIL OF DOORWAY TO TRIANGULAR LODGE, RUSHTON.

taste, as for instance, in the fantastic gables of the west elevation, and the fussy design of seven small Corinthian columns above the entrance bay on the south side of the courtyard. The details of Lyveden on the other hand are of singular severity, and the builder of this house and of the Rothwell market house evidently had more knowledge of Italian architecture than the builder of Kirby. To take one instance, the great pilasters at Kirby have no entasis or diminution, whereas the pilasters to Rothwell market house have both. Neither the plan of Lyveden House, nor that of Kirby in the same collection, is signed. The evidence therefore is internal, and rests with the buildings themselves, and if we take as our standard the monogram house, the most probable conclusion is that Thorpe may have had something to do with the design of Kirby, and possibly part of Rushton Hall, which is not unlike it, but that he had nothing to do with Lyveden new building, Rothwell market house, or the triangular lodge. The designs of these three latter buildings, which are very unusual, were probably due to Sir Thomas Tresham himself.[1]

Longford Castle, in Wiltshire, presents a similar difficulty. There is a plan and elevation of it in the Soane Collection. The building itself was begun in 1580 by Sir Thomas Gorges on the site of an older house, and at the desire of Lady Gorges, who was a Swede, the house was to imitate the castle of Uraniberg. It was probably finished by the beginning of the seventeenth century, since which date it has been considerably altered and enlarged. The peculiarity of its plan is that it is based on a triangle. At each apex stands a circular tower with buildings connecting the towers and inclosing a small triangular court. The three angle towers (or rather two of them, for the third has been rebuilt) are plain buildings of stone, and the wall face is divided into oblong panels by bands of white stone and black flints alternately. The towers are in three storeys, divided by string courses with a parapet wall above. The centre string course has a frieze with triglyphs set about four times their width apart. So far this work was English, and even local English, for the pattern formed by the mixture of stone and flint is characteristic of this part of Wiltshire. Moreover, the curious parapet course, and the profiles of the strings are not uncommon in English work of this date. But after the building of these towers there must have been an abrupt change in the plans. For instead of

---

[1] These buildings will be referred to again in the following chapter. A full account of them will be found in Mr. Gotch's "Buildings of Sir Thomas Tresham."

the simple gabled front of flint and stone which would have naturally followed these towers, Sir Thomas Gorges indulged himself in an extravagant stone façade of arches and pilasters and terminal figures in the worst manner of the Germans. This façade was built without any regard to the angle towers, the heights and mouldings of which are entirely ignored. It is known that there is a break in the history of the building, Sir Thomas Gorges' money having run out; but after the defeat of the Armada Lady Gorges obtained a grant of the wreck of one of the Spanish ships, which happened to contain a quantity of bullion, and on the proceeds of this the building was resumed, and very probably a fresh design was obtained on a more extravagant scale. The plan and elevation of Longford Castle in the Soane Collection do not tally with the present building. Either they were never carried out as shown in the drawings, or they have been altered in one of the many modifications of the building which have since been made, but in the original elevation the discrepancy between the design of the angle towers and the façade between is quite as glaring as in the building itself, and an examination of the building and comparison with these drawings leads one to the conjecture that John Thorpe, or at least an English designer, did actually design the ground plan, and that the towers and possibly the greater part of the fabric, were executed from this design, but that he had nothing to do with this entrance façade, which is later in date, and the design for which may have been made in Germany, or by one of the Germans then residing in England. On this view of it, the plan and elevation in the Soane Museum must be taken not as the designs for a new building, but as surveyors' drawings made after the building was completed.

Burghley House has already been referred to. No mention of John Thorpe occurs in any of the documents relating to this house, whereas Germans are mentioned in connection with the building, and I think their influence is distinctly indicated by the curious clock tower in the courtyard, with its unusual and quite foreign feature of a high square steeple above the clock. Burghley also shares with Kirby the absurdity of using the Doric order to form chimney-stacks, an affectation characteristic of the later work of the sixteenth century. If Thorpe was employed on this building, it could only have been in a subordinate capacity and not as architect.

Audley End was built for Thomas, 1st Earl of Suffolk. It was begun in 1603 and completed in 1616, and was one of the largest buildings of the kind in England. It is said to have cost £190,000 (in

50 RENAISSANCE ARCHITECTURE IN ENGLAND

the money of the time), mainly procured from Spanish bribes, and to have been built on a model obtained in Italy. As against this latter story we have the evidence of all the detail, which is obviously German where it is not English, and the evidence of the plan not only as it is, but as it was before two-thirds of it were pulled down, when it comprised three courts, the forecourt, the quadrangular court, and the three-sided court to the gardens. Moreover, it is doubtful if an Italian design would have included the great gallery, 226 feet long by 32 wide, and 24 high, which ran along the outer court. The house as it was before the destruction of the two courts (either in 1700, under Vanbrugh, or in 1749) is shown in the rare view by Winstanley. The details of the two entrance porches, and of the screen in the hall, are clumsy and vulgar, and resemble the designs given in De Vriese's pattern book. If Thorpe had anything to do with the design of this house, it is another piece of evidence against his having been the architect of Sir Thomas Tresham's buildings.

The collection also contains a plan and part elevation of Wollaton. This, however, was probably designed by Smithson. Thorpe seems to have spent some time in Paris about 1600. One of the drawings is inscribed " Queene mother's house, Faber St. Jarmin alla Parie, altered per J. Thorpe ;" and there is also a drawing of Monsieur Jammet's house in Paris. Thorpe's employment as surveyor at Ampthill old house, which belonged to the Crown, may have led to this work in Paris. The only other drawing which can be assigned to Thorpe with certainty is a plan drawn in different inks, with title " Sir Walter Coap at Kensington, perfected by me, J. T.," and it is probable that Thorpe had to do with the original design of Holland House, as built in 1606 ; but even here the phrase, "perfected by me," leaves it uncertain what part he actually took in planning the house as a whole. In the Cottonian MSS. (August 1. 1. 75.) there is a survey of Theobald's Park, drawn on vellum and tinted, said to have been made by Thorpe in 1611. The only other references as yet ascertained in regard to this obscure draughtsman are to be found in a MS. note by the late Mr. Wyatt Papworth appended to the Soane Collection. Mr. Papworth found mention of a plan of the Palace of Eltham made by Thorpe in 1590 (Calendar of State Papers, No. 78, p. 706), again in 1609 (Calendar of State Papers, No. 83, p. 515), where he is named as the King's Commissioner for surveying the Duchess of Suffolk's land, and, in 1611, of a warrant for the payment of £52 3s. to Thorpe, for certain repairs to the fencing of Richmond Park, which had been carried away

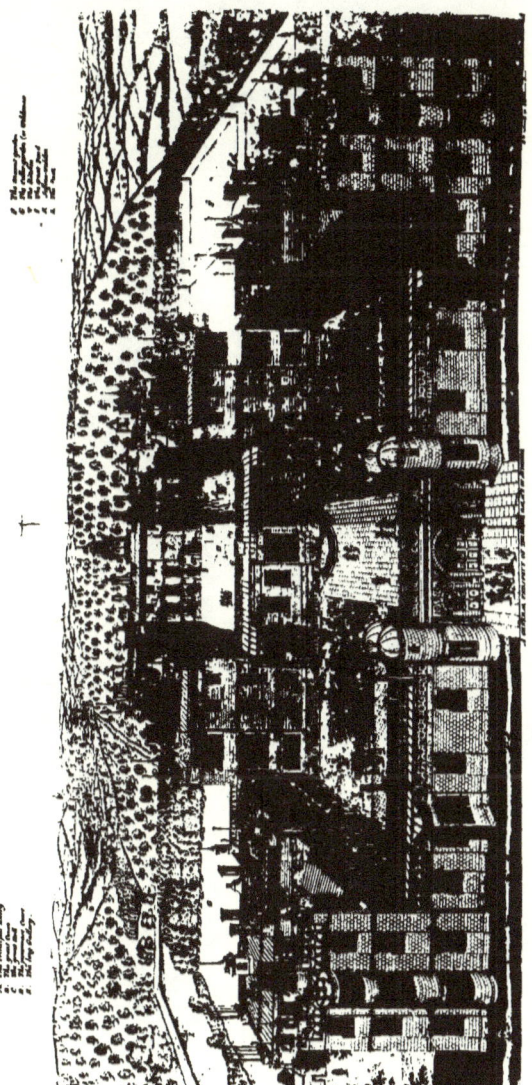

THE ENGLISH BUILDERS

by the flood. Cunningham discovered an important reference to Thorpe in Peacham's "Gentleman's Exercise," 1612. In describing a certain coat-of-arms, Peacham says, "it is now born by Master John Thorpe of the parish Saint Martins in the Fields, my especiall friend and excellent geometrician and surveior, whom the rather I remember, because he is not only learned and ingenious him selfe, but a furtherer and favourer of all excellency whatsoever, of whom our age findeth too few, and lastly the aforenamed master John Thorpe his sonne, to whom I can in words never be sufficientiy thankfull." Cunningham also mentions another unimportant reference to Thorpe. No other mention of him is known, and the net result of our examination is that he remains an almost unknown man. Indeed, it is not even certain that he was an architect at all. It is probable that most of his authentic drawings were made after the buildings were completed, instead of before, and that they are in the nature of surveys rather than working drawings, and if this was so, Thorpe would have to be classified with Norden rather than with Smithson. There is little doubt that the Soane volume is a collection of miscellaneous drawings by many different hands, such as Smithson for Wollaton, Bernard Janssen for Audley End, and other men connected with the buildings of this time, and it by no means follows that such drawings as that of Longford Castle were made by Thorpe. This drawing may have been made by the man who, on the theory given above, designed the façade in the centre. It is not likely that the designer of the angle towers would have drawn them with the string courses in the wrong place. The only drawings which can certainly be set down to Thorpe are the ones which he signed or initialled. Besides these, there are the drawings which may probably be his, such as Kirby, and from these it would appear that if Thorpe was a designer, he adhered to the English tradition of planning strictly, as, for instance, in the arrangement of courts, in the E-shaped plans, and in the relative position of hall and offices, and, with the exception of certain aberrations due to German influence, that he was fairly faithful to the idea of the English gabled house, with its plain sobriety of detail. North Mymms in Hertfordshire, though it is not known to have been designed by Thorpe, represents this phase of English architecture pretty closely, and Thorpe himself, assuming him to have been the architect of the older parts of Kirby and Holland House, may be taken as a fair instance of the class of men who worked in England, during the transition stage from the builder-designer of mediæval days to the academic architect of the following century. He

52 RENAISSANCE ARCHITECTURE IN ENGLAND

does not appear to have travelled abroad, with the exception of one visit to France, and his acquaintance with the Renaissance details of other countries was uncertain and probably derived mainly from pattern books. He seems, indeed, to have seen these details through mediæval spectacles,[1] yet he used them with much adventurousness, and the result was a manner of design of a somewhat informal character, which, though picturesque and lovable in a way, missed the essential quality of architecture—the distinction of severe restraint and single-minded purpose.

Smithson has already been referred to as the architect of Wollaton in Nottinghamshire.[2] His fame rests chiefly on the inscription in Wollaton Church to ." Mr. Robert Smithson, gent., architect and surveyor unto the most worthy house of Wollaton with divers others of great account" (ob. 1614). Wollaton in Nottinghamshire was begun in 1580 for Sir Francis Willoughby, Camden says, "at great expense, for a foolish display of his wealth," and this criticism is justified by the building, which is one of the very ugliest and clumsiest of those erected in England during the reign of Elizabeth. The front is overloaded with stale repetitions of the orders, and the great block of the hall which rises above the rest of the front overpowers the façade, and its general topheaviness is emphasized and insisted on by pepper-box turrets at the angles. The chimney-stacks, with their pediments on columns, are even worse than those of Audley End and Burghley. Smithson may have been an ingenious man and a skilful mason, but as a designer he was heavy handed, and seems to have had an instinctive leaning to ugliness and vulgar ornament. The idea of placing the hall in the centre of the house, and lighting it by windows above the adjacent roofs, shows a certain originality, but the effect is not satisfactory, inside

---

[1] It is curious that on the sheet of the five orders in the Soane Collection the titles "Corinthia," "Ionica," and "Composita" are written in black letter type, while "Tuscana" and "Dorica" are in ordinary Roman type.

[2] Mr. Gotch (vol. ii., p. 59-63) assigns this design to Thorpe on the strength of the plan and elevation contained in the Soane Collection. These, however, are not signed, and though generally they resemble the actual building, Mr. Gotch admits the existence of "considerable discrepancies" between them. The account of Cassandra Willoughby, Duchess of Chandos (1702), is that Sir Francis Willoughby sent for the master workmen that built the house out of Italy. There are thus three accounts of the designers. Smithson's name occurs in the building accounts as a mason, and as the work at Wollaton is very different in feeling from Thorpe's work, in so far as the latter can be identified, it seems probable that not Thorpe, but Smithson, was actually the designer of the house, and that, as in the case of Arnold at Wadham, and Grumbold at Clare, he not only supplied the designs, but worked himself on the building.

THE JERUSALEM-WALK-VALE, BERKSHIRE.

or out. Smithson's name occurs in the building accounts of Longleat as "Free master mason" of the works,[1] and there is indeed some resemblance in the use of orders above orders in both houses, which shows at least a common influence. It is probable that Smithson applied to Wollaton the lesson in ornament that he had learnt at Longleat, and by no means improved on the original. The pilaster treatment at Wollaton imitates that at Longleat, but at Wollaton an irrevelant band is introduced above the middle of the pilaster, and the sunk roundels for bust, which are comparatively plain at Longleat, are enriched at Wollaton with some florid cartouches. The designer of Longleat followed Italian models, and Smithson thought to improve on this by the later light of German ornament. But the natural man very soon shows himself in architecture, and the tradition of masonry on which Smithson must have been trained is evident in the outline of the hall block, and his constant tendency to slip back into Gothic terms of expression, as, for instance, in the tracery of the hall windows. There is a contemporary drawing of Wollaton in the Soane Collection.

Huntingdon Smithson, who died November 27th, 1648, and was buried in Bolsover Church, was probably a son of Robert; his epitaph calls him "gentleman." Huntingdon Smithson designed the "new house" at Bolsover, that is, the existing square castle and courtyard begun in 1613, and possibly the long gallery block,[2] begun in 1629-1630, along the brow of the hill which connects the castle with the riding-school. The riding-school is later, and is evidently by another hand. Bolsover Castle has many points of interest in regard to the development of English architecture.[3] Its details show a singular mixture of Gothic tradition, of classical ideas inspired by German examples, and of the individuality of Huntingdon Smithson himself, who, though evidently of a thoughtful and inquiring turn, was not able enough to fuse these three into a consistent and complete architectural design. The three elements lie side by side in unassimilated confusion. The pillar room, for instance, has a vaulted stone ceiling, the construction of which is Gothic in principle, and the section of the groining ribs is such

---

[1] "History of Longleat," by Canon Jackson. Devizes, 1868.

[2] Mr. Gotch thinks it doubtful whether these buildings were by the same man. There is, however, no very great difference of manner between the gallery and the castle, in spite of the variations of detail. The clumsiness of design referred to in Robert Smithson's work reappears in both these buildings by Huntingdon, whereas the riding-school, which is finely designed, suggests an altogether different influence.

[3] The peculiarities of its plan will be referred to in the next chapter.

as is found in late fifteenth century work. The pendants, corbels, and capitals to the pillars are of the ordinary German pattern book type, and the disproportion of scale and the combination of heaviness in design, with meagreness and tenuity in detail, are the personal failures of the architect himself. These faults reappear, though in a less degree, in the gallery block. Here, too, there is an evident effort after size, but the effect is only dullness, due to the absence of a fine architectural sense in the designer, and to his inability to realize that size in itself is nothing, proportion everything. The actual construction of the keep is by no means good ; a piece of masonry corbelled out next the right hand corner of the court has given way, and never could have stood for long, a defect in knowledge of building, by no means compensated for by a somewhat extensive acquaintance with German methods of ornamentation.

The work of both the Smithsons shows knowledge of architectural detail and a good deal of ingenuity. Where they failed was in attempting ambitious architecture, and it is in this regard that they, and such men as Thorpe and the builder-designers of the time, fall so immmeasurably below their great successor. The builders of such delightful houses as Littlecote, or Sydenham, or Ragdale old hall, were content with the slightest ornamentation ; they adhered to the local tradition of building as handed down from father to son ; their buildings entirely answered the purpose for which they were built, and hence they possess a quiet reasonable beauty, due to the well-considered use of materials, and the evident absence of any desire to amaze by technical dexterity. These buildings were the result of the work of many generations of simple-minded men, and as such they have the characteristic less of a single personality, than of a collective body endowed with the accumulated results of years of labour along familiar paths. As a result, we find in them the happy unconsciousness, the excellent fitness of buildings which have grown to their purpose, instead of the forced effort of men working with full consciousness on the one hand and inadequate capacity on the other. It is on this ground—on the ground of their reasonableness and distinct beauty of a humble order—that such buildings are more valuable, and more suggestive of the possible lines of development in architecture, than such essentially unartistic buildings as Wollaton or Audley End.

A few other names besides those of Thorpe and the Smithsons have reached us. Thomas Holt was a carpenter, and a native of York, and is believed to have come to Oxford about 1600, when Sir Thomas Bodley was beginning his new schools. He seems to have passed the

THE TOWER OF THE SCHOOLS, OXFORD.

56 RENAISSANCE ARCHITECTURE IN ENGLAND

remainder of his life at Oxford, where he died, September 9th, 1624, and was buried in Holywell Churchyard. His epitaph, which has since disappeared, is given in Sir John Peshall's edition of Wood's "Antiquities of Oxford."[1] It is on the strength of this epitaph that Holt has been credited with the design of the schools, that is to say, of Bodley's work there, and more particularly of the great tower. This remarkable composition shows, on the west side, the five orders ranged one above the other, without the slightest regard to the elevations on either side, which consist of a plain three-storey building with a moulded plinth, and a single string course below the battlements of the parapet. On the third storey of the tower was a seated figure of James I. under a canopy, supported by figures of Fame and the University kneeling.[2] The Bodleian as a whole was not completed till 1636, but this tower was finished earlier. Anthony Wood calls it an "eminent and stately tower," and it has a certain picturesque richness, though it can hardly be considered as serious architecture. The orders may perhaps be justified as buttresses, but they are little adapted for the purpose, and might probably be shorn off from top to bottom without affecting the fabric; and the designer certainly does not get over the difficulty inherent in this kind of composition, for when he got to the top of his Composite order there was nothing more for all this elaborate pile of columns to do, and they terminate tamely in a feeble little pediment. Moreover, the excessive and nearly equal elaboration of the four top orders defeats its own end, for the effect is not that of a building sumptuously ornamented,

---

[1] The epitaph is as follows:
"Thos. Holt. Ebor. Scholarum Public. Architecti
obt. Sept. 9. 1624.
"Mirare felix umbra felices domos,
Et mira tandem cernis æterni fabri
Laqueata tecta, ubi non recisas Africa
Magno paratas suspicis sumptu trabes,
Ebore lacunar nec superbit indico—
Hic videmus omnia.
Olim arte avita regiis Palatiis
Vestræ hæc (beate pulvis) aptarunt manus,
Sed tecta tantæ gloriæ quæ jam colis,
Cum struere tua diffideret mortalitas
Recte excolebas semper ad amussim omnia,
Erasque colere ut posse fortunæ fata." (*sic*.)
Wood's MS. must have been imperfect, for the last line is unintelligible.

[2] Anthony Wood states that these figures were at first double gilt, but that when King James came over from Woodstock to inspect the schools he declared that the glare dazzled his eyes, and ordered the sculpture to be painted white.

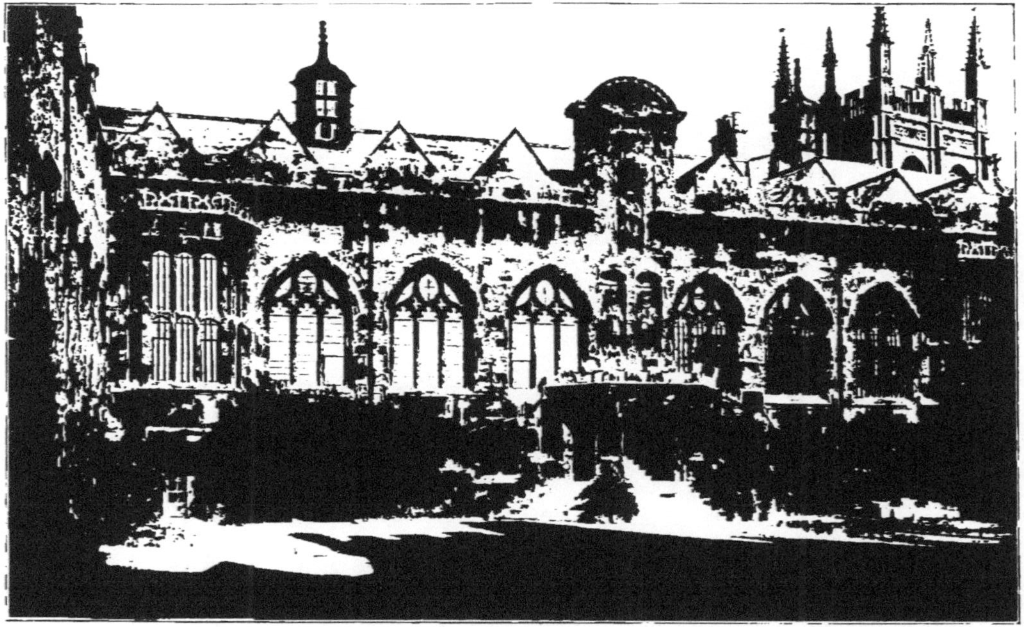

Wilson, Aberdeen, Photo. *Face p. 50.*

ORIEL COLLEGE, OXFORD.

but of a building covered with a confusion of sumptuous ornament. The quatrefoil tracery which appears in the parapet, in combination with strap-work, and the crocketed finials, show how fictitious was this assumption of classical architecture. The latter was not yet grasped as a broad principle of design, but its detail was arbitrarily adopted as a new fashion in ornament.

The tower of the schools has been referred to on the assumption that Holt was the architect; but the whole story of Holt's connection with the schools rests entirely on the words of the epitaph, and is otherwise doubtful. It is at least remarkable that in the whole of Bodley's correspondence with Dr. James, his first librarian, a correspondence relating entirely to the business of the library, and written while the buildings were in progress, there is no mention of Holt at all. Yet Holt survived Bodley by twelve years, and if connected with the Bodleian building at all, Holt must have been employed by the university to carry on Bodley's work. The latter had already employed Yorkshire masons for his building, John Acroyde, and J. and Michael Bentley whose names appear in the Oxford register of deaths in 1613, 1615, and 1618 respectively, and the business details of the building, including such matters as the provision of wainscot oak for the library fittings, were directed by Bodley himself, though the design was left to the workmen. Thus in Letter 77 he writes: "In the fashion of the antikes and pendents, I refer myself wholly to the workmen, together with yourself, Mr. Gent, Mr. Brent, and Mr. Principal (Hawley) having herewith returned your patterns again, which I can like of well enough if they be to your liking." The contracts were made by Bodley through his workmen; thus he writes: "If Bal— College lead be very good, and a reasonable peniworth to be had, I pray you speak to Jo. Acroyde to bargain for it." No reference is made to any system of architect's certificates, and it appears that Bodley kept the entire finance of the business in his own hands. Thus, when the work got behindhand, Bodley would have none of the workmen's "lewd excuses," and writes in Letter 138, "I pray God Jo. Bentley keep touch in amending the building, whereof I stand the more in doubt for that I am informed he maketh that which was naught a great deal worse with his very unrightly daubing, which I trust Mr. Brent or Mr. Gent will cause him to forbear or else I will forbear to him his wages." The inference suggested by these letters is (1) that Bodley had nothing to do with the design of the building, (2) that Holt had nothing to do with it in Bodley's lifetime, (3) that during the latter's lifetime the only design

58 RENAISSANCE ARCHITECTURE IN ENGLAND

there was of the building was given by the masons, Acroyde and the Bentleys, who submitted to Bodley patterns, or rough models, of what they proposed to do. The whole character of the work suggests a mason's idea of architecture, rather than the work of a trained designer. John Acroyde also contracted for the new stonework in the south quadrangle at Merton, in 1608, for £570. Here, as at the schools, he probably supplied the designs as well, and Holt made a separate contract on his own behalf for the woodwork, for which he was paid £430 and the expense of his journey.

To Holt is also attributed the design of buildings at Exeter, including probably the old chapel,[1] Oriel, and Jesus, and the charming library of Merton. All this work was done at about the same time. He has also been credited with the design of Wadham. The façade opposite the entrance to the quadrangle at Wadham resembles the tower of the schools in the use of the orders above orders. Wadham, however, was designed before the schools, and Mr. Jackson has shown conclusively[2] that though Holt was employed at Wadham, he was only employed as a carpenter, *faber lignarius*, on the roofs of the hall and library, and did not appear on the scene at all till three sides of the quadrangle were practically finished. Probably all that Holt did at Oxford was to contract for the design and execution of· the woodwork in the buildings mentioned above; and his work, to judge by the panelling of Merton Library, and the woodwork of the old Exeter Chapel, was fair Jacobean, reasonable in design and excellent in workmanship.

Ralph Simons was employed at Cambridge about the same time as Holt at Oxford. Simons was a native of Berkhampstead in Hertfordshire. At Emmanuel he adopted the remains of the Dominican Convent and built the Founders' Range. (The charter of foundation is dated 1593.) At Sidney-Sussex, he built the three-sided court, forming the original building. At Trinity he was employed by Dr. Nevill in the

---

[1] The old chapel was built by the rector of the college early in the seventeenth century. It was destroyed to make way for the present chapel designed by Sir Gilbert Scott. The chapel was full of fine oak panelling, and in excellent preservation; but the rector and fellows were informed at the time that the fabric was unsafe. When, however, its destruction was begun, the walls were found to be so solidly constructed that they had to be blown up with gunpowder.

[2] Mr. Jackson, in his history of Wadham College, has shown that the real designer of Wadham College was a certain William Arnold, a Freemason, who worked on the buildings, and carried out the work by verbal instructions to his men, rather than by any drawings to scale.

GATEWAY AT COBHAM COLLEGE.

scheme of alterations, begun in 1593 and carried on till 1615, which resulted in the great court and the dining-hall. Simons gave the design for the latter in 1604, but does not appear to have been employed in carrying it out. The inscription on his picture in Emmanuel College calls him "*architectus sua ætate peritissimus, qui (præter plurima ædificia ab eo præclare facta) duo collegia, Emmanuelis hoc, Sidneii illud Extruxit integre, magnum etiam partem Trinitatis reconcinnavit amplissime.*"

Emmanuel was finished by Sir Walter Mildmay in 1584. Sidney Sussex, by Frances, Countess of Sussex, in 1588. It is probable that in every case Simons supplied the design besides contracting for the work; and in the case of St. John's, Cambridge, the original drawings, consisting of three "plotts" (plans) and three "uprights" (elevations), signed "Raf. Simons" and "Gilbart Wigge," still exist in the college library. The building at St. John's consisted of a court 137 ft. by 165 ft., but it was an unfortunate affair for both of them. Simons lost a hand on the works, and was involved in a lawsuit about the winding up of the accounts, which lawsuit eventually landed Wigge in prison in 1605. Simons appears to have left Cambridge, and is not heard of after this date. Wigge, who was released from prison on petition and humble amends to the college, afterwards built a range of buildings in Walnut Tree Court, at Queen's College, 1616-19. Both men worked in a plain unambitious manner, with little affectation of Renaissance detail.

The designs of buildings seem to have been supplied indifferently by carpenters, masons, or bricklayers. Simons, Acroyde, and Arnold were masons; Westley, of Cambridge, died 1656, who built part of Clare and the new buildings of Emmanuel at Cambridge, in 1634, was a bricklayer; Holt was a carpenter; and about the time of Holt's death, a young Herefordshire carpenter was already making his reputation in the west country. The development of building crafts naturally followed the staple building material of the district. Yorkshire was a stone country and consequently abounds in characteristic masonry, whereas Lancashire, Cheshire, Shropshire, and Herefordshire, were at one time thickly wooded, and accordingly developed a half timber style with well marked peculiarities. John Abel was a Herefordshire man, born in 1597. So far as his buildings can be identified he worked entirely in half timber, and is said to have designed and built the market-halls of Hereford, Leominster, Kington, Brecon, and Weobley. The market-hall at Weobley was pulled down about forty-five years ago and sold as old materials. It is described as having been built in

Frith & Co., Photo. ST. JOHN'S COLLEGE, CAMBRIDGE. Face p. 60.

half timber, with a large upper hall carried on wooden pillars, richly carved. The ground floor was open, and it no doubt followed the

PORCH AT WEOBLEY IN HEREFORDSHIRE.

regular treatment of west country market-halls. The building stood at the head of the triangular square in the centre of the village, but not a vestige of it remains except the weather-cock on the turned oak

62 RENAISSANCE ARCHITECTURE IN ENGLAND

baluster, which was transferred to the half timber house close by. The wooden porch at Weobley, which closely resembles the detail at Abbey Dore, was probably by Abel. The Shire Hall at Hereford was destroyed about thirty-five years ago. Duncombe, writing in 1804, says: "The old Shire Hall of Hereford was constructed mainly of wood, and rests on three ranges of pillars, having nine pillars in each range; the length is 84 feet, the breadth 34; at present it consists of one floor only. . . . In its original state there was a second floor divided into apartments for the accommodation of the fourteen trading

CARVING IN BUTCHER'S ROW, HEREFORD.

companies of the city. . . . The Shire Hall was built in the latter part of the reign of James I. by John Abel." After the second floor was taken down, the first floor was covered in with a three-gabled roof, and it is so shown in old drawings. There are now no remains of it whatever. In fact the only half timber building now standing in Hereford is the old house which once formed part of Butcher's Row, built in 1621, which is not unlike Abel's work. The old hall at Leominster has fared rather better. It was built in 1633, and was pulled down in the present century, but rebuilt as "The Grange," and is now inhabited as a private house. Unfortunately, the intercolumniations on the ground floor have been filled in with windows, which make it impossible to form any adequate opinion of the value of the original design. The details are not without a certain ingenious fancy, but they are very coarse in execution and show a merely rudimentary acquaintance with the models they professed to imitate.[1]

THE GRANGE, LEOMINSTER

In 1634, John, Viscount Scudamore, having some misgivings as to his right to the tithes of his estate, and acting under the influence of Laud, obtained a special licence to restore the Church of Abbey Dore, and employed the famous west country carpenter to carry out the work. No architect appears in the transaction at all.[2] Scudamore supplied the wood, Abel the design and labour. About £1,000 (money of the time) was spent on the work, which included a new roof with oak

---

[1] A more complete account of this building will be found in the Portfolio for 1888. The accounts and contract for this work have been discovered by Mr. Blashill.

rafters and brackets, a new gallery, seats, reading desk, and pulpit, some painted glass, and the great oak screen under the chancel arch. The latter is in five bays, divided by columns with rough Ionic capitals, carrying a frieze with a curious Latin inscription: "Vive Deo gratus, toti mundo tumulatus, crimine mundatus, semper transire paratus." This inscription also occurs at Leominster. Above the frieze are the royal arms, with two small coats-of-arms on either side, set in open strapwork and divided by pierced obelisks. The general design of the screen is bold and effective, and the scale is well preserved throughout, but the workmanship is exceedingly rough. The marks of the axe and the chisel are everywhere apparent; even the carpenters' numbers scratched on the different pieces of wood were never removed, and the columns and pedestals are made out of one solid baulk of oak from top to bottom.

Abel was employed once more by Scudamore, when the Civil Wars had put a stop to building. In 1645 Hereford was besieged by the Scotch army, and Abel was employed to keep their mills in order. Scudamore, who was governor of the town, writes of him to Lord Digby as an expert carpenter, and "the only man in all the county to make mills." He died in 1694, at the age of ninety-seven, and was buried at Sarnesfield in Herefordshire. Abel's buildings, in their rude vigour of design and coarseness of execution, closely resemble the half timber work of Lancashire and Cheshire to the north, and of Somerset and Devon to the south. Nearly all this west country work is crude as compared with the half timber work found in the east of England, in the home counties, and particularly in the Weald of Kent; and the superior refinement of the latter, a superiority found also in brick and stone buildings, is probably due to the presence of Flemings, who taught the English builders some of their own unexampled skill in craftsmanship. We have already seen how local was the influence of the Italian artists introduced by Henry VIII., and it is probable that the immaturity of west country work is due to the absence of any such influence, and to the comparative inaccessibility of this part of England.

Work such as Abel's is interesting as showing the result of the new movement in out-of-the-way districts. Abel, it is clear, had received no training in architectural design. The details of his work abound in blunders of scholarship and errors of taste. His acquaintance with Renaissance detail appears to have been entirely at second-hand, and derived from those insidious pattern books to which I have already referred. These pattern books never gave working drawings

THE ENGLISH BUILDERS 65

of details, and very seldom any intelligible scale. The country carpenter was therefore left to his own devices, and the results of his mother wit and the atrocious models given in his pattern books were something

THE SCHOOL AND ALMSHOUSE, CORSHAM.

altogether childish. On the other hand, the actual construction is good, the immediate result of local tradition. It is honest and straightforward, and essentially wood construction, not a construction borrowed from stone or metal. We thus have the two streams meeting, that of the

K

building tradition of the country side, and that of the new fashion of ornamentation, filtered through hardly intelligible pattern books ; the two run side by side at present, not yet fused into a complete and reasonable method of design. So far, what is good in this Herefordshire carpenter's architecture was the result of the older Gothic tradition. What is bad, and the ornament as a rule is wholly bad, was the result of fashion ill-understood. It by no means follows, however, that anything more could have come of the old tradition by itself. The various attempts made in the seventeenth and eighteenth centuries to rehabilitate Gothic design were failures, and the facts of history show that the spirit which had hitherto expressed itself in Gothic art had exhausted the range of its language and had to find vent in some new idiom of architecture. For it seems sounder, both on historical and philosophical grounds, to consider the actual details of the architecture of any given period as so much language, capable of expansion or modification amounting almost to a total change of expression; and it by no means follows that, because a fashion of language can be superseded, the spirit which once expressed itself through that language is dead. Gothic architecture, as a language, was dead, but the keen artistic spirit which had once expressed itself in mediæval architecture, and inspired its admirable craftsmanship, was as vital and active as ever, only it was finding its course in new channels, and seeking fresh methods of expression for its ever-varying thought. This motive power, this creative and informing spirit, was neither Gothic nor Renaissance, but simply the instinct of the nation and the race, and as such we shall find it re-asserting itself with a vigour as characteristic, as entirely national, as any that it had ever displayed in mediæval times. Within a hundred years from the date of the screen of Abbey Dore we shall find the tradition of sound and skilful handiwork re-established in England, and country workmen capable of executing woodwork, masonry, and brickwork of delicate refinement and unsurpassable workmanship; we shall find in work of the seventeenth and eighteenth centuries the independence of thought, the sober taste and kindliness of manner which has throughout stamped our architecture, whether mediæval or Renaissance, with a character unmistakably English.

CHAPTER IV.

SIXTEENTH CENTURY HOUSE PLANNING AND ARCHITECTURAL TREATISES.

ABEL was not the last of the builder-designers, or master builders, as they might fairly be called. John Westley and Thomas and Robert Grumbold carried on the tradition at Cambridge throughout the seventeenth century, but meanwhile a race of architects had sprung up, perhaps of less practical knowledge of building materials, but of wider scholarship and greater attainment as designers; and before discussing these forerunners of the modern architect with his complete professional equipment, it will be desirable to consider the state of English architecture before this new era was started by Inigo Jones.

Throughout the sixteenth century rapid strides were taken towards the perfecting of house planning.[1] Few important churches were built in that century, and no attempt was made to depart from the traditional methods in this regard, but the whole ingenuity of the builders of the sixteenth century seems to have been concentrated on the house. Owing to the decay of feudal power, and to the proportionate increase in the strength of the monarchy, the necessity for strongly fortified houses had ceased to exist by the beginning of the sixteenth century, and we find two main types of house in common use. On the one hand, for larger houses, there was the house built round one or more courts, and on the other, what we may, for convenience, call the yeoman's house, consisting of a hall in the centre, with kitchen and offices at one end and a solar and living rooms at the other. This second and smaller type of house was the direct survival of the smaller mediæval dwelling-house. It was altered and adapted in many ways, but throughout the sixteenth century it continued to be the typical form for small and moderate sized houses, and can easily be

---

[1] The plans given in this chapter, with the exception of the plans of the fishing house at Meare and the garden house at Amesbury, have been traced from the originals in the Soane Museum. They have been hatched to make them clearer, and to avoid confusion, owing to the considerable reduction necessary, the original writing has been replaced by lettering and printed descriptions of the rooms.

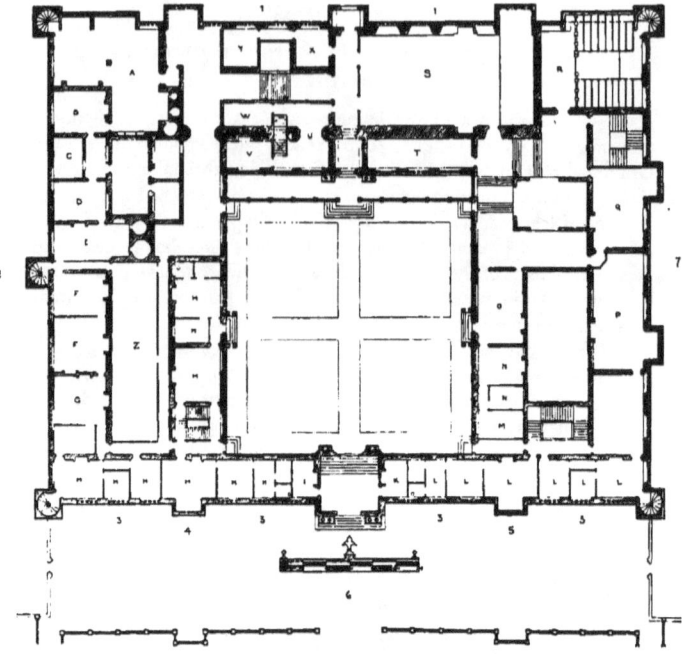

PLAN OF BUCKHURST HOUSE IN SUSSEX. (SOANE COLLECTION.)

- A. Kytchen.
- B. Dry larder above wett under.
- C. Scullery.
- D. Bolting.
- E. Bakehouse.
- F F. Lodgings heare.
- G. Offices.
- H H H. A noblemans lodging.
- H H H. A noblemans lodging.
- H H H. A noblemans lodging.
- I. Porters.
- K. Lodg.
- L L L. A noblemans lodging.
- L L L. A noblemans lodging.
- M. Servants lodging.
- N N. A noblemans lodging.
- O. His ante camera.
- P. Parlour great chamber over.
- Q. Wayters chamber.
- R. This chapell is below. [*Note.* The part figured R is probably the gallery, the chapel floor for the servants being below.]
- S. Hall.
- T. Wine cellar underneath terrace above throughout.
- U. Buttry.
- V. Breakfast room.
- W. Butlers lodging.
- X. Pantry.
- Y. Pantlers lodging.
- Z. A tennis court 65 fo. long.
- 1 1. The garden and orchard syde.
- 2. Woodyard heare, bakehouse, brewhouse, &c.
- 3 3 3 3. The gallery over these lodgings.
- 4. For my ladys syde.
- 5. For my lords syde.
- 6. Terrace heare.
- 7. Garden house.

SIXTEENTH CENTURY HOUSE PLANNING 69

traced in their various modifications. From these two sources the characteristic features of the Elizabethan house were developed by a double process, that is to say, the plans of the larger houses resulted from the gradual modifications of the earlier house with inclosed courts, and the plans of the smaller houses from the natural extension of what has been called above the yeoman's house.

Of the courtyard house, which speedily developed into the simple quadrangular house, the earlier part of Haddon Hall, or South Wingfield Manor House, built in the reign of Henry VI. by Ralph, Lord Cromwell, are good examples. These houses must be taken as the immediate precursors of the Tudor house in historical development. They were built with a view to defence, yet with some regard to comfort of living. Instead of the grim impassable keep, there were courtyards, with solid walls, it is true, on the outer side, but with sufficient space within the court to admit of some reasonable amount of light and air to the rooms of the surrounding buildings. The necessity of a symmetrical court was as yet unthought of. The inclosing buildings followed the conditions of the site, with the result that the court was seldom exactly rectangular, and as the idea of defence was still urgent enough to induce the builder to place his house on a rock, differences of level and all kinds of irregular angles were accepted with indifference. But under the long "King's Peace" of Henry VIII. this necessity of treating the house as a fortress disappeared, and when houses were placed on level sites and on low-lying ground, there was no occasion for any awkward angles, and the rectangular court was adopted as a matter of course. Layer Marney and Sutton Place (1521-1527) are good early instances of the quadrangular arrangement.[1] Generally speaking, the quadrangular house of the early part of the sixteenth century consisted of an inclosed court with an entrance under a tall gatehouse, rising higher than the adjacent buildings, as at Hampton Court and Nonesuch. To one side, or on the side opposite the gatehouse, were the hall and offices, with living and sleeping rooms round the remaining sides, which rooms, except when arranged *en suite*, could only be entered from the court.[2]

---

[1] The court at Sutton was originally quadrangular, measuring internally 81 ft. 3 in. by 81 ft. 3 in. It was entered by a gateway on the north side under a tower flanked by hexagonal turrets. This tower is said by Mr. Harrison ("Annals of an old Manor House," Macmillan, 1893) to have been about 70 ft. high. It was standing in 1750, but has since been destroyed.

[2] The instances given above were, however, anticipated in a certain sense by Wykeham at Oxford more than a hundred years before. The earliest example of a quadrangular plan, designed without any idea of defence, is Wykeham's buildings at New College, Oxford, 1379-1393, a precedent which was followed at Lincoln, 1456-1475, St. John's, 1436,

70 RENAISSANCE ARCHITECTURE IN ENGLAND

Out of this quadrangular plan speedily grew the various types of the larger Elizabethan house. In these houses the quadrangular plan with one or more courts was adhered to through the sixteenth century, as at Kirby, Burghley, and Audley End. The plan of Buckhurst in Kent (since destroyed), and which is preserved in the Soane Museum, is a characteristic example of the arrangements of a great nobleman's house in the middle of the sixteenth century. Buckhurst was completed about 1568. The plan, as shown in the drawing in the Soane Collection, was rectangular, about 270 ft. in front by 214 ft. at the sides. The entrance was under a projecting gateway, with my lord's lodgings on the right and my lady's on the left, and opened on to a principal court about 105 ft. by 105 ft., with a raised terrace and balustrade on the opposite side, and entrance to a lobby communicating with the screens and the great hall, about 70 ft. by 38 ft., with the kitchen and multifarious offices to the left of the screens, and the chapel beyond the upper end of the hall. On either side of the main courtyard were ranges of buildings occupied by noblemen's lodgings; to the right was a small internal court, 55 ft. by 28 ft., with parlour and other rooms on the outer side. To the left of the court, beyond the noblemen's lodgings, a tennis court, 65 ft. by 25 ft., occupied the whole of the internal court, and beyond this, on the outer side, were offices and lodgings. Newel staircases, at each of the four external angles, communicated with the upper floor. An additional newel staircase in the centre of the left hand façade, and four internal staircases, were provided, at least two of the latter appearing to be grand staircases. A corridor led past the hall to a broad passage-way and flight of stairs 15 ft. wide, going across to

All Souls', 1437-1442, Magdalen, 1473-1479, and in the following century by Wolsey in his great quadrangle at Christchurch. These buildings, however, were based on the idea of providing distinct sets of tenements, attached, but each provided with its own separate access, a theory of collegiate building which was tenaciously adhered to at both universities. As such they are distinct from conventual houses of the same date, which provided series of cells, communicating with a common corridor, and from domestic buildings. Gradually, however, the collegiate buildings approached the domestic type; towards the end of the sixteenth century the college and the country house were planned on very much the same lines, and there can be little doubt that, as Professor Willis maintained, the quadrangular collegiate plan was directly connected with that of the contemporary manor house. The ground plan of Queen's College, Cambridge (1448), nearly resembles that of Haddon Hall, and the plan of Sidney-Sussex (1596-1598), with its hall and screens, offices and kitchens occupying the centre, and sets of rooms in the wings, is hardly to be distinguished from that of an ordinary Elizabethan manor house. Professor Willis has been so far followed that in this general survey of sixteenth century domestic architecture colleges are classified with the larger country houses of the period.

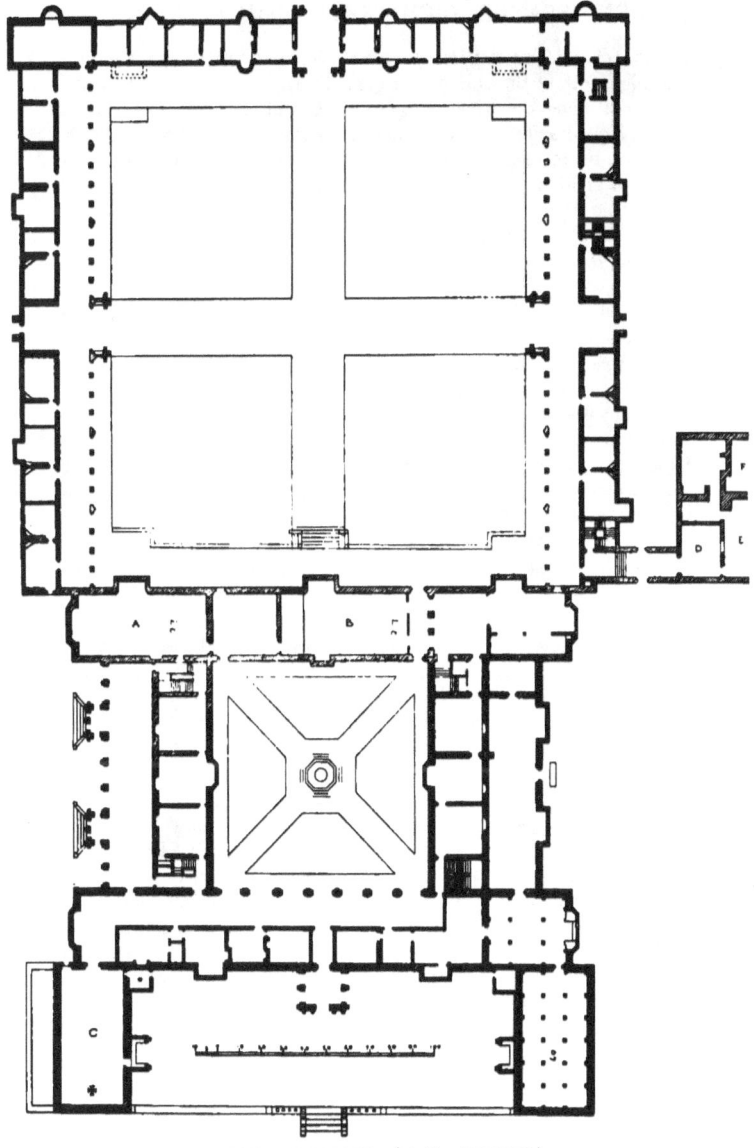

AUDLEY END IN ESSEX. (SOANE COLLECTION.)
A. Parlour 57 feet long.   C. Chaple.   E. Kytchen 52 feet long.
B. Hall.   D. Survery.   F. Dry larder.

the chapel and grand staircase, and above this corridor was a terrace the full length of the side of the great court. A broad terrace, 55 ft. wide, ran along the whole length of the main façade. For smaller houses a quadrangular plan was sometimes employed, with a small court in the centre merely for purposes of light and air, and in no way as a means of architectural effect. Instances of this are found at Chequers' Court, near Tring, Godinton in Kent, Burton Agnes and Barlborough in Yorkshire, and Chastleton in Oxfordshire.

The tendency, however, was to break away from the quadrangular plan inclosed on all four sides. When Dr. Caius built his New Court at Caius College, Cambridge, in 1565, he expressly forbade the closing in of the court on the south side, "lest the air from being confined within a narrow space should become foul;" and it was probably on this ground that the plan of a three-sided court came into general use. This meant the removal of the gatehouse side with its tall tower. The entrance was set back, either as a projecting bay in the centre of the main façade which gives the familiar E-shaped plan, or towards one end of it, with a corresponding bay at the opposite end, and was usually carried up the full height of the building. The side left open was treated in various ways. At Rushton a corridor of one storey was built between the two wings; elsewhere the front was fenced in with a simple balustrade of stone, as at Charlton House in Wiltshire, before the alteration of 1779, or the side walls of the wings were extended and returned opposite the house to inclose a forecourt with a gatehouse, in one or more storeys, in the centre, opposite the main entrance. As part of this change, the gatehouse had now detached itself from the house, and had become a separate building of more or less importance. The most famous instances are the gatehouses of Tixall in Staffordshire (1580), a three-storey building of stone, with four octagonal turrets at the angles, and a remarkably correct design of the orders above the entrance archway; Burton Agnes in Yorkshire (1610), a three-storey building of brick and stone, with two octagonal turrets at the sides; Lanhydrock in Cornwall (1651); Charlecote, Cranborne in Dorsetshire, and the remarkable instances of Westwood in Worcestershire, and Stanway in Gloucestershire. The Westwood gatehouse consists of two two-storey pavilions of brick with a gateway between, surmounted by a cupola on a boldly designed framing of open timber work. The Stanway gatehouse stands at one end of the forecourt, instead of in the centre, owing to peculiarities of the site.

Thus, by the removal of one side of the court, the re-arrangement

SIXTEENTH CENTURY HOUSE PLANNING

of the porch in the centre of the arm connecting the two side wings, and the shortening of the side wings, all of which resulted from the transformation of the quadrangle into a three-sided court, open in front, we arrive at the E-shaped plan, frequently found in large Elizabethan houses, as, for instance, North Mymms in Hertfordshire (early seventeenth century), and Corsham Court, near Bath. That the E-shaped plan had nothing at all to do with any fanciful compliment to Elizabeth

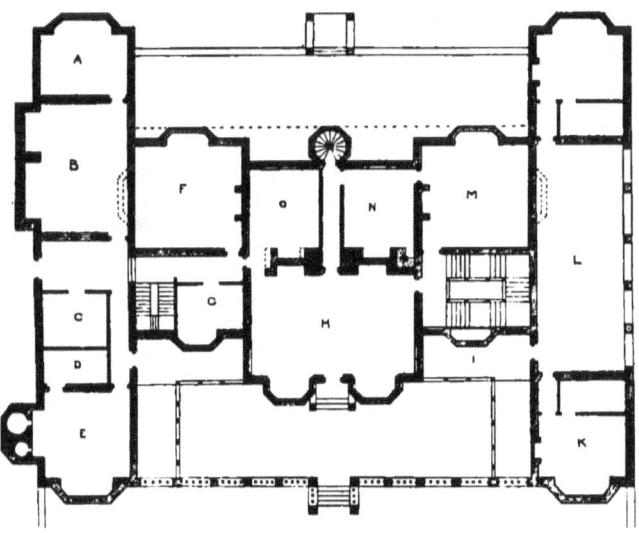

PLAN OF HOLLAND HOUSE. (SOANE COLLECTION.)

A. Wet larder.
B. Kytchen.
C. Dry larder.
D. Bolting house.
E. Pastry.
F. Winter parlour.
G. Pantry.
H. Hall—great chamber over.
I. Walk terrace above.
K. Lodg.
L. Terrace and gallery above.
M. Parlour.
N. Parlour.
O. Bed.

is proved by houses built on this plan before she came to the throne, or was even within sight of it, such, for instance, as Barrington, built by Sir Thomas Phelips, probably the man who was appointed by Henry VIII., in 1539, chief supervisor of the buildings in the town and marches of Calais. By extending the side wings to the back as

74 RENAISSANCE ARCHITECTURE IN ENGLAND

well as the front, another common form of sixteenth century plan was obtained, the H plan, as at Shaw House, near Newbury, 1581, and the plan of Holland House given in the text.

All the plans that we have considered so far belong to the class of the larger Elizabethan house, and are, in my opinion, directly descended from the larger fortified houses with internal courts of the Middle Ages. The court was extended and made symmetrical, and finally one of the inclosing sides was abandoned in order to gain increased light and air. At this stage of development their characteristic is their complete and deliberate symmetry. Gable answers to gable, even chimney-stack to chimney-stack; and this quality, and their more intricate planning and greater scale, seem to me to differentiate them from houses which might also be classified as belonging to the E plan, but which, probably, have arrived at the result in another way, such as the manor houses of Lancashire and Cheshire, and buildings in which, though the general plan is symmetrical, or nearly so, there is no obvious and deliberate attempt at symmetry in detail. The plan of these houses seems to be directly derived from the yeoman's house, which, to all intents, is identical with the small unfortified mediæval dwelling-house, consisting of a common hall in the centre, with offices and one or two small rooms ranged at either end, or at one end only. Instances exist in the original part of Cranborne, the priest's house at Muchelney, the fishing house at Meare, and in the ordinary plan of the half-timbered yeoman's house in the Weald of Kent, such as Beavor House, or Singleton, near Ashford. This plan, being in fact about the simplest arrangement of rooms and offices possible, was derived from remote antiquity, and survived with extraordinary pertinacity in England. It appears again and again under varying forms. The plan of Fountains Hall, for instance, in Yorkshire (1611), consists of a hall, dividing the two sets of apartments at either end, with two separate staircases thrown out at the back. Except for the position of the staircases, the general outline of this plan, on the first floor, very nearly resembles the ordinary plan of a small fifteenth century house, and there can be little doubt that the smaller E and H-shaped houses of the sixteenth century were merely modifications of this traditional plan. By bringing forward the buildings at either end of the hall, an E or H, or half E or H, plan is obtained; and the process of development is so natural that Mr. Taylor ("Old Halls of Lancashire and Cheshire") inclines to think that this modification of the small mediæval house is the real and only origin of the E-shaped plan. This appears probable enough in the case of smaller houses. A very shallow form of H plan is actually to be seen in some of the sixteenth century half timber houses in the Weald of Kent. And plans such as that of Montacute (1580-1601), which might be classified as either of the E or the H plan, rather bear out this view. Here the hall, which occupies half the centre block, separates the wing containing the living rooms of the family from the kitchen offices and servants' rooms, and so far the derivation from the mediæval dwelling-house seems direct. But though there can be little doubt that the smaller houses built on an E or H-shaped plan were derived by direct development from the small rectangular mediæval dwelling-houses, the weight of evidence makes it probable that the more elaborate Elizabethan plans were arrived at by a gradual modification of the old inclosed courtyard.

This opening-up of the house, the importance attached to the

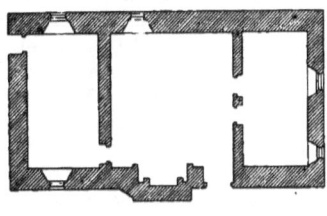

PLAN OF THE FISHING HOUSE AT MEARE.

admission of light and air, were not the only advances in planning made in the sixteenth century. In the earlier houses built on a courtyard plan the builders appear to have been content if they got separate access to each room on the ground floor, directly from the courtyard, and on the upper floor either by doors from room to room or by long galleries running all round the court, and usually open on the courtyard side. The last survivals of this method were to be found in the old inns, such as the "White Hart," the "George," and the "Queen's Head" in Southwark, and in many an old coaching inn. This manner of building was, however, found to be intolerable, and the next step forward was to provide corridors and passages for purposes of communication between the different rooms without going in and out of the house. In order to reach the upper rooms, staircases were provided in every part of the building, much on the system that may still be seen in the seventeenth century college buildings at Oxford and Cambridge. An attempt to deal with this problem is found in the south block of Kirby Hall, as shown in John Thorpe's plan, though the inmates of the rooms on either side the court had to be content to cross the court to get to the hall, or else go through each other's rooms, and, in fact, no serious attempt was made to grapple with the difficulty in the sixteenth century. People were content, apparently, to pass from room to room, with such additional assistance as might be gained from an occasional narrow passage or newel staircase. It was not till Inigo Jones introduced an entirely new system of house design that the problem was squarely met and the lines laid down on which modern house planning has proceeded more or less steadily ever since.

Inconvenient, however, as some of these plans appear to be, the ingenuity displayed is sometimes very great, more especially in the less common examples and those eccentricities of planning which were probably either experimental or due to some caprice on the part of the owner. Besides the quadrangular, the E and the H-shaped plans, there are occasionally found houses planned as a solid square, such as Barlborough (1583-4) and Bolsover (1613). The latter may have been due to a desire to fit the house to the lines of the Norman keep, as is suggested by Mr. Gotch, or may have been suggested by Barlborough. The hall is reached by a small corridor from the porch, and the principal stairs occupy a square tower in one corner on the opposite side to the porch. The plan is picturesque, but exceedingly inconvenient. Barlborough Hall in Derbyshire was built by Francis Rodes in 1583-4. Considering the date, the plan is very remarkable. The kitchen and offices were placed on the ground floor, and the hall and principal living rooms on the floor above; a small staircase led up from the kitchen, but the chief entrance to the principal floor was reached by a long external flight of stairs. In the centre of the house was a small court, or rather, well, for purposes of light and air, measuring about 26 feet by 22 feet.[1] The noticeable point in this plan is that the architect has simply turned his back on the traditional arrangement of the hall as a common living room, dividing the offices from the rooms of the family. The hall here is planned specifically as an entrance hall, and nothing more, with the great dining chamber beyond it, the latter having separate access from the hall and from the stairs from the kitchen. The plan has a singularly modern feeling, and though it can be traced to the courtyard type, the court here is little more than a well, and we get an approximation to the

[1] This has since been covered in and converted into the principal staircase.

SIXTEENTH CENTURY HOUSE PLANNING 77

next advance in planning, when architects grasped the idea of combining under one roof two or more sets of rooms, with a corridor between.

There is no doubt that the house builders of the latter part of the sixteenth century were quite as fond of experiments in planning as they were of unholy and inordinate combinations of the orders. The symbolical plans of Longford Castle and the triangular lodge at Rushton Hall are instances in point. Both plans seem to have been intended

GARDEN HOUSE AT AMESBURY.

as an exposition in stone of the doctrine of the Trinity. A key plan is attached to the plan of Longford Castle in the Soane Collection, which is almost exactly similar to a diagram given in Sir John Peshall's edition of Wood's "Athenæ," 1773, as then existing in one of the windows of St. Peter's Church, Oxford. This diagram has words running to the various points, which concisely state the doctrine of the Trinity. The resemblance to the plan is singular, and whether the key plan attached to the drawing in the Soane Collection is merely an ingenious after-thought

78 RENAISSANCE ARCHITECTURE IN ENGLAND

of some seventeenth century mystic, or actually represents the intention of the original designer, it would have been quite in accordance with certain phases of thought in the early part of the seventeenth century to make a house or a building symbolical of some recondite idea. There can be no doubt that such was the intention of Sir Thomas Tresham when he built the triangular lodge at Rushton. The curious garden house at Amesbury, designed on a system of pentagons, is another instance.[1] In Northamptonshire there are examples of buildings planned as a cross, such as Gayton Manor House and Lyveden new building; but these, and other vagaries of planning, have mainly an archæological interest, and had little or no influence on the development of English house planning.

By the end of the sixteenth century the idea of the hall as a common living room was going out of fashion.[2] It was used for Christmas revels and great entertainments, but the master and mistress had their private dining-room, and even as early as 1460 a "privy-parlour" was attached to the hall at Wanswell Court in Gloucestershire. Moreover, the long galleries, characteristic of the Elizabethan house, tended to diminish the importance of the hall, and the latter gradually came to be used rather as a means of communication between the different parts of the house than as a place in which the household lived. What the hall lost in importance the grand staircase gained. The fact that the gallery and the chief living rooms of the house were on the upper floors suggested that the staircase should become one of the most important features of the house, and the fancy of the Elizabethan nobleman indulged itself here in a profusion of carving, mouldings, balusters, and plaster work, which remain as monumental evidence of their exuberant taste in ornament.

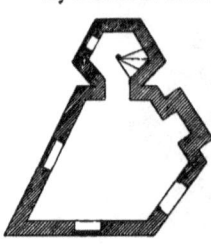

PLAN OF GARDEN HOUSE AT AMESBURY.

The long gallery, the great staircase, and a superabundance of windows were the main contributions of the sixteenth century to domestic architecture. The gallery was placed on the upper floor and usually ran the whole length of the house or of one side of the court.

[1] It is built of stone and dressed flints. Over the entrance is inscribed "Diana her house 1600."

[2] See plan on page 79, in which a dining parlour and a winter parlour are provided, in addition to the hall.

SIXTEENTH CENTURY HOUSE PLANNING 79

The original idea must have been little more than an inclosed walk for use in bad weather. Professor Willis considered it to be directly derived from the mediæval cloister. Beyond, however, a possible identity of function, it is difficult to see any connection between the two, and it is more probable that the gallery was suggested by the long covered passage devised for internal communication between the various parts of the house. Probably the earliest instance was the gallery at Hampton Court. This was begun by Wolsey, and was completed in 1536. It was destroyed by Wren in 1689. It measured 180 ft. long by

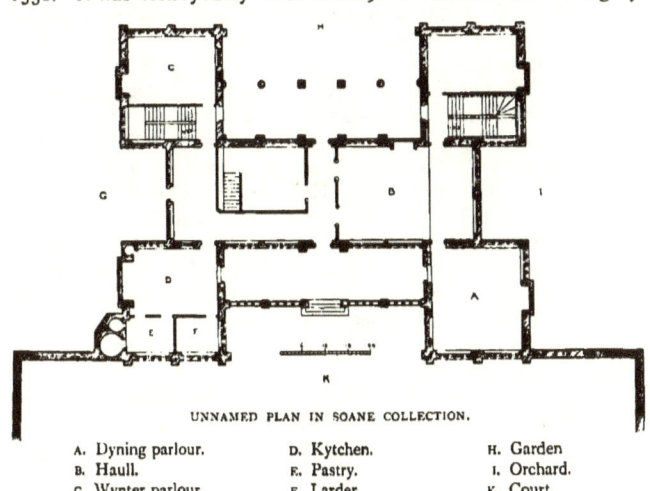

UNNAMED PLAN IN SOANE COLLECTION.

A. Dyning parlour.
B. Haull.
C. Wynter parlour.
D. Kytchen.
E. Pastry.
F. Larder.
G. Woodyard.
H. Garden.
I. Orchard.
K. Court.

25 ft. broad, and had a large semicircular bay in the centre. Mario Savorgnano,[1] a Venetian who visited England about the date of this building, was struck by these galleries, "which are long porticoes or halls, without chambers, with windows on each side, looking on gardens or rivers, the ceilings being marvellously wrought in stone with gold, and the wainscot of carved wood representing a thousand beautiful figures." No galleries of this date with stone roofs exist, and the writer must have mistaken plaster for stone. Later in the century galleries

[1] Quoted by Mr. Law in his "History of Hampton Court." Calendar of Venetian State Papers, 1527-1533, No. 688.

80 RENAISSANCE ARCHITECTURE IN ENGLAND

were nearly always provided, even in moderate sized houses. The gallery at Audley End (destroyed in the last century), which John Evelyn pronounced to be "most cheerful, and one of the best in England," measured 226 ft. long by 32 ft. wide and 24 ft. high. The gallery at Montacute is 170 ft. long by 20 ft. 6 in. wide, and runs the whole length of the building, with semicircular oriels at each end. The gallery at Hardwick (1590-1597) measures 166 ft. long, 22 ft. 5 in. wide, and 26 ft. high; that at Parham in Sussex, 160 ft. by 18 ft. by 13 ft. high; the gallery at Bolsover (1629) was 220 ft. long; and the plan of the old Royal House at Ampthill, in the Soane Collection, shows a gallery 243 ft. long and 26 ft. wide. Of smaller galleries that at Charlton in Wiltshire measures about 130 ft. by 22 ft.; and the gallery at Haddon Hall 109 ft. by 18 ft. wide. The gallery of Queen's College, Cambridge (1537-1541), measures 80 ft. long by 12 ft. broad by 9 ft. high; that of St. John's, Cambridge, is now 93 ft. long, but was originally 148 ft., with an oriel at one end. This formed part of the building by Simons and Wigge. The gallery of Astley Hall, near Chorley in Lancashire, measures 72 ft. by 12 ft. 6 in. by 9 ft. high; that of Moreton Hall (1559) 75 ft. by 12 ft. 6 in. Oriel windows were commonly placed at the ends, and two or more bays at the sides, carried up from the ground floor; where the gallery was open on both sides, the bays, as a rule, were not set opposite each other. The sides were wainscoted, and the ceilings, whether flat, or coved, or segmental, were usually enriched with elaborate plaster work.

At Old Wimbledon House, built by Sir Thomas Cecil in 1588, and destroyed by the Duchess of Marlborough, there were two galleries, which are described in the survey of the Commissioners of 1649. One was of stone, 108 ft. long, "seeled over head (with parge work), pillored and arched with gray marble, wayscotted round with oak, varnished with green and spotted with stars of gold." The great gallery on the second floor was 109 ft. 8 in. long and 21 ft. 1 in. wide, "floored with cedar boards, casting a pleasant smell, seeled and bordered with fret work well wrought, very well lighted, and wayscotted round with well-wrought oak, 13 ft. 6 in. high, garnished with fillets of gould on the pillars, and starrs and cross-patches on the panes, in the middle whereof is a very fayre and large chimney piece of black and white marble, engraved with coates of arms, adorned with several curious and well guilded statues of alabaster, with a foot pace of black and white marble."

The galleries and principal rooms in the greater houses were

SIXTEENTH CENTURY HOUSE PLANNING

profusely decorated with colour. Wallop, writing to Henry VIII.,[1] November 17th, 1540, mentions that Francis I. had told him that he "heard saye that your majestie did use much gilding in your said houses, and especially in the rooffs, and that he in his building used little or none," preferring the natural colours of wood, such as ebony, brasel wood, etc., as "more rich than gilding, and more durable." "The antike work," that is, modelled ornament, at Hampton Court, was covered with gold and byse (light blue). The ceiling of the hall at Theobalds was decorated

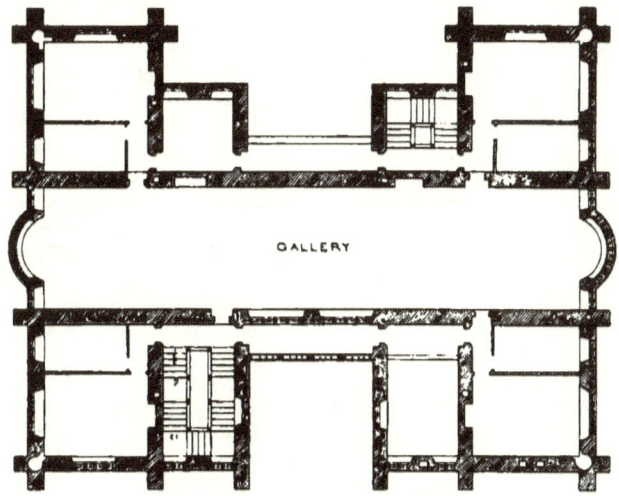

THORNTON COLLEGE, SIR VINCENT SKYNNER'S. SECOND STOREY, SHOWING THE GALLERY. (SOANE COLLECTION.)

with the signs of the zodiac, and by means of some ingenious mechanism the sun performed its course across the ceiling, and the stars came out at night. Another hall at Theobalds was painted with designs of the towns, mountains, and rivers of England; and most of the ceilings were painted blue, with gilt roses. At Boughton Malherbe in Kent (1573), there were, till recently, considerable remains of red, blue, and yellow colour on the plaster work, and heraldic bearings were emblazoned to the full wherever used. Perhaps the most remarkable example of coloured

---

[1] "State Papers," Henry VIII., viii. 523.

and modelled plaster work in England is the exceedingly beautiful frieze in the state room at Hardwick Hall. The taste, however, for colour decoration, as opposed to painters' painting, seems to have lost ground in the first half of the seventeenth century. The plaster work of about that date, as used by Inigo Jones, was not as a rule coloured at all. Instead of modelled and coloured plaster, large panels of painted allegorical figures became the accepted method of decorating interiors ; and it is a fact which throws a suggestive side-light on the brotherhood of the arts, that in proportion as the painters advance, the other arts have to quit the field. The taste was lost for that exquisite craftsmanship which made the rooms of Henry VIII.'s palaces the admiration even of the fastidious Venetians ; and with it disappeared that fine sense of decoration which was satisfied with the harmonies of the tapestries of Hardwick, and with the quiet play of light and colour over the soft modelled surface of its plaster work. The magnificent audacity of Rubens's brushwork seems to have bewitched the taste of the Court. It was forgotten that each art has its limits, and not yet realized that the instinct of the painter, in so far as it is simply graphic, is the most insidious enemy of architecture. Though Rubens's genius could carry all before it, Nemesis was not slow to follow in the blatant allegories of Verrio and Laguerre, and the rapid degeneration from their art to the pitiful nonsense of Kent and Zucchi, and Angelica Kauffmann, in the following century.

The great staircase, with its carved oak newels, is another familiar feature of sixteenth and early seventeenth century domestic work. The abandonment of the stone staircase in favour of wooden stairs of twice the width, easier ascent, and adequate light, shows the higher standard of comfort which accompanied the growing wealth of England. Stone ceased to be used as the inevitable material for staircases, and wooden stairs of solid and elaborate construction were built in most new houses, and were often added to old ones. The position of the staircase varied. It was usually in close proximity to the hall, but the use of the hall as a living room was still sufficiently important to keep the staircase distinct from the hall. At Littlecote the main staircase is to the right of the hall as you enter, and separated from it by the entrance passage. At Canons Ashby the staircase is to the right hand further corner of the hall; but it was more commonly placed to the left of the hall as you entered, as at Aston Hall, Hatfield, and Sydenham. At Fountains Hall there are two staircases, placed in square projecting bays at the back of the hall; and at Godinton

NEWEL, HATFIELD HOUSE.

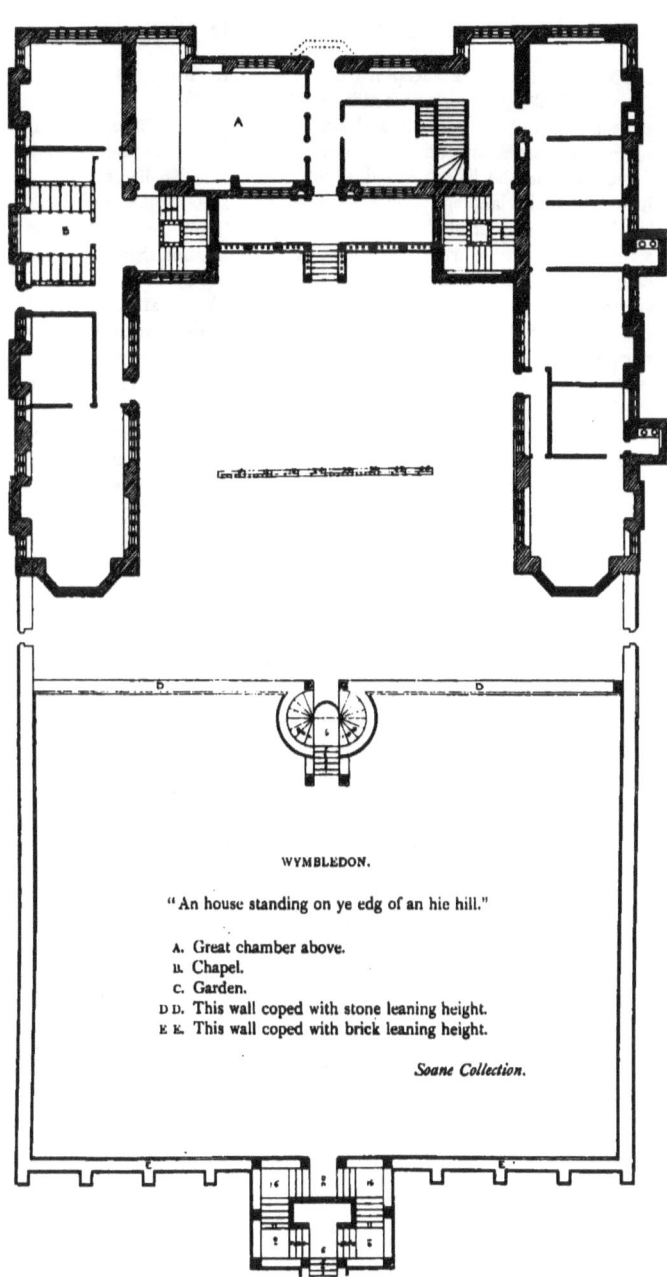

WYMBLEDON.

"An house standing on ye edg of an hie hill."

A. Great chamber above.
B. Chapel.
C. Garden.
D D. This wall coped with stone leaning height.
E E. This wall coped with brick leaning height.

Soane Collection.

in Kent the staircase is placed in a square bay at the back, and separated from the hall by an open wooden screen. Blickling is a somewhat unusual example: the hall and staircase are placed in the central range that divides the two courts from each other, and instead of being detached from the hall a broad flight of stairs leads directly out of it to the half landing, and thence by returning flights on either hand bringing up on the first floor landing. Of the treatment of the stairs in detail there were two main variations. First, there were the cases built in a quadrangular compartment, with a well of considerable size in the centre, and detached newels, as at Aston Hall (1618-1635) and Hatfield (1607-1611); secondly, the staircase built in narrow oblong spaces, with either single newels, or newels coupled together with wooden arches or brackets, as at Burton Agnes (1602-1610), Audley End, Cranborne, and the single newel staircase of Sydenham. The newels and strings were elaborately carved, and small figures instead of terminals were often placed on the newels, as at Hatfield and Blickling,[1] and the example from the old college at Wye in Kent. However picturesque these staircases may be, and in spite of the historical interest of their associations and vicissitudes, their artistic value is small. In the larger examples, every inch of the newels, strings, and balusters, is covered with carving or mouldings: the carving is ill-considered, and seldom shows much regard for the structural intention of the member it decorates. The whole work shows an evident inability in the designer either to stay his hand or to conceive of a large architectural effect, apart from elaborate details. It is probably this absence of idea, this entire confidence in mere detail for effect, that has commended this particular form of staircase as an easy model to the modern copyist. No considerable deviation was made from it till the introduction of Palladianism by Inigo Jones more or less revolutionized building design in England.

The architecture of the hundred years, from 1520 to 1620, was in fact tentative. The builders were losing their old tradition, and had not yet replaced it by a new one, and on the other hand a certain sense of expansion and intellectual enfranchisement in the air at the time tempted them to bold experiments for which they were ill-equipped. So long as they adhered to plain building their work was admirable, but directly they attempted what they probably considered

---

[1] It is evident, however, from the costumes, that several of the figures at Blickling were added later.

SIXTEENTH CENTURY HOUSE PLANNING 85

to be serious art they were on uncertain ground, and the result might be an elaborate and costly building, but it was seldom architecture. The specialization of building had already begun : the builder, instead of being an artist who built and designed in one and the same process,

H

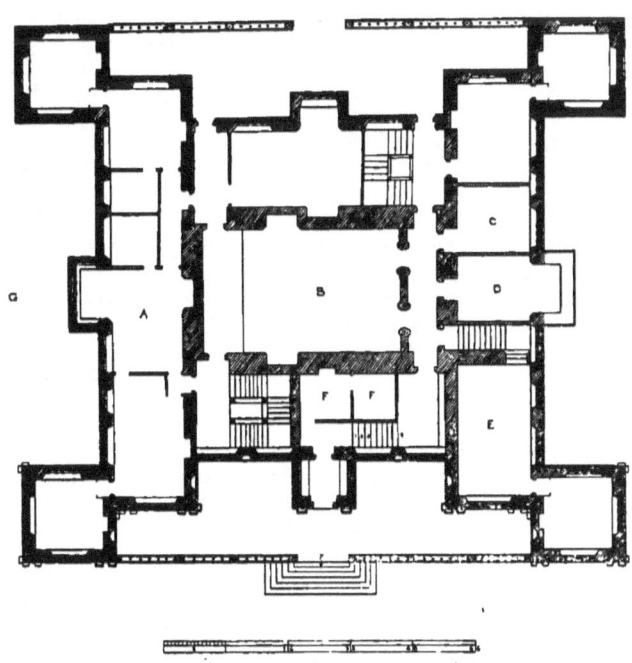

WOLLATON HALL. (SOANE COLLECTION.)

A. Gallery above 100 feet.
B. Hall—35 feet to the sills of the windows.
C. Pantry.
D. Buttery.
E. Kytchen under the servery.
F F. Porter's lodgings.
G. Orchard heares.
H. Garden heares.

was already becoming a person who built buildings, and then thought it necessary to adorn them with ornamentation borrowed at random. This conclusion is borne out not only by the buildings themselves, but by the rapid increase in architectural treatises and pattern books, a sure sign of the increased demand for novelty, and of the recognized inability of the builder to meet it. Soon after the middle of the sixteenth century, a vague consciousness of the orders, as some terrible mystery at the root of all architecture, had begun to present itself to the mind of the English builder-designer. It is indeed at once comic and pathetic to think of some good mason, who could build a building well, but sign his name with difficulty, wrestling laboriously with all the intricate terminology involved in the system of the five orders, as elaborated by scholarly Italians.

The first systematic attempt to deal with architecture as a fine art was John Shute's "First and Chief Grounds of Architecture," published in 1563. Dr. Andrew Boord, who died in 1549, had already written "A Boke for to lerne a man to be wyse in buildyng of his house for the health of his body, i to holde quiyetness for the helth of his soule and body. The Boke for a good husband to lerne." Boord describes generally the arrangements of the house of the time (which, he takes it for granted, is to be "quadryngall"), but, much in the manner of Bacon's subsequent essay, makes no attempt to treat of architecture as the art of beautiful building, and only professes to deal with his subject as a layman. John Shute's "First and Chief Grounds of Architecture" was an attempt to handle the matter from a technical standpoint, and with such special knowledge as the writer had gained by personal study in Italy. Shute, who is described as a painter and architect, was one of the first English architects to study in Italy, and he mentions incidentally that "there are many which name this order of building to be of the new fashion." In the dedication of his book he says that he was sent to Italy by the Duke of Northumberland about 1550, "to confer with the doings of the skilful masters in architecture, and also to view such ancient monuments hereof as are yet extant." The notes which he made were submitted by the Duke of Northumberland to Edward VI., and were finally published by Shute in 1563 in a collected form, consisting of translations from Vitruvius, with extracts from Sebastian Serlio and Philander, and observations made by Shute himself in Italy. The book contains an account of the five orders, with rules for their proportions and use, and diagrams. Subsequent editions appeared in 1579 and 1584, but only two copies of the first edition are known to exist. Shute died in 1563. His work is by no means original, being, in fact, mainly a series of translations from Vitruvius ; but it is interesting in the quaintness of its style, as, for instance,

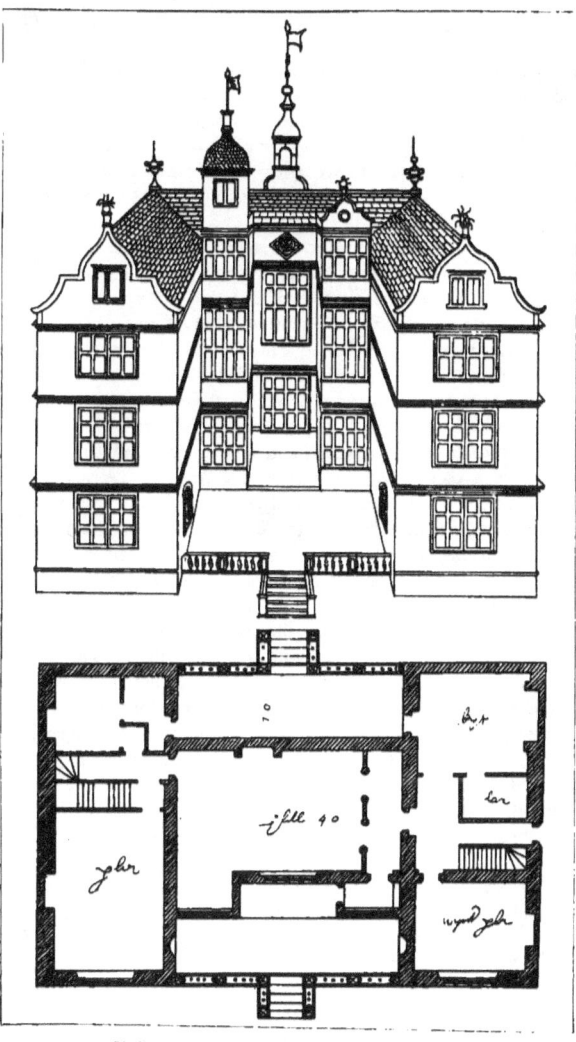

PLAN AND ELEVATION FROM SOANE COLLECTION.

88 RENAISSANCE ARCHITECTURE IN ENGLAND

in this admirable paraphrase of the famous passage in Vitruvius, *nec musicus ut Arixtoxenus sed non amousos, nec pictor ut Apelles, sed graphidis non Imperitus*, etc. Here is Shute on architecture: "Surely such is the amplitude and largeness, I may well say perfection of this facultie, that without some acquaintance with many other artes ye shall not enter into ye deepe secrets . . . by reason of its kinship to the mathematical it is the basis of all the arts . . . so that without a meane acquaintance or understanding in it, neyther paynters, masons, goldsmyths, embroiderers, carvers, joyners, glasyers, gravers in all manner of metals, and divers others more can obtayne any worthy praise at all . . . all these arts are only branches of that aforesaid stock." The next English treatise was Richard Haydocke's "Tracte containing the arts of curious paintinge, carvinge and buildinge," translated from Lomazzo's treatise. This was printed at Oxford in 1598, and is described as "Englished by R. H., student in physick." Haydocke, who was educated at Winchester, and a fellow of New College, refers to Shute as a painter *in tempera*. His translation deals with the orders in much the same manner as Shute's "First and Chief Grounds." More important than either of these books was the translation of Serlio's five books on architecture, translated from Italian into Dutch, and from Dutch into English, "at the charges of Robert Peake, bookseller," in 1611. The book is folio, printed partly in black letter and partly in Roman type, with fine illustrations taken from the Italian original. The first book deals with geometry, the second with perspective, the third with "Antiquity," very fully illustrated, the fourth with the orders in detail, the fifth with "diverse formes of Temples." This translation is important in the development of English Renaissance architecture. It must have largely extended the knowledge of genuine Italian detail, and helped to put a stop to the disastrous aberrations introduced by the German pattern books, which pretty well held the field from the middle of the sixteenth century till the time of Inigo Jones.

The best known of these German treatises are Hans Bloome's folio on the five orders, published at Zurich, 1550, and translated in London, 1608; Vriese's "Perspective," 1559; "Fountains," 1568; "Architectura," Antwerp, 1577; Rivius' "Oder Architectur aller Furnensten Baukunst," Basle, 1582, of whom Wotton says that, besides his notes on Vitruvius, he published "the most elaborate translation that I think is extant in any vulgar speech of the world;" and Wendel Dietterlin's "De Quinque Columnarum," etc., 1593, and "Architectura," 1594.

SIXTEENTH CENTURY HOUSE PLANNING 89

Dietterlin was a mason of Strasburg; his book on architecture contains a few explanatory remarks, and thirty-nine plates illustrating the five

STAIRS, WYE COLLEGE, KENT.

orders, according to Dietterlin's notion of them, with a good deal of bizarre and heterogeneous ornament. The designs are freely drawn, but

90 RENAISSANCE ARCHITECTURE IN ENGLAND

none of them show any refinement, and the majority are extraordinarily ugly. Their relation to what is usually called Elizabethan work is clear. Most of the ornamentation of buildings erected between 1550 and 1610 was borrowed directly from the illustrations to these publications, though here and there may be found details of much refinement, evidently based on Italian examples. Fortunately this German fashion was abandoned as easily as it was assumed; and the value of Peake's translation was that it put within the reach of English designers some account of Italian architecture, drawn direct from the fountain head, and not filtered through the impurities of German taste. In 1615 Walter Gidde published his "Booke of Sundry draughts," "principally serving for Glasiers and not impertinent for Plasterers and Gardeners, besides Sundry other professions." This book was reprinted by Henry Shaw in 1848. It is practically a pattern book of designs for glazing, and a builder's price book, "giving choice to the Builder, both for price and draught of work, which by no understanding can the Glasyer so securely demonstrate his feat as by having his examples of Draught," and so on, for Gidde, having got into a sentence, finds very great difficulty in getting out of it. Bacon's essay is too well known to need description. Scarcely inferior in literary charm, and far more valuable in its sound sense and practical insight into the subject is "The Elements of Architecture, collected by Henry Wotton, Knight, from the best authors and examples," published in 1624. This is not a mere précis of Vitruvius, but an attempt by an amateur of much experience to set down concisely the result of his reading and observations on architecture in Italy. Wotton never affects to be an authority on the subject. He calls himself a "speculative writer," and "a plain Kentishman;" details "must be committed to the sagacity of the architect;" and all he offers is "the wisdom of the ancients, with such reasonable notes of his own as are likely to help his fellows and countrymen." Wotton's work, however, is truly original. He classifies his subject with precision, and, though fully alive to the necessity for scholarship in architecture, he never lost sight of the basis of architecture in reasonable building. His robust common sense declined to be daunted by the pedantry of professors, "as if the very terms of architraves and friezes and cornices, and the like, were enough to graduate a master of this art." The book begins with a statement of the object of architecture, namely, "to build well, both for commoditie, firmness, and Delight." The site must be chosen with care and reason, and in the placing of the parts, use is to be followed. Thus, "the Principle chambers of Delight, all studies and

SIXTEENTH CENTURY HOUSE PLANNING 91

Libraries" should face east, "for the morning is a friend to the Muses." Offices which require warmth (in which, by a curious slip, he includes

STAIRCASE TO HOUSE IN WHITECROSS STREET AS EXISTING IN 1888.

the kitchen) should face south; those which have to be cool, north. In regard to actual building, the two points to be considered are—first, the materials; secondly, their use. The knowledge of materials is very necessary, but Wotton, having in his consciousness the Italians, who were scholars first and architects afterwards, inclines to think that this knowledge is rather the business of the "officinator," or clerk of the works. As to the form or disposition of materials, circular plans should be avoided, "as of all most chargeable" and "fanciful figures, such as pentagons, and the like, do more aim at rarity than commoditie" (a sly hit at Sir Thomas Tresham). Enormous heights of six or seven storeys are on no account to be allowed. Entering into detail, Wotton then deals in order with foundations, walls, openings, compartition (plan and elevation), and roofs. For foundations he quotes Vitruvius, the practice of the Italians, rules of Philibert de l'Orme, and Palladio's rule that they should be carried down one-sixth of the total height of the building. Under the head of walls he includes piers or pillars, which gives him occasion for a general discourse on the five orders and their usual proportions. He condemns "licentious inventions of wreathed and vined and figured columns," and "the practice, grown too familiar, of making pillars swell in the middle as if they were sick of some Tympanie or Dropsie." The entasis to which Wotton refers was often used at the time in complete ignorance of its true intention; and, in fact, owing to a misunderstanding of Alberti's, there was some authority for its misuse even among the Italians; but if Wotton had been familiar with Greek architecture he would hardly have written so disrespectfully of this most delicate refinement of abstract form. Though gifted with sound sense and considerable power of observation, Wotton was quite uncritical in regard to history. For instance, in his next section, dealing with arches, he says that three-centred or four-centred arches "ought to be exiled from judicious eyes, and left to their first inventors, the Goths or Lombards, among other reliques of that barbarous age." In point of fact the four-centred arch had only come into use about 150 years before Wotton wrote. As to openings, notes from Alberti and Vitruvius are given on doors and windows, and some "vulgar cautions" in regard to staircases, as that they should have liberal light, plenty of headway, half paces at comfortable intervals, and a fair width—say 10 feet—the treads to be 12 to 18 inches wide, with 6-inch risers. Chimneys and drains are classified under openings. Some practical remarks as to smoky chimneys are quoted from De l'Orme, and it is suggested that drains should be put in the lowest part of the foundations, with secret shafts in the walls for ventilation, "to the wild air aloft."

Wotton's remarks on "compartition," that is planning, are interesting, in view of the change which was shortly to be introduced from

STAIRCASE AT HAWKHURST, KENT.

Italy into the system of English house-planning. He describes the Italian plan of collecting the offices in a basement, with the principal rooms on the floors above, and further of arranging the rooms *en suite*. He points out several disadvantages of this, as, for instance, that the butteries and kitchen would be too far removed from the dining place, the rooms would be draughty, and there would be very little accommodation for guests. Dealing with "lodging chambers," he takes leave to reproach a fashion prevalent in Italy, namely, "that they so cast their partitions as when all doors were open a man may see through the whole house, which doth necessarily put an intolerable servitude upon all the chambers save the inmost, where none can arrive but through the rest." Notwithstanding Wotton's protest, the very plan which he condemns "as unsuitable to the natural hospitality of England," became the established practice within a few years of his death. There is much good sense in Wotton's criticism, but it is evident that, though fully sensible of the beauty of Italian architecture, he regarded it merely as an affair of detail, to be plastered on to the traditional plan, where a fine porch or a showy façade were considered desirable. From insufficient acquaintance with the practical conditions of architecture, he did not know that a given plan necessitates a particular treatment. Inigo Jones was the first English architect to realize that, if justice was to be done to Italian architecture, plan and elevation must go together as a homogeneous whole. A few remarks on roof coverings complete the first part of Wotton's treatise. The second part deals briefly, but shrewdly, with the ornaments within and without the building, painting and sculpture, and their allied arts, mosaic, and plaster work. Wotton would admit no painting outside, except in black and white, and figures at least 9 or 10 feet high. He seems to have had a wholesome fear of the vagaries of the decorator, and intended his limitations to be more or less prohibitive. As to "grotesques" or "antique work," he would confine "such medley and motley designs" to friezes and borders. For internal decorations, he still contemplated pictures rather than frescoes, and offers as rules: (1) That no room be furnished with too many; (2) that rooms lighted at both ends, or double-lighted, are bad for pictures; (3) that the point of sight intended by the painter should be considered; (4) that pictures be arranged in rooms according to their subject. Sculpture should be used with reserve and regard to its position. In regard to proportion in general, Wotton adds, " Let me only note this, that the least error or offence that can be committed against sight is excess of height, yet that fault is nowhere of small

SIXTEENTH CENTURY HOUSE PLANNING 95

importance, because it is the greatest offence against the purse." Wotton was the first English writer to attempt a practical manual of architecture; and, on the whole, and within his very limited scope, he succeeded better in his attempt than any subsequent writer. The

STAIRS, CHRIST'S COLLEGE, CAMBRIDGE.

writers of the Restoration tended to become entirely academical, without the redeeming humour and penetration of this plainspoken, keen-witted Englishman.[1]

[1] For the convenience of the reader I give the dates of the principal architectural treatises published in Italy before the time of Inigo Jones.

RENAISSANCE ARCHITECTURE IN ENGLAND

EDITIONS OF VITRUVIUS, LATIN TEXT.

"Editio princeps," Rome, about 1486, printed by George Herolt under the supervision of John Sulpitius. Second edition, 1496.

Next edition, Florence, 1496, with a "panepistemon" and an essay entitled "Lamia," by Politian.

Next edition, Venice, 1497. Jocundus' edition, Venice, 1511, the first with woodcuts. Small edition of the same, called the Giunta edition, 1513; and reprint of same at Florence, 1522.

Translations and Commentaries on Vitruvius. First translation by Cæsar Cæsarianus, Como, 1521, with plates.

1544, Philander's notes, published at Rome. The Lyons edition of 1552 was brought out under Philander's own directions; the edition of 1586 has good but rather florid illustrations. Daniel Barbaro's Commentaries, published at Venice, 1567, with excellent woodcuts. Barbaro was Venetian Ambassador to England, 1548-1550. Fresh editions were published in 1584, 1629, and 1641.

Vitruvius was also translated by Jan Martin, Paris, 1547, by Rivius, Nuremberg, 1548, and into Spanish, 1602. A list of subsequent editions of Vitruvius will be found in Gwilt's translation.

OTHER TREATISES.

Alberti's "Architettura," Florence, 1485.

Seb. Serlio, "Architettura," Venice and Bologna, 1540; Paris, 1545; London, 1611. "Perspectiva," 1547.

Antonio Labacco, "Appartenente all' architettura," etc., Rome, 1552.

Pietro Cataneo, "i quattro primo libri d'architettura," etc., Venice, 1554.

Vignola, "Le due Regole delli V. ordini d'architettura," Siena, 1563.

A. Palladio, "i quattro libri dell' Architettura," Venice, 1570; Paris, 1642; London, 1663.

Lomazzo, "Trattato, dell'arte, della Pittura, scultura, e architettura," etc., Milan, 1588.

Scamozzi, "L'idea dell' architettura Universale," Venice, 1615.

FRENCH WRITERS.

Philander, "Notes on Vitruvius," Lyons, 1552. (See above.)

Jean Cousin, "Perspective," Paris, 1560.

Philibert de l'Orme, "Nouvelles inventions," Paris, 1561. "Le Premier Tome de l'architecture," Paris, 1568.

Jean Bullant, "Règle Générale d'architecture," 1564.

Jacques Androuet de Cerceau, "Des plus excellens Bastiments," Paris, 1576 and 1579.

Julien Mauclerc, "Le premier Livre d'architecture," Rochelle, 1600.

CHAPTER V.

INIGO JONES.

INIGO JONES was born on July 15th, 1573, in the parish of St. Bartholomew's, Smithfield. His father, also named Inigo Jones, was a clothworker, and though his name does not occur in the Freedom Book of the Clothworkers' Company, Mr. Horne[1] suspects that the name Hugo Jones, entered in 1569, is probably a clerical error for Inigo. The father was not in very prosperous circumstances, as appears not only from his suit in the Court of Requests, 1589, in regard to the repayment of a loan, but more especially from his will, dated 1596, whereby he left to his son Inigo, and his three daughters, Joane, Judith, and Mary, "all the debtes, Billes, Bondes, and Bookes that I leave in wrytinge to receave and to paye my debtes so farre forth as they maie be receaved." It would seem from this that he left little or no ready money to his children, and no light is thrown on the education of his son, and it is not known by what means he was enabled to travel and to reside in Italy, as he certainly did between the date of his father's death and the year 1604.

Little in fact is known of the first thirty years of Inigo Jones's life. The anonymous memoir prefixed to "the Most Notable antiquity of Great Britain, vulgarly called Stonehenge," etc., 1725, states that he was "early distinguished by his inclination to drawing and design, and was particularly taken notice of for his skill in the practice of landscape painting." There is a picture attributed to him at Chiswick, a classical landscape, not unlike a Gaspar Poussin, which shows some feeling for style, and a considerable mastery of the brush, and among the drawings at Chiswick there are some vigorous pen-and-ink sketches of landscapes drawn for the scenery of masques. These, however, he more probably made during his second journey to Italy; and the only clue to his early training is a tradition which Vertue heard from Dr. Harwood, who received

---

[1] I am indebted to Mr. Herbert Horne for several particulars, hitherto unpublished in regard to the life of Inigo Jones.

98 RENAISSANCE ARCHITECTURE IN ENGLAND

it of Sir Christopher Wren, that Inigo Jones was apprenticed to a joiner in St. Paul's Churchyard, a tradition which is supported by Ben Jonson's allusions to his humble antecedents :

> "And he nam'd me In-and-Inn Medlay : which serves
> A joiner's craft, because that we do lay
> Things in and in, in our work. But I am truly
> Architectonicus Professor rather :
> That is, as one would say, an architect."—
> *Tale of a Tub*, Act IV., Scene 1.

Towards the end of the sixteenth century he paid his first visit to Italy. The first paragraph of his "Stonehenge Restored" (1655) opens with the words " Being naturally inclined in my younger years to study the arts of design, I passed into foreign parts to converse with the great masters thereof in Italy." The anonymous memoir says that "he travelled over Italy and the politer parts of Europe," at the expense of William, Earl of Pembroke, Sir Christopher Wren says, of the Earl of Arundel. Both these noblemen employed him on his second journey, but their connection with the first is uncertain. In the " Vindication of Stonehenge Restored" (1665) Webb states, that "Christianus IV., King of Denmark, first engrossed him to himself, sending for him out of Italy, where, especially at Venice, he had many years resided ;" and there is a tradition that while in the service of the Danish Court, he designed several important buildings, such as the Castle of Fredericksborg, the Rosenberg Palace, and the Bourse at Copenhagen. There are, however, several suspicious points about this story. Andersen Feldborg[1] ascribed the design of Fredericksborg to Inigo Jones on the ground of its resemblance to the inner quadrangle of St. John's, Oxford, and to Heriot's Hospital. In point of fact there is little reason to suppose that Jones had anything to do with either St. John's or Heriot's Hospital, and there is very little resemblance between the three buildings. The Fredericksborg Castle is in much the same manner as Cronenburg Castle, of which the architect was a certain G. F. Stahlmann, as appears from two drawings at Chiswick. In one point Webb's account is clearly inaccurate. He says that Inigo Jones accompanied Christianus to England in 1606, whereas it is known he was in England in 1604-5 ; for on Twelfth Night, 1605, " the Masque of Blacknesse," composed by Ben Jonson, was performed at Whitehall, "of which the bodily part was of Master Inigo Jones's design and art." At this time he would have been thirty-one years of age ; if, therefore, as Webb states, he resided

[1] " Denmark Delineated."

many years in Italy before he was summoned by Christianus, not many years are available for his stay in Denmark. Webb wrote in a large manner without any too particular regard for accuracy. At the same time he would hardly have made an absolute misstatement of a fact which must have been within the knowledge of his contemporaries, and we may take it from his account that Jones was in the service of the Danish Court for some time previous to 1604, but probably was employed in a subordinate capacity, perhaps as draughtsman to Christian, who had a weakness for designing himself.

It seems clear that when Inigo Jones returned to England in 1604 he had some reputation as a traveller, but was not yet known as an architect. For instance, when in 1605 the University of Oxford desired to entertain King James with three plays in the hall of Christ Church, they obtained the assistance of two of "his Majesty's master carpenters" and of the controller of his works for the construction of the stage. "They also hired one Mr. Jones, a great Traveller, who undertook to further them much, and furnish them with rare Devices, but performed very little of that which was expected. He had for his pains, as I heard it constantly reported, £50."[1] It is evident from the account of the fee paid that Jones already enjoyed a considerable reputation as a man of knowledge and resource, but there is no evidence that he was employed on any building at all prior to his appointment as Surveyor to Henry, Prince of Wales, in 1610. Up to that date he seems to have been regarded as a man of ready invention and versatile capacity, and when he was not engaged in designing and superintending the scenery for the constant succession of masques at Court, he was employed on miscellaneous duties, such as that of a King's Messenger. Thus in 1609 he was employed to carry the King's letters into France. After his appointment as Surveyor-General to Prince Henry in 1610, he superintended certain repairs and alterations at St. James's, Richmond, and Sheen, and in May, 1611, together with Francis Carter, Prince Henry's clerk of the works, he drew up an estimate "of the charge of the pyling, plancking, and brickwork for the three islands at Richmont," in order to carry out the design of Solomon de Caux, so that as late as the middle of 1611 it appears that he was not yet employed purely and simply as an architect.[2] Walpole's speculation that to the

[1] As a matter of fact this was the first occasion on which shifting scenery was used in England.
[2] Mr. Horne, who discovered this estimate, signed by Inigo Jones, and Francis Carter and others, in the Record Office, has printed it in full in "The Hobby Horse" for

100 RENAISSANCE ARCHITECTURE IN ENGLAND

period between his first and second journeys to Italy are to be assigned "those buildings of Inigo which are less pure, and border too much upon that bastard style which one calls King James's Gothic," is not supported by any evidence whatever. The earliest signed architectural design by Inigo Jones in existence [1] is dated 1616, and there are drawings in the Worcester Library, dated 1617, for certain works in the Star Chamber; and the conclusion suggested by all the evidence at present discovered is that he did not settle down to the practice of architecture as his one absorbing art till after his return from his second visit to Italy.

Meanwhile he had already established his position at Court. He was on intimate terms with the Earl of Shaftesbury and other noblemen, and with most of the men of letters of the time,[2] who were mainly dependent on him for the setting of their masques. The important work done by Inigo Jones in this regard hardly belongs to a history of architecture; but the fact that the best part of his energies for nearly ten years of his life (1604-1613) was devoted to designing for masques is a sufficient reason for a short account of his work,[3] and of the entirely new departure which he introduced into stage scenery and management.

The masques played at Court and elsewhere in the early part of the seventeenth century were on a scale of great magnificence. The most brilliant noblemen and ladies of the Court were the actors, and the pieces were mounted at prodigal cost. In the "Hue and Cry after Cupid," by Ben Jonson, with scenery by Inigo Jones (1608), the actors were such men as Lord Arundel, Lord Pembroke, Lord Montgomery, and the Duke of Lennox; and in 1630 the king himself acted in the masque of "Love's Triumph through Callipolis," and the queen returned the courtesy by acting the principal part in the masque of "Chloridia" in the same year. Shirley's "Triumph of Peace," presented by the Societies of the Middle and Inner Temple, Lincoln's Inn, and Gray's Inn, at Whitehall, on February 3rd, 1634,

---

October, 1893. Mr. Horne says that he has been unable to discover any evidence that Inigo Jones had carried out any considerable architectural work prior to the death of Prince Henry in 1612.

[1] In the Duke of Devonshire's collection.

[2] I am indebted to Mr. Horne for reference to a Latin poem by Tom Coryat describing a supper at the Mitre, where, among the list of distinguished guests, occurs, "nec indoctus, nec profanus, Ignatius architectus."

[3] For more detailed information I must refer to Mr. Horne's study of Inigo Jones in "The Hobby Horse" for 1893 et seq., and to three papers contributed by myself to "The Portfolio" in 1889.

A DESIGN BY INIGO JONES FOR THE SCENERY OF A MASQUE.

was estimated by Whitelock, a contemporary, to have cost £20,000. A good deal of this money went on sumptuous dresses, usually designed by Inigo Jones, but the greater part must have been spent on the scenery. The masques were played on improvised stages, and it is probable that on each occasion fresh mechanical appliances were furnished by the ingenuity of Inigo Jones, for he completely revolutionized the scenery of the stage. As is well known, the mechanical resources of Shakespeare's stage were quite primitive. No such thing as movable scenery existed. Its place was supplied by the "nuncupations, only in text letters," and the very form of the playhouse, in which the stage projected into the house, with galleries in front and at each side carried up to the back line of the stage, made such scenery impossible. The great improvements made by Inigo Jones were all developed from his initial change in the form of the stage itself. The stage which he used for the masques was set back behind the extreme ends of the side seats, and inclosed by an architectural or other border, much in the manner of the gigantic picture-frames which inclose the stages of modern theatres. Behind this, and out of sight of the spectators, he was able to provide the necessary room for scene-shifting. He worked his changes by means of painted slips, or, as he calls them, "shutters," with a large painted scene filling in the background. There are several sets of designs for these shutters at Chatsworth, all in sets of four, and each shutter carefully drawn in perspective in relation to the rest. Among the Lansdowne MSS. in the British Museum are eight drawings by Inigo Jones of the machinery for shifting his scenes, including a plan and section with written directions for the machinery of "Salmacida Spolia," Whitehall, 1639-40. It appears from these that the shutters were rolled backwards and forwards on runners fixed at top and bottom, and pulleys were arranged at the sides to raise and lower the clouds. The floor of the stage was raised at the back eight feet above the floor of the house, with a fall of one foot to the front, and under the stage were placed windlasses and other contrivances for raising platforms, on which the masquers were introduced. Movable scenery was the most important improvement brought by Inigo Jones from Italy, and there can be little doubt that he greatly developed the mechanical resources of the stage all round. Lighting, for instance, was very carefully considered. Instead of the hanging candles and half-a-dozen footlights of the public playhouse, the stage for the masques was brilliantly lighted. In " The Masque of Queens " the friezes both above and below were filled in with various coloured lights "like emeralds,

INIGO JONES

rubies, sapphires, carbuncles, etc., the reflex of which, with our lights placed in the concave upon the masquers' habits, was full of glory."[1] The sumptuous magnificence of the Renaissance, its pride of colour and glory of display, is surely indicated in this account. The years which Inigo Jones spent in Italy were not in vain. He returned to England filled with the very spirit of the great Italian artists of the Renaissance, and lifted the art of his country on to an altogether different plane. The homely fancy, the lovable humility, as one might say, of its traditional art were laid aside; the art of this country was to be no longer an affair of happy instinct, but completely conscious, dependent on scholarship almost as much as on capacity in design. Henceforward abstract thought, and imagination under rigid restraint, were to supersede the poetry of mediæval fancy.

Inigo Jones was employed to design the scenery of the masques at

---

[1] The following list includes most of the masques in which Inigo Jones was employed:
"The Masque of Blacknesse," by Ben Jonson, 1604-5.
Three plays at Christ Church, Oxford, 1605.
"Hymenæi," Ben Jonson, 1605-6.
"The Hue and Cry after Cupid," Ben Jonson, 1607-8.
"Masque of Queens," Ben Jonson, 1608-9.
"Tethy's Festival," by Daniel, 1610.
"Love freed from Ignorance and Folly," Ben Jonson, 1610. In this masque, for the first time, Jonson omitted any mention of Inigo Jones, and so began their lifelong enmity.
"Oberon," Ben Jonson, 1610-11.
"The Lord's Masque," Thomas Campion, and a Masque by George Chapman, 1612-13
"Christmas Masque," Ben Jonson, 1617.
"Masque of Augurs," Ben Jonson, 1622.
"Time Vindicated," Ben Jonson, 1622-23.
"Neptune's Triumph," Ben Jonson, 1623-24.
"Pan's Anniversary," Ben Jonson, 1624-25.
"Pastoral Play," Ben Jonson, 1625-26.
"The Fortunate Isles," Ben Jonson, 1625-26.
"Albion's Triumph," Aurelian Townsend, 1630-31.
"Love's Triumph through Callipolis" and "Chloridia," Ben Jonson, 1631.
"Tempe Restored," Aurelian Townsend, 1631-32.
"Triumph of Peace," James Shirley, 1633-34.
"Cælum Britannicum," Thomas Carew, 1633-34.
"Temple of Love," Davenant, 1634-35.
"Florimen," 1635.
"Love's Mistress," Heywood, 1636.
"The Royal Slave," Thomas Cartwright, 1636.
"Britannia Triumphans," Davenant, 1637-38.
"Liminalia," 1637.
"Salmacida Spolia," Davenant, 1639-40.

Court in each year from 1605 to 1612, the year of Prince Henry's death. Except possibly in 1617, he was not employed again till 1621, after which he was regularly called upon to design the scenery whenever a masque was presented at Court. It is possible that his quarrel with Ben Jonson may have had something to do with the neglect of him between 1612 and 1621. Ben Jonson was irritated by the increasing interest attached to the scenery, and the consequent diminution in his own importance, and Inigo Jones, who seems to have considered the poetry as an occasion for magnificent spectacle, is not likely to have been content with anything less than complete control of the *mise en scène*. Ben Jonson showed his resentment by omitting any mention of Inigo Jones in the description of his masques, and by satire so virulent that it was suppressed by order. The last masque for which Jones designed was the "Salmacida Spolia," by Davenant, 1639-40, the object of this masque being to express the king's anxiety "by all means to reduce tempestuous and turbulent natures into a sweet calm of civil concord." On September 2nd, 1640, appeared the ordinance of both Houses of Parliament for "the suppressing of public stage-plays through the kingdom during these calamitous times."

After the death of Prince Henry in 1612, Inigo Jones's appointment of Surveyor of the Works lapsed, and early in the following summer he started on his second journey into Italy. The dates of his visit to Italy are surrounded with uncertainty. The only authorities are the entries in his annotated copy of "Palladio" in Worcester College Library. In Book I., folio 52, is an entry "London, Jan. 18th, 1614," and in Book II., folio 8, "Vicenza, Jan. 18th, 1614," and by a comparison of the dates and places entered in his "Palladio," it would appear that he was in Rome on January 2nd, 1614, in London, January 11th, in London or Vicenza on January 18th, and in London, January 26th. This confusion of dates casts some doubt on the meaning of these entries. However, there is little doubt that he stayed in Italy from the middle of 1613 till the autumn of 1614, chiefly at Rome, Vicenza, and Tivoli, with perhaps a flying visit to England in January, 1614. His second visit to Italy was taken partly in the service of the Earl of Arundel, for whom he collected works of art, and he was also employed in this capacity by the Earl of Pembroke and Lord Danvers; but the main object of his journey was further training in painting, and a thorough study of classical architecture. He spent long days amid the ruins of Rome, with his "Palladio" in hand, verifying illustrations, correcting errors, making notes on the buildings, and bitter comments on the

INIGO JONES

Vandalism of the time. It is evident from his notes that he had studied the writings of Serlio, Vignola, Fontana, Labacco, and Philibert de l'Orme, and was acquainted with the most famous architects then living in Rome. He mentions a conversation he had with Scamozzi on August 1st, 1614, in reference to a point in Palladio. He had, however, a very

CEILING, WILTON.

poor opinion of Scamozzi, for in another note he accuses him of ignorance, and malice against Palladio, and notes that "in this, as in most other things else, Scamozzi errs." In the Worcester Collection there are some leaves of a MS. treating of windows numbered 162 *et seq.*, and studies of the orders and temples, executed with a degree of care which makes it probable that they were intended for publication. There is, however, no record that Inigo Jones ever carried out this intention.

In 1615 Inigo Jones succeeded Simon Basil as Surveyor-General of the Works, at a fee of 8s. a day for his entertainment, £80 per annum for his "recompense of availes," and 2s. 8d. a day for riding and travelling expenses. A warrant for his living at £12 15s. 10d. is dated March 16th, 1615, and in 1629 a yearly grant of £46 was made him for the rent of his house in Scotland Yard.[1] Out of these fees he agreed to forego his fee of entertainment owing to the embarrassed state of the exchequer. In 1617 he prepared designs and a model for a new Star Chamber, and began the Queen's House at Greenwich. In the same year he began the new Chapel of Lincoln's Inn,[2] which was consecrated in 1623. This chapel is the one certain instance of a design by Jones in Gothic architecture, and Mr. Horne thinks it likely that the design was made in 1610, when the old chapel was pulled down, that is before Inigo Jones had arrived at his mature manner. There is no evidence beyond a vague tradition that he had anything to do with the Church of St. Catherine Cree (1628-30), but St. Albans, Wood Street, which was burnt in the Great Fire, is known to have been in the Gothic manner,[3] and this has always been attributed to Inigo Jones.

In 1618 he was appointed one of the commissioners to lay out Lincoln's Inn Fields, with instructions to prepare a plan for this purpose. The picture at Wilton is a view of Lincoln's Inn Fields in the eighteenth century, and is certainly not Inigo Jones's original draft. It shows, however, Lindsay House and the houses on the west side, with the rose and fleur-de-lis which were designed by Inigo Jones some years later, and which are now the best examples left of his street architecture. Shaftesbury House (No. 55, Aldersgate Street, now destroyed) was another example. In the year 1619 he was ordered to design the new buildings at Whitehall. There are several variations in the published designs. Campbell published his set of plates in the "Vitruvius Britannicus," 1717-1725, and states that he obtained the originals, which he dates 1639, from Mr. William Emmet of Bromley. These drawings are now in Worcester College Library. Campbell, however, is by no means to be trusted, for he also says that the Banqueting Hall was built in 1617, that is, two years before Jones was commissioned to make the designs. Moreover, it is pretty certain that the drawings from which he published his plates were not by Inigo Jones, but drafts by

[1] Authorities quoted by Mr. Horne in Article *Inigo Jones*.
[2] Since altered by Lord Grimthorpe.
[3] Wren's "Parentalia."

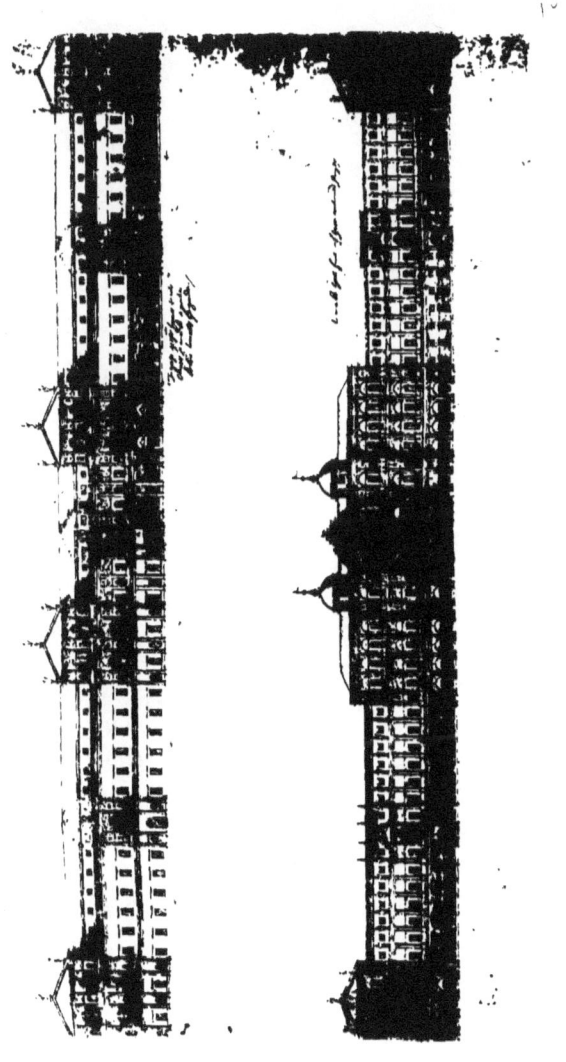

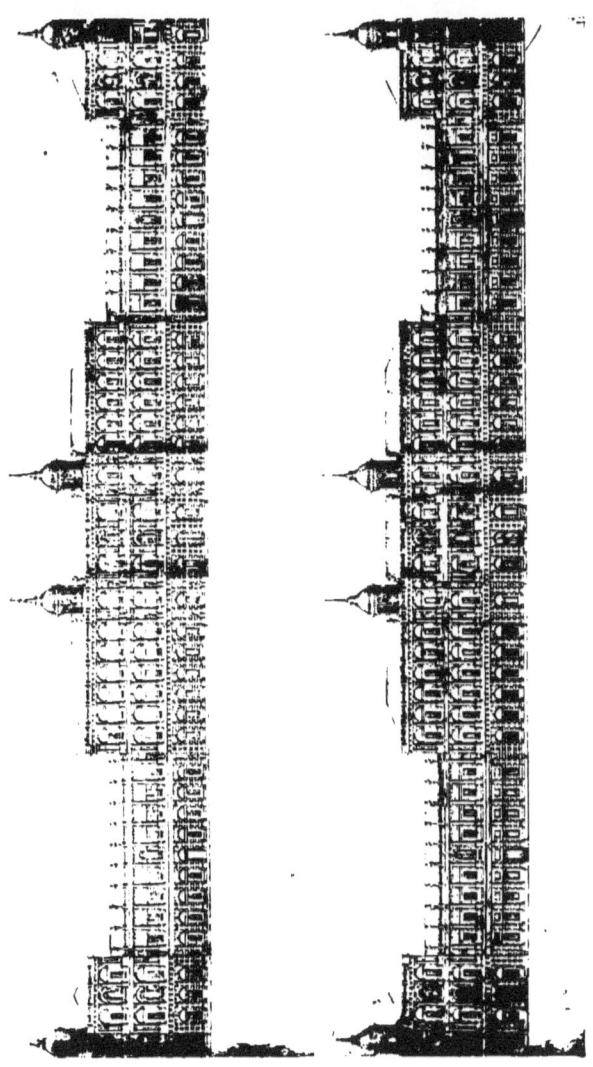

John Webb from the original designs made by Inigo Jones in 1619.[1] William Kent published a set of plates in 1727, from drawings in the possession of the Earl of Burlington; these drawings also appear to have been made by Webb, and many of them are now in the collections at Chiswick and Chatsworth. Besides the numerous variations in detail, two distinct sets of designs appear to have been made by Inigo Jones. The first (1619), and this is the set figured in Campbell from the drawings in Worcester College Library,[2] was only about half the size of the subsequent design, the total dimensions being 630 ft. by 460 ft. The second, which is given by Kent from originals now at Chatsworth, was to be double the size, 1,280 ft. long by 950 ft. wide. The Chatsworth drawings are entitled "The ground plant for the palace of Whitehall for King Charles ye first taken. John Webb,[3] architect," and the elevation, "upright for the palace of Whitehall, for King Charles the first taken, but the front is to be arranged (?)

DOOR, WHITEHALL.

[1] Several of the Whitehall drawings are signed "John Webb, architect," and were evidently made up by Webb from Inigo Jones's sketches. With the exception of a drawing entitled "Skizo of the great door, Ban. Ho. 1619," there is no drawing for Whitehall which can with any certainty be assigned to the hand of Inigo Jones.

[2] The large plan on a folding sheet in the chest at Worcester, signed "John Webb," is a plan of the larger (and in my opinion later) scheme. The other drawings in this chest belong to the earlier design.

[3] John Webb was pupil to Inigo Jones, and assisted him in most of his later works.

according to ye ground Plott. John Webb." The meaning of this last provision was that it was to include Inigo Jones's Banqueting House, which was already built. It seems certain from this express reference to Charles I. that the original design was almost exactly doubled in size when Charles I. took up the Whitehall schemes.[1] For instance, the great central court was 392 ft. by 198 ft. in Jones's original design for James I., whereas in the plan prepared by him for Charles I., and accepted, this court becomes about 800 ft. by 400 ft. So again, the circular court which in the first design had a diameter of 140 feet, has a diameter of about 280 feet in the later design preserved at Chatsworth. The astonishing thing is that, in spite of this heroic increase in scale, the original plan was to be preserved throughout. Roughly speaking, the site was to occupy the whole of the space from Whitehall Gardens to the ground at the back of the Treasury; the north side passing through the Horse Guards; the south following a line through the middle of the Home Office; and the plan was to consist of a huge rectangular block, 1,280 ft. long by 950 ft.[2] wide. This was divided into three parts, the central division was to be occupied by an immense court, 800 ft. long by 400 ft. wide,[3] running north and south; the division to the west was subdivided into three courts, of which the centre was the famous circular or Persian court, 280 feet in diameter, with oblong courts on either side; the division to the east, with front to the river, was also divided into three courts, the centre one square corresponding to the circular court, and the two end ones oblong. In one of the alternative schemes, the central court was to be occupied with buildings, but this idea was abandoned. The elevation was symmetrical, the composition consisting of a regular façade, with projecting blocks in the centre and at the ends, carried up above the intermediate range of buildings. The height to the top of the centre block was to be about 110 feet.

The work was begun in haste. The old Banqueting House had been burnt in January, 1619. Inigo Jones's design for the new hall and estimate

[1] Mr. Loftie, in his able account of Inigo Jones ("I. Jones and C. Wren," 1893), following the hasty summary of Ferguson, exactly reverses this, no doubt on the evidence of Campbell, who describes his set of plates "as it was presented to his Majesty, King Charles I., by the famous Inigo Jones, 1639." Campbell, however, is quite untrustworthy as to dates, and the definite inscription by Webb on the drawings of the larger design, quoted in the text, seems to place it beyond doubt that Charles, instead of reducing the original design proposed for James I., very greatly enlarged it.
[2] These dimensions are taken by scale from the drawings at Chatsworth.
[3] Parliament Street runs over the site marked out for this court.

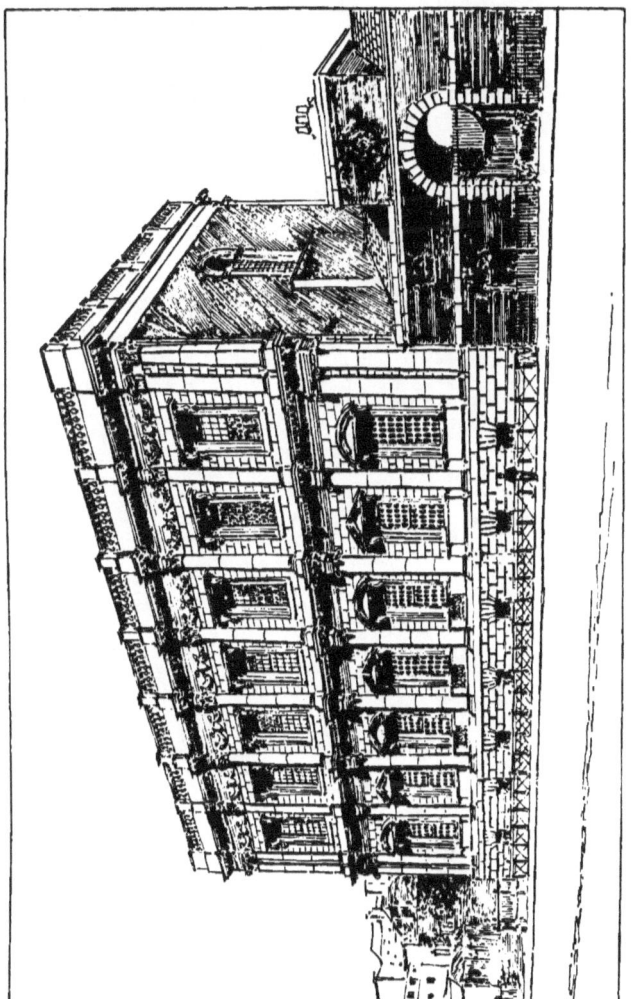

THE BANQUETING HOUSE, WHITEHALL, NOW THE ROYAL UNITED SERVICE INSTITUTION.

Face p. 108.

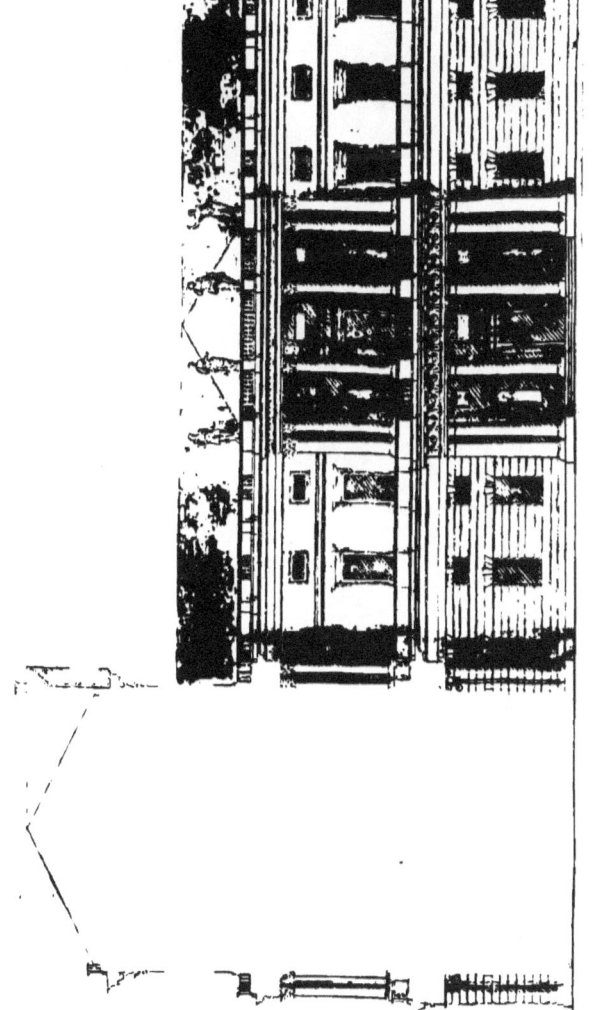

DETAILS OF WHITEHALL
(Worcester College Collection)

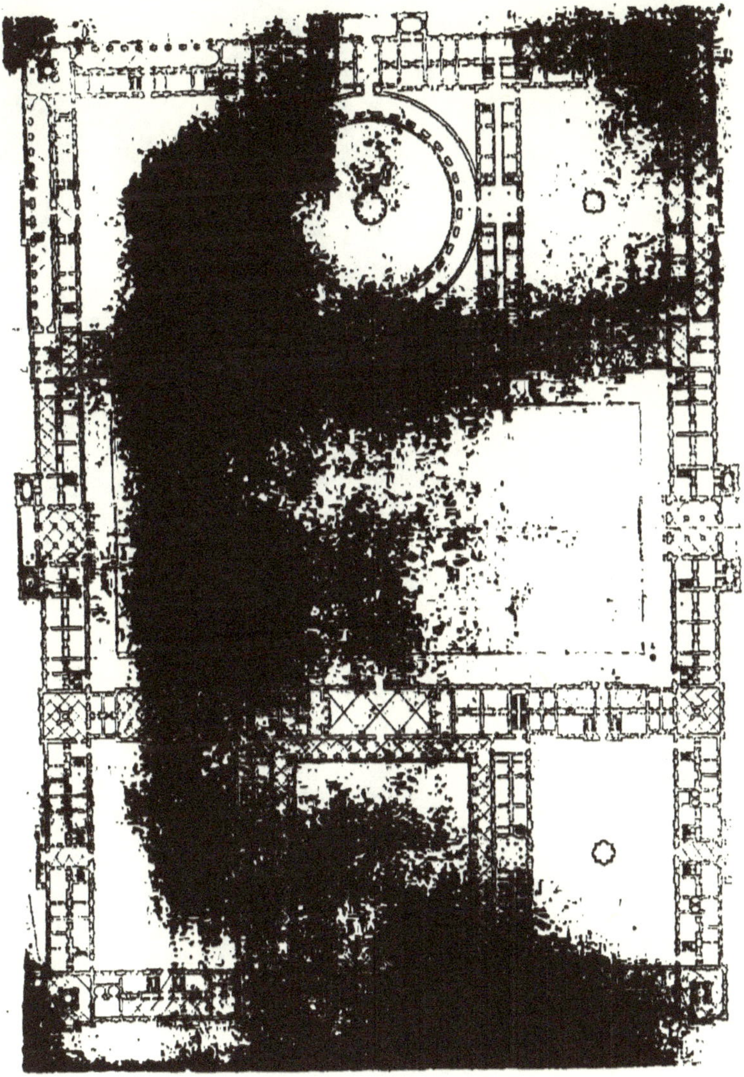

of cost (£9,850) were completed in the spring, and the first stone was laid on June 1st of the same year. The new Banqueting House was completed March 31st, 1622, at a cost of £15,653 3s. 3d. This building, sumptuous as it is, was only intended as a subordinate feature of a vast façade,[1] but it is the only part of the design that was ever carried out. Charles I. revived the scheme on a colossal scale, apparently between 1630 and 1640, but there was no money available, and the increasing difficulties in which the king became involved, put a stop to any possibility of carrying out this magnificent design.

The boldness and originality of Inigo Jones's conception is amazing. It has appeared, from our survey of English architecture in the sixteenth century, how utterly wanting this art had been in what may be called architecture in the grand manner, that is, architecture on a great scale, and depending for its effect upon proportion and orderly distribution, that is, on the abstract and essential qualities of architecture, rather than on the accidents of detail. Throughout the Elizabethan age costly palaces had been built, such as Wollaton and Audley End, but not one of these great houses can be said to embody any large architectural idea. They are more or less picturesque masses of building, tricked out with adventitious ornament, which might be shorn away without materially injuring the architecture; the detail itself is usually wanting in refinement and distinction, and though these houses arrest our sympathy by their associations, considered from a purely critical standpoint they only rank as second-rate work. There was, in fact, no precedent whatever in England for such a building as Inigo Jones designed for Whitehall. The force of his genius is shown in the fact that almost at one effort, and without previous failures, he was able to create a finished masterpiece of design in a manner that was as yet quite unfamiliar in England. The Banqueting House, mere fragment though it is of a stupendous design, is to this day the most accomplished piece of proportion in England, and not inferior to the finest work of Palladio and the great Italian masters.

From this time forward till the outbreak of the Civil War, Inigo Jones was constantly employed by the king. Mr. Horne has discovered in the Record Office an account of money disbursed for his riding expenses, which shows that much of his time must have been spent in the saddle, travelling up and down England in the superintendence of his work. In 1620 he was made a member of a commission to

---

[1] The exact position it was to occupy was on the east side of the great central court.

inquire into all new buildings erected in London since the beginning of the reign of James I., and to enforce compliance with certain building regulations. In 1623, on the occasion of a visit to Southampton to prepare for the reception of the Infanta, he was made a burgess of the town, and in 1630 a justice of the peace for Westminster. In 1626 he designed the water-gate of old York House, which was executed by Nicholas Stone. The gateway is still standing in an obscure hole at the foot of Buckingham Street, Strand, but its fine proportions are concealed by the alterations in the ground. A fine gateway, designed for Lord Weymouth, in Oatlands Park, near Weybridge, was pulled down about thirty years ago. The gateways of the Botanical Gardens at Oxford were designed, as well as executed, by Nicholas Stone; but it is possible that Inigo Jones gave the design for the south entrance porch of St. Mary's at Oxford. His next important work was the Church of St. Paul's in Covent Garden, and the laying out of the square. This church was begun in 1631, and consecrated by Juxon in 1638. It was burnt to the ground in 1795, but rebuilt on the old lines, and though it has been tampered with since, we have to this day, substantially, the original elevation; and, in fact, no architect but Inigo Jones could have made such an extremely powerful design. The elements are very simple. A plain Doric portico, with a triangular pediment and a cupola above it, form the east elevation; but, as usual with Inigo Jones, his genius is shown in his superb treatment of these simple elements. Hawksmoor, with the same problem before him, would have blundered into clumsiness, but, as handled by a master, the great shadows of this portico, and the exact proportions of its parts, make it one of the most impressive façades in London. Historically, it is interesting as anticipating the great porticoes to churches, introduced by Hawksmoor, Gibbs, and James in the eighteenth century, though, as Mr. Loftie points out in the case of St. Paul's, Covent Garden, the portico, owing to the necessity of placing it at the east end, belongs to the square rather than to the church.

A comparison of this authentic building with such buildings as the inner court of St. John's, Oxford, and St. Catherine Cree, make it very improbable that the latter can have been designed by Inigo Jones. At St. Catherine Cree the south doorway is the only detail that bears any resemblance to his manner. The work at St. John's, Oxford, was first attributed to Inigo Jones by P. Heylyn ("Cypriacus Anglicanus," 1688, quoted by Willis and Clark, iii. 277), who describes the new buildings at St. John's, begun by Laud in 1631, as "fashioned in an

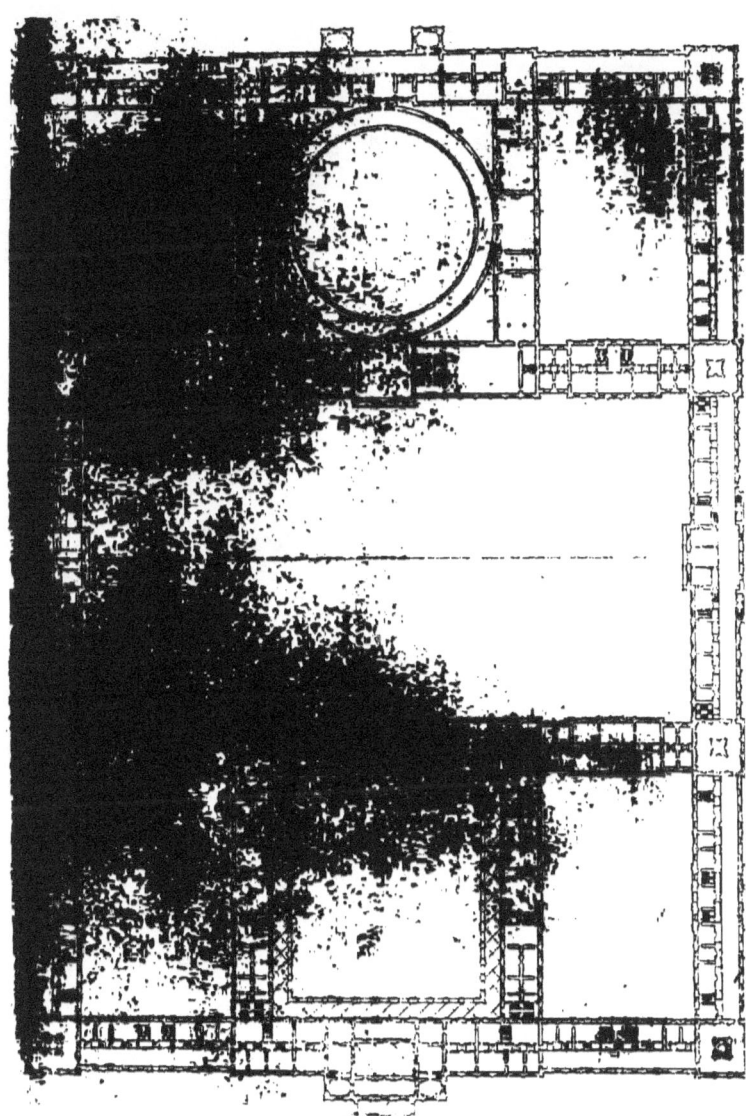

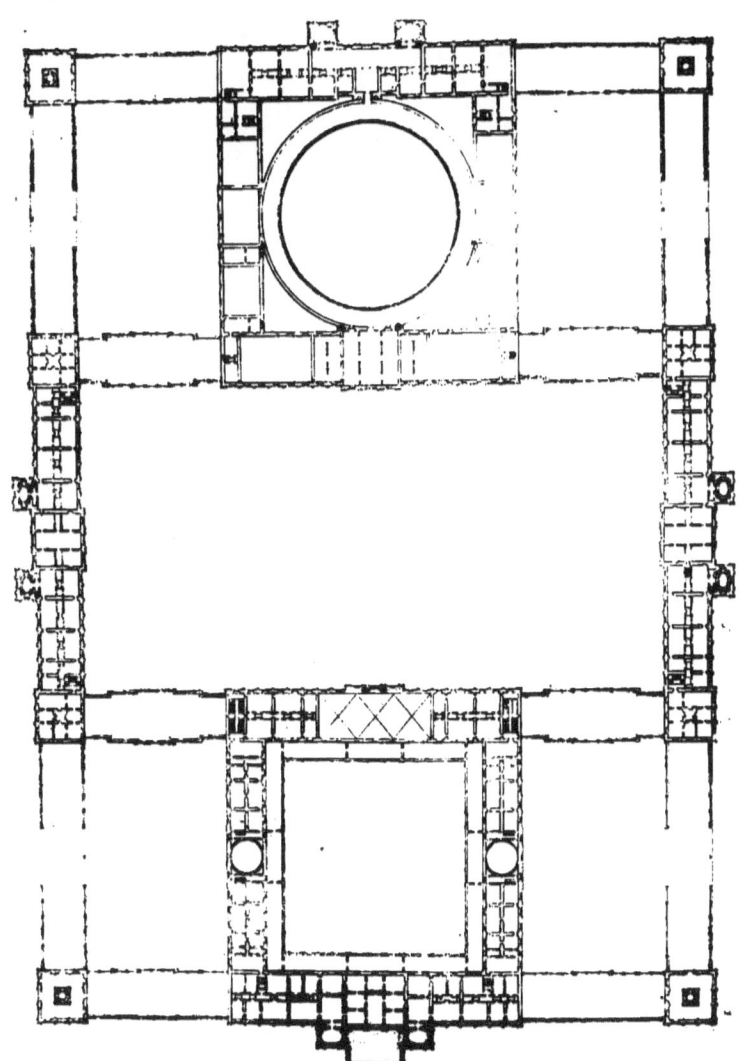

GREENWICH HOSPITAL.

excellent symmetry according to the exactest rules of modern architecture." St. Catherine Cree was consecrated by Laud in 1630. The two buildings have one feature in common : the arches are brought down direct on to the abacus of the columns; but there is no evidence whatever, beyond a vague tradition, that Inigo Jones had anything to do with either of these buildings. In regard to St. John's, there is no reference to Inigo Jones in the college books, whereas Lesueur, who made the two bronze figures, is mentioned, and it seems most unlikely that an architect so steeped in Palladianism as Inigo Jones could have had anything to do with the detail of the St. John's work, which is evidently Flemish in feeling. It is possible that the work was designed and executed by Lesueur himself, or some foreign artist about the court. It is essentially sculptor's work, that is to say, the central frontispiece of the inner court has no relation to the main architectural lines of the rest of the building.[1] The detail is rather exuberant, but exceedingly well executed, and approaches in feeling the details on the Weston tomb at Winchester by Lesueur. The architecture of the east quadrangle of St. John's (excepting the arcade) is ordinary English work, such as might have been done by Acroyde or Arnold of Wadham, and the garden front is almost Tudor in its low simple lines. The only features that differentiate it from ordinary Jacobean work are the arcade and the elaborate ornamentation of the east side of the quadrangle, which is Flemish, and rather rococo in character, and of an order which Inigo Jones rarely used in any of his buildings. This legend may, I think, be dismissed with the equally unauthenticated tradition that he made the designs of Heriot's Hospital and the Bourse of Copenhagen. It is singular that, with the possible exception of two gateways, there is no evidence that Inigo Jones was employed at either Oxford or Cambridge. It is almost certain that the buildings at Christ's, Cambridge, erected in 1642, are not by him.

Somewhere about 1620 Jones was ordered to survey old St. Paul's. The cathedral was in a state of disgraceful dilapidation, but nothing was done till Laud became Bishop of London. In 1631 a commission was issued for the repair of the building. Laud succeeded in raising £101,300,[2] and the works were begun in 1633, and continued till the outbreak of the Civil War, when the balance in hand was annexed by the Parliament. The scheme, it appears, was to gradually rebuild the cathedral, and Inigo Jones got as far as the south transept

[1] There is an excellent plate of this building in Mr. Gotch's series (plate 133).
[2] See Note p. 122.

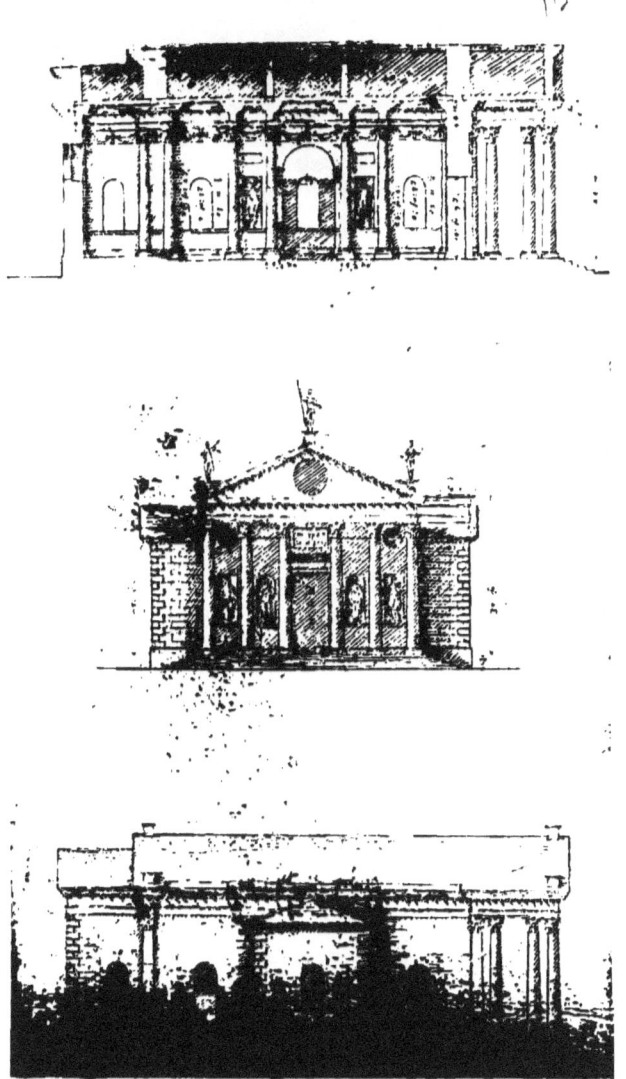

DESIGN FOR A CHURCH, BY INIGO JONES
(PROBABLY A SKETCH FOR ST. PAUL'S, COVENT GARDEN)
(*Worcester College Collection*)

Valentine, Photo. *face p. 112.*
ST. MARY'S CHURCH, OXFORD. GATEWAY CARVED BY NICHOLAS STONE,
THE DESIGN ATTRIBUTED TO INIGO JONES.

INIGO JONES

when the works were stopped. There is a view of the west front by Hollar, and a drawing of it at Chiswick. The design is inferior to Wren's, but it was much admired at the time, and Webb is enthusiastic over his "magnificent portico." It must be pointed out, however, that the steep-pitched pediment, flanked by two obelisks which terminated the nave, was necessitated by the pitch of the old nave roof. It is to be noticed, moreover, both in regard to Wren and Inigo Jones, that there

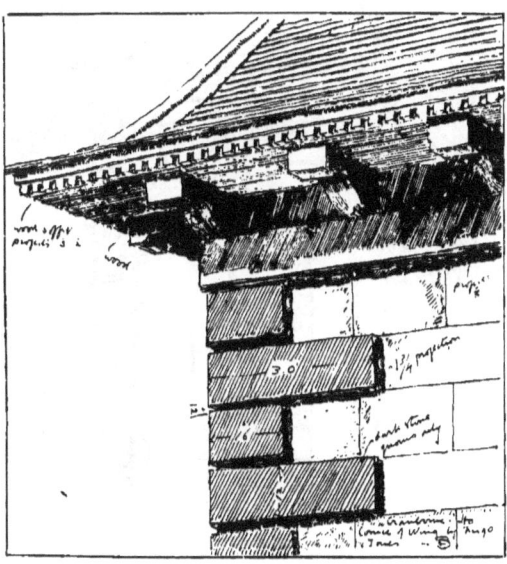

EAVES, CORNICE, AND QUOINS, CRANBORNE.

is always a vast improvement in the building as executed, compared with the building as shown in their drawings. There can be little doubt that both men trusted far more to their actual supervision of the work, and to directions to be given as the building proceeded, than to their original draughts; and further, that they possessed a more intimate knowledge of building materials, and a keener insight into their artistic possibilities than is possible to a modern architect, who, by the nature of his calling and the exigencies of contracts, is prevented from standing over his building from start to finish, and, so to say, shaping and

114 RENAISSANCE ARCHITECTURE IN ENGLAND

moulding it on the spot into what he believes to be the most perfect form attainable. Jones's designs for the rebuilding of St. Paul's involved the destruction of St. Gregory's Church, and, in spite of the protest of the parishioners in 1637, he pulled down part of the church, and

PORCH, WEST WOODHAY.

threatened that they should be laid by the heels if they did not take down the remainder. He was summoned for this conduct before the House of Lords, and had to hand over his materials to the parishioners for the rebuilding of their church.

The Queen's House at Greenwich was finished in 1635, the date

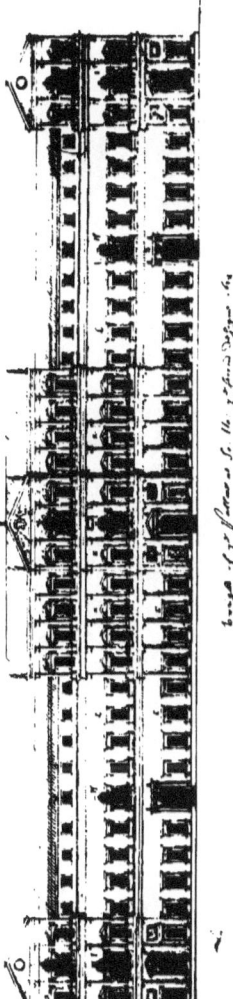

UPRIGHT OF YE PALLACE AT SO(MERSET) HOUSE, 1698
(*Worcester College Collection*)

INIGO JONES

carved on the building. Some of the designs for Greenwich at Chiswick are dated 1637, but most of these drawings were made by Webb for Charles II. In the Soane Museum there is a large folio of miscellaneous designs by Inigo Jones, Wren, and others, containing designs for Greenwich, which will be referred to in my account of Wren. Folios 8 and 9 show the river front and side elevation of what is called King Charles block, which were undoubtedly designed by Inigo Jones, and these drawings may have been by his own hand. The masterly completion of this superb building is due to Wren, but to Inigo Jones belongs the credit of the original designs, and of having initiated a scale, which Wren alone was able to follow. In the same year (1637) the chapel of Old Somerset House was finished from designs by Inigo Jones, and in 1638 he prepared designs for additions and alterations to "the palace at Somerset House," three of which are preserved in Worcester College Library. One of the designs, which is marked "not taken," shows a fine elevation in three orders, each order including two storeys; the total height to the top of the cornice being 110 feet. At Chiswick there is a drawing for "the chimney-piece," for the gallery of Somerset House, dated 1636, which shows that he had already designed the great gallery. In Kip's view of Somerset House,[1] Inigo Jones's block occupies the centre of the river façade, and behind it stood the older building of Protector Somerset, which seems to have resembled in style Wolsey's buildings at Hampton Court. There are two drawings at Chiswick for the gateway at Temple Bar, dated 1636 and 1638, which do not appear to have been carried out. The older parts of West

CAPITAL TO PORCH, WEST WOODHAY.

[1] "Britannia Illustrata."

Woodhay House, including the entrance porch, built 1635, are probably by Jones. In 1636 he designed the Barber Surgeons' Hall in Monkwell Street, the greater part of which is now destroyed, including the oval lecture theatre, shown in the drawing in the Worcester Library. This theatre was pulled down in 1782. In 1637-8 he designed the choir screen of Winchester Cathedral, since destroyed. One of his latest works in London seems to have been Lindsay House in Lincoln's Inn Fields, a fine stone built house, completed in 1640. Two of the piers in front of the forecourt remain, but Hatton says that four of "the fine spacious brick piers" had been removed in his time, 1708. The date given for Shaftesbury House in Aldersgate Street is 1644, but Inigo Jones was then at Basing House, and it was probably completed at about the same time as Lindsay House (1640-1642). Shaftesbury House is now destroyed. It resembled Lindsay House in its general design, and consisted of a basement storey supporting a single large Ionic order in five bays, which included two storeys. The centre bay was flanked by coupled pilasters, and had a broken circular pediment above the first floor window. The house was built for the Earl of Thanet, but was sold by him to Anthony Ashley Cooper, Earl of Shaftesbury.

On the outbreak of the Civil War, Inigo Jones left London, having, according to the tradition, buried his money in Lambeth marshes, with the help of his faithful sculptor, Nicholas Stone. He was attached to the Royal Cause, and his arbitrary action in the matter of St. Gregory's Church made him exceedingly unpopular with the citizens. In 1643 "he was thrust out of office for his loyalty, and fled to Basing House in Hampshire, where he remained with Peake and Faithorne, Hollar, and Robinson the player, till the house was taken by Cromwell in 1645, after a siege of over two years. Inigo Jones was taken prisoner with the others, and in 1646 was condemned to pay a fine of £545, and a further sum of £500 for his fifth and twentieth part."[1]

After this stormy passage in his career he seems to have resumed his work unmolested, and to this period belongs his work at Wilton. Aubrey's account is that Charles I. persuaded Philip, 1st Earl of Pembroke to build the garden front, intending Inigo Jones to design it, but as the latter was at this time (1633) occupied with the work at Greenwich, "he recommended it to an ingenious architect, M. Solomon de Caux, a Gascoigne, who performed it very well,"—that the south side of

[1] Mr. Horne, "Dict. Nat. Biog.," Art. *Inigo Jones*.

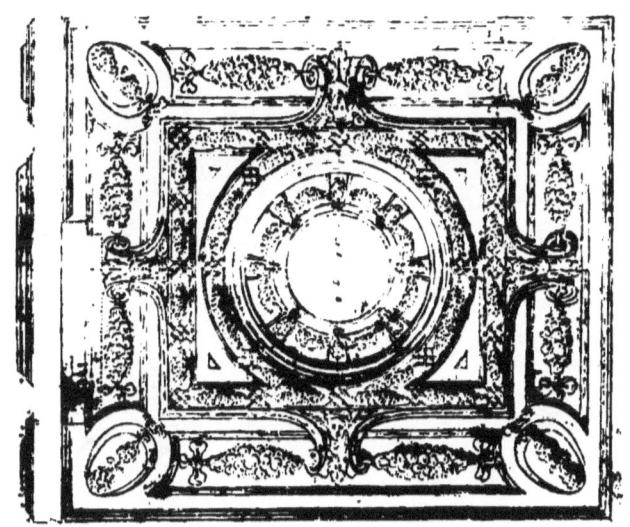

CEILING, COUNTESS OF CARNARVON'S BEDCHAMBER
(*Worcester College Collection*)

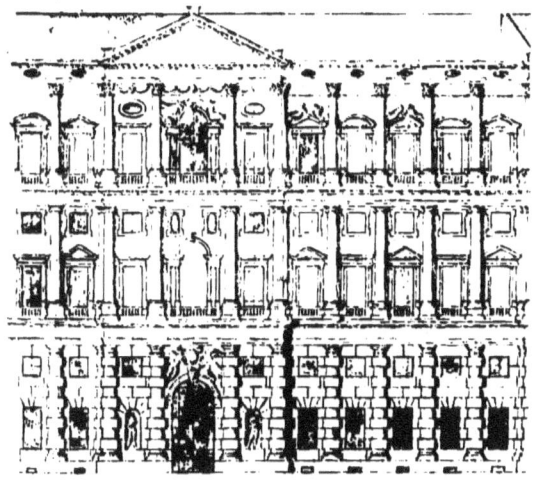

DETAIL OF ELEVATION OF OLD SOMERSET HOUSE
(*Worcester College Collection*)

CHIMNEY-PIECE TO THE DOUBLE CUBE ROOM, WILTON.

this house was burnt about 1647, and that it was then rebuilt from the designs of Inigo Jones, under the superintendence of John Webb. The fine drawing at Chiswick of the ceiling of the Cabinet room is dated 1649, and is undoubtedly by Inigo Jones, and there can be little doubt that the interior of the south block was entirely designed by him, for Webb, as appears by his other work, was quite incapable of such admirable proportion and exquisite detail. There is a view at Wilton of the house as it was left by Inigo Jones, which shows a rectangular block of building with an oblong court, and towers at the four corners raised above the adjacent building. The sixteenth century gateway tower on the east side was preserved by Jones on account of its excellent workmanship, but brought into his design by a flat steeple-roof, so that the elevation of this east side, which faced the forecourt and the principal approach, consisted of a raised block in the centre, joined by a lower range of buildings on either side to the two raised blocks at the angles, a favourite composition with Inigo Jones. De Caux's work on this east façade

PANELLING IN DOUBLE CUBE ROOM, WILTON.

was allowed to remain. Part of the building was burnt down early in the eighteenth century, and a great part of it destroyed towards the end of that century, when James Wyatt rebuilt the north front and a great part of the east and west sides in an abominable travesty of Gothic. The position of the forecourt appears to have been shifted to the north side before this date, probably when Chambers built the triumphal arch as an entrance from the north. As the building now stands, the only remains of De Caux's work are two niches on either side of the east gateway, and probably the grottoes and garden houses, in his barbarous German manner. Aubrey also assigns him the stables, a good reasonable piece of architecture which is more probably by Inigo Jones or Webb. Of Inigo Jones's work there remains the south block (partly altered on the south façade), including the suite of rooms on the first floor, which appear to be in much the same state as they were left by him, for there is no finer example of his mature manner in existence in England. The great room, a double cube of 60 ft. by 30 ft. by 30 ft., with its superb mantlepiece, and panelling designed by Jones to receive Vandyke's portraits, is probably the most beautiful room in any house in this country; as the Banqueting Hall, also a double cube, of 110 ft. by 55 ft. is unquestionably the finest state room. Even Wren could never match their surpassing dignity and perfection of proportion. Wilton is a peculiarly valuable example, inasmuch as parts of it, at any rate, are undoubtedly by Inigo Jones. Tradition assigns to him a great quantity of buildings in England, but for many of these there is no authority, and the internal evidence of the actual design of the buildings is the only test which it is possible to apply. Raynham Park, in Norfolk, is an instance where the tradition is verified by the building itself, and the design of it is indeed the most distinguished example of seventeenth century domestic architecture in England. It is peculiarly refined and accomplished. Quiet, reserved, and dignified in the highest degree, it stands by itself, apart alike from the mere picturesqueness of Jacobean work, and from the genial yet coarser manner of Wren. The house was built about 1636. The outside starts with a basement storey above ground of Portland stone; above this the walls are of brick with stone quoins, strings, cornices, and dressings. An unusual entablature with engaged balusters in the frieze is carried across the central block between the wings on the west side. The plan consists of an oblong block with slightly projecting wings at the sides. The principal floor is raised on a basement above ground, and a grand flight of stairs on the west side leads to the front entrance to the hall, round which are ranged the living rooms *en suite*, with several staircases to the right and left communicating with the upper floors, and there is no grand staircase at all inside. On the second floor on the west side is the grand salon, a superb rectangular room, very lofty with a rich plaster ceiling, lighted by a Venetian window on the east side. Towards the end of the seventeenth century certain alterations were made in the internal decoration, overmantels were added to the chimney-pieces, and it is possible that the central pediment

CENTRE BAY TO SOUTH FRONT, WILTON.

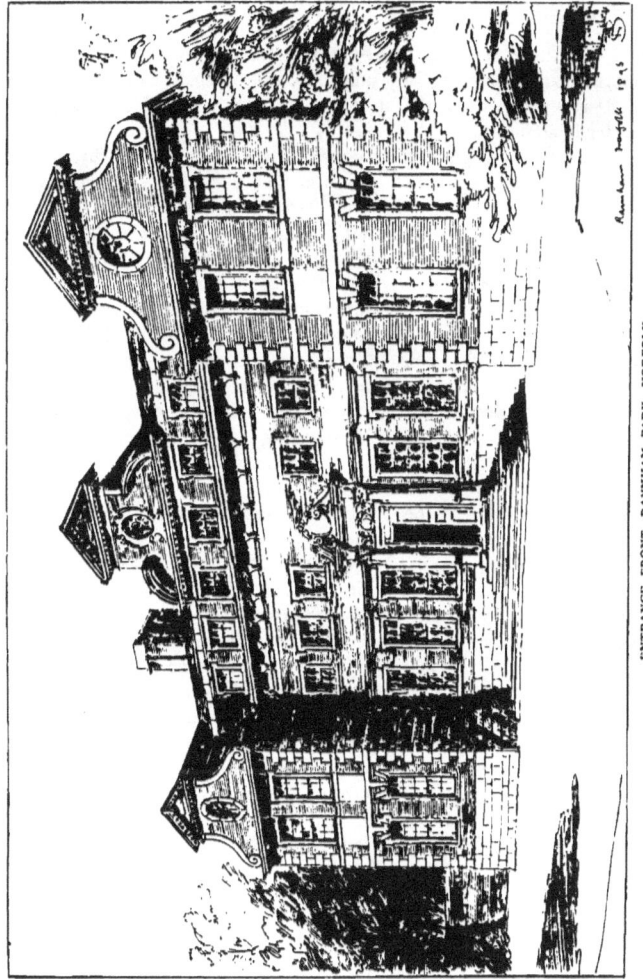

ENTRANCE FRONT, RAYNHAM PARK, NORFOLK.

and Corinthian order on the east side was added about this date; but the house is substantially unaltered, and abounds with refinements of design which show the strong unfaltering touch of a truly great master in architecture.

About 1647 Inigo Jones designed certain additions to Kirby, which closely resemble his work at Wilton in their austerity of manner; and he prepared designs for re-building Durham House, of which there are draughts by Webb in Worcester College Library. There is also in this collection a drawing by Webb, entitled "Purfyle of ye Duke's Pallace at Cobham, 1648," which is probably the origin of the story which attributes to Inigo Jones the centre bay of the garden court of Cobham.[1] It is possible that Inigo Jones did some work at Cobham, but this particular façade as it now stands cannot have been designed by him. It is a poor piece of work, coarsely designed, and was perhaps by Webb; the explanation of much unsatisfactory work throughout the country which vague tradition has assigned to Inigo Jones. There is no doubt that he did design many additions and alterations to existing houses, of which no documentary record exists, but in the case of such traditions the evidence of the building itself is the only clue. This at once eliminates the Jacobean work at Cranborne Manor, executed for Cecil soon after 1604, but will include among the list of his works the west wing with its great quoins and boldly projecting eaves, which in scale can only be compared with St. Paul's, Covent Garden. This wing was built in 1647, and is almost certainly by Inigo Jones. It is also probable that he designed the stairs and some of the ceilings at Ford Abbey,[2] Coleshill in Berkshire (1650), and the Grange in Hampshire, since entirely altered by Wilkins. Castle Ashby in Northamptonshire was begun by Inigo Jones, but interrupted by the Civil War. He is also said to have superintended the building of Stoke Park, Northamptonshire (1630-1634), but the design was brought from Italy by Sir Francis Crane. Brympton, Amesbury, and Gunnersbury were by Webb, the two last possibly from designs by his master.

[1] Mr. Gotch, ii. 37, says this part "was rebuilt in 1662, under the direction of Inigo Jones," but the latter had died ten years before. The date on the pediment is 1667. The Worcester drawing has no sort of resemblance to any part of the existing garden court at Cobham.

[2] Woolfe and Gandon ("Vitruvius Britannicus," vol. v., p. 86-7) say: "It is perhaps the most perfect work now remaining of that great architect Inigo Jones, having undergone no alteration since the year 1650, when it was compleated." Ware, who measured up this house for Lord Burlington, published sections of the hall and staircase in his "Complete Body of Architecture," plates 70, 71.

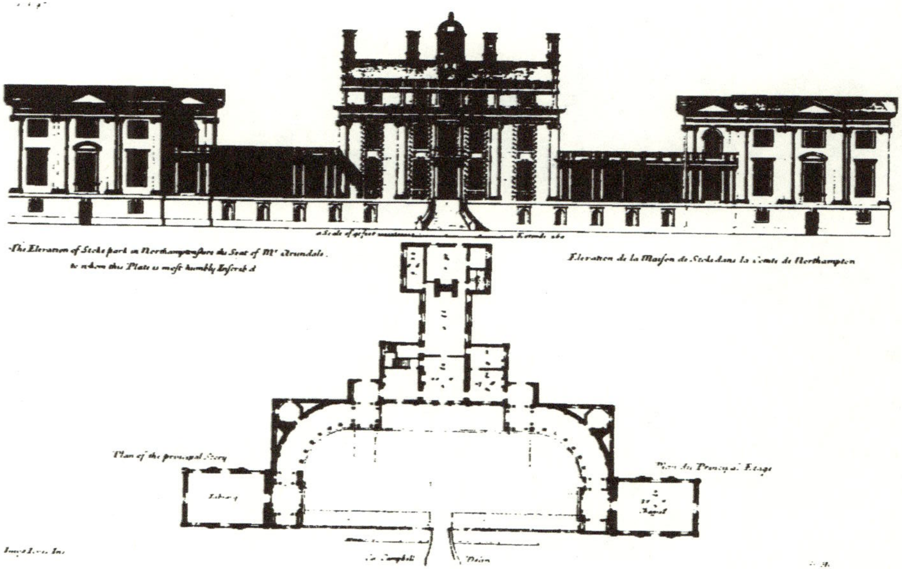
The Elevation of Stoke park in Northamptonshire the Seat of Mr Arundale.
to whom this Plate is most humbly Inscrib'd
Elevation de la Maison de Stoke dans la Comte de Northampton
Plan of the principal Story
Plan du Principal Etage
Library
Chapel
C. Campbell Delin

KIRBY, NORTHANTS. THE DOORWAY AND BALCONY, PROBABLY BY INIGO JONES.

INIGO JONES

The admirable staircase and other details at Ashburnham House were probably designed by Jones, but carried out by Webb with variations just sufficient to miss the distinctive quality which Inigo Jones impressed on all his work.[1] His latest design is probably one for the re-building of the College of Physicians, now preserved in Worcester College Library, dated 1651, and marked "not taken." He died June 21st, 1652, and was buried by the side of his father in the Church of St. Bennet, Paul's Wharf.

Inigo Jones was on the whole the greatest architect and one of the most accomplished artists that this country has ever produced. No man has mastered more completely the scholarship of his art; but to this range of knowledge he added a power of design and a quality of imagination which place him, as an artist, higher even than his great successor Wren. " It was *vox Europæ*," says Webb, "that named Inigo Jones Vitruvius Britannicus, being much more, than at home, famous in remote parts, where he lived many years, designed many works, and discovered many antiquities, before unknown, with great applause." The "antiquities" refer to his studies at Rome, for his theory of Stonehenge is not among his most memorable achievements. His extraordinary capacity is shown by the success with which he freed English architecture from the imbecilities of the German designers, and started it on a line of fresh development, borrowed it is true from Italy, yet so successfully adapted to English traditions, that it was at

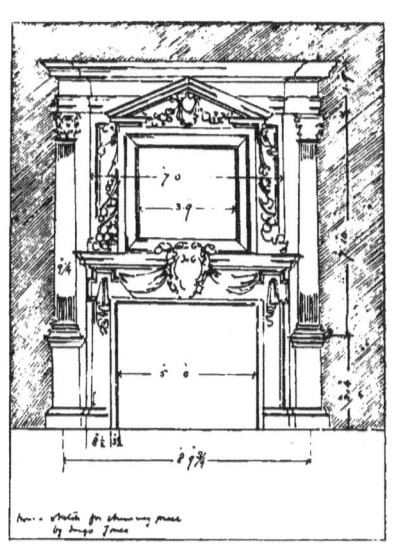

SKETCH FOR CHIMNEY-PIECE, BY INIGO JONES.

---

[1] A list of other buildings which have been assigned to Inigo Jones is given by Mr. Horne in his article in the " Dictionary of National Biography."

once accepted and followed by the best intelligence of the country for the next hundred and fifty years. His especial strength lay in his thorough mastery of proportion, his contempt for mere prettiness, and the rare distinction of his style. His own theory of architecture was that, in his own words, it should be "solid, proportional according to the rules, masculine and unaffected." No man has ever more completely realized his own ideal of his art.

NOTE p. 112. The figures given by Mr. Longman in "The Three Cathedrals dedicated to St. Paul," p. 72, are as follows :—Up to Oct. 29, 1639, £89,489 4s. 5d had been received, and between this date and 1643 a further sum of about £14,000 was raised. In this year Paul's Cross was pulled down, and all work stopped by order of Parliament. It appears that of the sums received, about £79,080 was spent on the Cathedral, and in compensation "unto several persons for houses demolished and other necessary charges."

CHAPTER VI.

JOHN WEBB, MARSH, AND GERBIER : THE LAST SURVIVALS OF GOTHIC.

THERE can be little doubt that an architect of the reputation and constant practice enjoyed by Inigo Jones, must have had some sort of staff of assistants. His only known pupil, however, is John Webb, and, in fact, with the exception of Webb, and the doubtful work of Gerbier and Marsh, the period of the Commonwealth is practically a blank in the history of architecture. A few houses were built, but, with the exceptions mentioned in the text, they were probably designed by the builders, and indeed it is clear that, in spite of the brilliant example of Inigo Jones, the architect had as yet hardly disentangled his calling from that of the builder.

John Webb was born in 1611,[1] and educated at Merchant Taylors' School. He seems, on leaving school in 1628, to have been apprenticed to Inigo Jones, with whom he worked as assistant till the death of the latter in 1652. How far he also worked on his own account during any part of this period is uncertain. There is no doubt that he superintended the execution of many of the designs of Inigo Jones both during his lifetime and after, as at Ashburnham House (probably between 1650 and 1660), Wilton, Amesbury (rebuilt), Gunnersbury, and Greenwich. The brick houses on the south side of Great Queen Street have been assigned to Webb by Walpole, who mentions that Gerbier condemned the lions' heads on the pilasters. There are no lions' heads on the pilasters in their present state, but the houses are of about this period, and were probably built by Webb while he was still working with Inigo Jones. Though by no means badly designed, they have none of the distinction of his master's work, and the capitals are very careless. The front is divided into five bays by Corinthian pilasters on a basement storey, the order including the first and second storeys ; a bold modillion cornice terminates the order. The roof is brought right down to the

[1] In the registers at Butleigh, in Somerset, the home of the Webbs, there is a doubtful entry : " John, filius Thomæ Webb (?) baptizat fuit 24 die Augusti, 1603." The surname is almost illegible, and is possibly Webb.

cornice without either parapet or blocking course. Whether this was the original intention or not, the effect is very picturesque, but it is hardly orthodox, and the curious brick cartouches suggest the fancy of John Webb rather than that of Inigo Jones. During the Civil War Webb sent plans of the fortifications of London to the king, at Oxford, a service which might have cost him his head, but he was able to resume work with Inigo Jones after 1645, and during the latter's lifetime he married his niece, and was appointed his executor. In 1655 he edited Jones's notes on Stonehenge, and in 1665 wrote "A Vindication of Stonehenge Restored," a loyal, if ineffectual defence of his master's archæological theories. In 1653 he designed some mantelpieces for Drayton, and in 1654 a large portico and summer-house with some other alterations, including the removal of the base-court at the Vyne near Basingstoke, for Chaloner Chute, Speaker of the House of Commons. One or two of the mantelpieces of this date at the Vyne show plainly the influence of Inigo Jones, and are well designed, though poor in detail, but the portico is very ugly. The proportions are bad, and the pediment heavy without being impressive, a fault which is also seen in the entrance piers to the park at Amesbury.

ENTRANCE PIER, AMESBURY.

In 1656 he designed Thorpe Hall, near Peterborough, for Oliver St. John. The date on a lead head to the stables is 1656, and the house was probably begun soon after the death of Inigo Jones. Standing on rising ground above the Valley of the Nene, Thorpe Hall is a singularly dignified building, and the most perfect instance now existing of that very interesting phase of architecture which extended from about 1640 to 1670, an architecture directly inspired by Inigo Jones, and as yet uninfluenced by Wren. On the north side is the forecourt, approached by an avenue. To the left are the gardens, all walled in, and extending along the south side of the house till they meet the kitchen garden to the south and west. To the west of the house are the stables. A raised terrace runs along three sides of the gardens, with a gateway in the centre. The house, which is constructed entirely of stone up to the cornice, is very boldly designed. In plan it is oblong, divided into four quarters by wide corridors, running north and south, and east and west. The grand staircase occupies the eastern arm of the corridor and leads to the principal rooms, which are, as usual, on the first floor, and arranged *en suite*. The north elevation is in seven bays, and has three storeys up to the cornice, above a basement storey with windows

DOORWAY AT THE VYNE, NEAR BASINGSTOKE, BY JOHN WEBB.

STONE MANTELPIECE. THE VYNE, NEAR BASINGSTOKE.

ENTRANCE PORCH, THORPE HALL.

128 RENAISSANCE ARCHITECTURE IN ENGLAND

in the plinth. The ground floor windows have plain architraves, and the chief ornament is reserved for the first floor windows, which have alternate straight entablatures and pediments, the centre light over the entrance porch having a segmental pediment. Square windows with stone architraves on the second floor bring up under a heavy modillion cornice executed in wood with plaster soffit. Above this is a steep pitched roof with dormers, covered with Collyweston slates. The interior of the house is richly decorated with panelling and plaster work; the latter is coarse, but extremely vigorous, and the fine carved open work balustrade to the staircase anticipates the delicate panels by Grinling Gibbons, used afterwards by Wren for his internal woodwork with such admirable effect. This staircase has been partly restored and altered. The stables are more plainly designed than the house, but the same masculine scale is maintained throughout. The big centre gable closely resembles the gables of the riding-school at Bolsover, a resemblance which makes it probable that the designer of the latter was also a pupil of Inigo Jones. Thorpe Hall shows Webb's peculiarities in every detail, such as his affection for returned and mitred architraves, and other variations on the simpler methods of design. He had learnt from his master the value of bold simple details, the necessity of avoiding fussiness of design, even at the cost of ugliness, but he had not attained that clear-headed strength of intelligence which can see its way through a design from start to finish, and, in consequence, his work is sometimes violent without being strong. Yet Thorpe Hall is a fine design; in spite of a certain heaviness, it has the rare quality of maintaining its scale throughout, and that in a very exacting style. The extent of the advance, or if it is preferred, the alteration in English architecture brought about by Inigo Jones can be gauged by comparing Thorpe Hall with the charming little manor house of Stibington about six miles off, finished in 1625, where the scale is, by comparison, that of a cottage, and the detail, in so far as it is intended for classical detail, is quite rudimentary. In 1657-8 Webb was doing work for the Earl of Northumberland at Northumberland House. There are drawings at Chiswick for some of the mantels, and a drawing for a house at Bishop's Burton in Yorkshire. In June, 1660, Webb made a petition for the place of surveyor of works, which the late king had designed for him in succession to Inigo Jones.[1] The post, however, was given to Sir

---

[1] A summary of this petition is given in the Calendar of State Papers, Domestic, 1660-1661, p. 76:
"1660, June. Petition of John Webb, architect, to the King, for the place of

THE STABLES, THORPE HALL.

John Denham, and the reversion granted to Webb. In 1666 he was appointed assistant-surveyor to Denham, but on the latter's death in 1668, Wren was appointed surveyor, and Webb, perhaps in disgust at this discreditable abuse of patronage, seems to have retired soon afterwards to Butleigh in Somerset, where he built himself a house, since destroyed, and died on October 30th, 1674.[1] His principal works, besides the above, were Gunnersbury, from designs by Jones, 1663 (rebuilt by Smirke in 1834), Burlington House, 1664-1666 (remodelled for the Earl of Burlington in 1720), Horseheath Hall, Cambridgeshire, 1665, destroyed in 1777, Bedford House, on the north side of Bloomsbury Square, since destroyed, Lamport Hall, Northamptonshire, Ramsbury in Wilts, Ashdown Park (shown in Kyp), and the execution of Inigo Jones's designs at Greenwich (1661-1666), forming the western part of the river front.[2] There are at Chiswick numerous drawings by John Webb for the details and plaster work of Greenwich, dated 1663-66-68. These designs are freely drawn in Indian ink and cross-hatched, and, as executed by the admirable plaster workers trained by Inigo Jones, would no doubt have been effective, but Webb's taste was uncertain. In some 1 in. scale details of capitals to the doors of the king's cabinet at Greenwich, lions and unicorns are substituted for the volutes under the abacus, an anticipation of what Adam called his Britannic order, and a piece of originality which would have been intolerable to the stricter Palladians. The atrocious design[3] for an alcove for His

surveyor of works, designed for him by the late King, (he) being brought up under Inigo Jones in the study of architecture, and appointed his deputy, till thrust out for loyalty in 1643, is now by instruction of Parliament preparing a survey of his Majesty's houses for his reception, the cost of which will be £8,140 5s. 2d., for which he is engaged in credit, having received only £500." Annexed to this is a paper containing "arguments in behalf of Mr. Webb, that under his uncle, Inigo Jones, he not only studied architecture, but masques and triumphs—was his deputy and executor, and has £1,500 due to him in Jones's board wages. He sent to the King at Oxford designs of all the fortifications in London, with instructions how they might be carried,—prepared Whitehall in a fortnight for his Majesty on his own credit—and though Mr. Denham may, as most gentry, have, some knowledge of the theory of architecture, he can have none of the practice, but must employ another, whereas Webb has spent 30 years at it, and worked for most of the nobility."

[1] The entry in the registry is "John Webb, Esq., was buried the 4 day of November, 1672," but a note at the bottom of the page says, "John Webb, esq., dyed the 30 of Oct. 1674."

[2] It is not known who was the architect of the Town Hall at Abingdon. The design is a very fine one, and marked by certain qualities which are also found in Thorpe House and Ashdown. It is possible that this building was designed by Webb.

[3] This design is given by Kent as the work of Inigo Jones, but the original drawing is dated 1663.

F. H. Ault, Aldbourne, Wilts.

ASHDOWN HOUSE, BERKSHIRE.

To f. 139.

JOHN WEBB, MARSH, AND GERBIER

Majesty's bedchamber at Greenwich shows how impossible it is for the greatest of masters to instill into their pupils their own essential qualities, unless the latter are exceptionally able men.

Webb appears to have been a conscientious architect, intelligent, but not profoundly original. He worked in the manner he had learnt from Inigo Jones, a manner admirable in itself, but most difficult to handle, and there is little trace in his work of the learning and consum-

PART OF A DESIGN FOR A CEILING AT GREENWICH, BY JOHN WEBB.

mate reticence of his master. Yet he came of a splendid school, and nowhere is the saving influence of tradition more clearly seen than in the work of pupils of great masters in architecture.

Vertue, in Walpole's "Anecdotes" (ii. 175), mentions an architect of the name of Marsh, who designed the "additional buildings at Bolsover, erected after the Restoration," and Nottingham Castle. The "additional buildings" are the riding-school block at Bolsover, by far the finest part of the building, and a very powerful design. The bold rustication of the archways, the quoins to the dormers, and the breadth and vigour of the entire façade, suggest the influence of Inigo Jones, in spite of certain lapses here and there; and it is possible that this architect may have worked with Inigo Jones, though hitherto nothing further has been discovered about him.

Sir Balthazar Gerbier credited himself with a fine building near the York Stairs water-gate, and published a small treatise on magnificent buildings, and another with the title of "Counsel and Advice to all Builders," both in 1662. In the preface to "The 3 chief principles of Magnificent Building," Gerbier says that the place of Surveyor-General was intended for him after the death of Inigo Jones. Walpole says that he gave the designs for Hempstead Marshall (since destroyed), begun in 1662, and finished by his pupil, Captain Wynne; but this appears to be inaccurate, as Gerbier was in utter disgrace at the Restoration, and died in 1662. Gerbier is said to have designed the original house for Lord Craven in 1620, in imitation of Heidelberg. This house was burnt, and it is not known that he had anything to do with the second house, which was designed and carried out by Wynne. Gerbier's work, however, is unimportant, and only of interest in so far as Gerbier, who was employed under both James and Charles I., lived till after the Restoration, and in this way forms a link between the times of Inigo Jones and Wren. He died in 1662.[1]

Meanwhile the Gothic style had lingered on in the country, in spite of the example set by the Church of St. Paul's in Covent Garden. Bath Abbey Church, which was begun in 1499, was not completed till 1616, without any deviation in style from the original design. The best traditions of the style were lost before the end of the sixteenth century; yet almost down to the time of the Restoration, a mason, when called upon to build a church window, fell naturally into the ways of late Perpendicular Gothic. It is, indeed, possible that the disappearance of Gothic as a distinct style was partly due to the check given to all church-building by the Reformation. Very few churches were built in the last half of the sixteenth century, and the records of any of the larger parish churches indicate clearly the tendency of national feeling

---

[1] Some interesting details of Gerbier's career are given in Walpole's "Anecdotes," i. 273-282. He was a restless but unsuccessful adventurer, who handled architecture merely as one among his many other methods of speculation. He was deprived of his post of Master of the Ceremonies, and died in 1662 (not 1667, the date given in the "Dictionary of Architecture," art. Gerbier). On August 24th, 1663, a petition for relief was presented by his three surviving daughters, in which they state that they were left in extreme poverty; that £4,000 of arrears had been owing to their father from Charles I., and that they had been praying for relief for the last six months.

in this regard. At Rye, Sussex, for instance, in 1547, there was expended, "for cleaning the Church from Popery," £1 15s. 4d.; this consisted of the removal of all the images, altars and rood lofts, and the sale of the church plate for £99 14s. 10d. An ordinance of Edward VI. enacted that the Royal Arms were to be substituted for a cross above the rood lofts of parish churches, and though at Mary's accession, in 1553, an attempt was made to restore the old religion, money was short, and the shabbiness of the outlay is almost pitiful. When Elizabeth came to the throne, in 1558, the church at Rye was again adapted to Protestant notions, that is, texts were painted on the walls, and pews were made for the mayor and jurats and their wives. The days of that lavish self-sacrifice, which gave to this country churches which are still among its most beautiful achievements in architecture, were past for ever; and though churches were still to be built in the older manner, they were built with rigid parsimony, as a necessity, no longer as an occasion for the enthusiastic devotion of pious men. The artistic value of this later work is in consequence very slight. Its interest is mainly historical, as showing how intimately Gothic architecture was associated

DESIGN FOR A MANTELPIECE AT GREENWICH,
BY JOHN WEBB.

with the older religious motives, and how deeply rooted this tradition was in the minds of the English people.

During the reign of Elizabeth the money, which a hundred years before would have been spent in building new chapels and chantries, or in rood loft and reredos, was, so far as church-building was concerned, devoted to sumptuous monuments of marble and alabaster. The existing churches were probably sufficient for the population, and the question was rather that of preserving the old than of building any new. In 1560 a proclamation was issued at Windsor against breaking or defacing monuments of antiquity set up in churches, and converting church bells to private uses;[1] and, in consequence of the fire of June 4th, 1561, a commission was appointed[2] to consider the repairs of St. Paul's, and to procure funds. A considerable sum of money was raised, and the roofs were restored and covered with lead, but the steeple was not rebuilt; in fact, the church work of this time consists chiefly in repair and maintenance. Sometimes specific additions were made, such as the gallery at the west end of St. Peter's, Wolverhampton, built at the cost of the Merchant Taylors' Company in 1610, but of actual church-building very little was done in the reigns of Elizabeth or James. The porch of Sunningwell Church, near Oxford, with Ionic columns and Gothic tracery, was built in 1562, and the tower of Probus Church in Cornwall, in 1570; Brancepath, Durham, in 1577, and Lower Peover Church in Cheshire in 1580. Quarendon Church in Bucks was restored by Sir Henry Lee about 1600; and Fulmer in Bucks in 1610. In all these churches Gothic details were used, though often intermixed with strange variations of Renaissance motives, faint echoes of that far-away movement of which the country builder had heard, but as yet had no understanding.

On the other hand, the Puritan ideal was rapidly gaining ground throughout the country; the meaning of the great Gothic churches was becoming a sealed book to the majority of Englishmen. The architecture, which had once been the familiar language of a people with faith and imagination, was already regarded by the Puritan as mysterious and incomprehensible, the symbol of a doctrine which he hated, no longer as the centre of all the most sacred and intimate associations of life. Moreover the Court of James I. was greedy, and indifferent to religion. In 1617 and 1618 licences were granted to search for treasures in abbeys and priories, such as St. Albans, Glastonbury, and

---

[1] Cal. Dom. State Papers, 13 Eliz., September 19th, 1560.
[2] Cal. Dom. State Papers, 17 Eliz., June 24th, 1561.

JOHN WEBB, MARSH, AND GERBIER

Romsey; and probably much of the injury to shrines and monuments, attributed to Cromwell's soldiery, was actually done by the persons who

SOUTH PORCH OF GROOMBRIDGE CHURCH, KENT, BUILT 1625 BY WILLIAM CAMFIELD.
"OB FELICISSIMUM CAROLI PRINCIPIS EX HISPANIS REDDITUM."

obtained these licences. The poetry and mysticism of religion was lost to all but a few devoted men of exceptional imagination, and it was only the singular pertinacity of one great churchman which breathed fresh life into this dying spirit. This is not the place to discuss Laud's views of government, ecclesiastical and temporal, but there is no doubt of his sincere desire to make the services of religion orderly and comely, and to make the church a building worthy of such services. By the Puritan mind, intolerant of ideas and insensible to beauty, this was interpreted as a desire to introduce superstitions; but it is clear to us that nearly everything that was done to keep churches in decent maintenance, and whatever activity there was in the way of church-building during the twenty years that preceded the Civil War, must be attributed mainly to the personal influence of men such as Laud and Matthew Wren. In 1621 Laud was appointed Bishop of St. David's, and in 1626 Bishop of Bath and Wells, and between these years several of the west country churches were added to and repaired. Stalls and a new aisle roof were added to Sandbach Church in Cheshire, in 1620-1633 and 1638. A new roof was constructed in Astbury and Barthomley Churches in Cheshire about 1620, and galleries were put up in Nantwich Church in 1624. About the same time some of the midland churches were repaired. In 1626 Sir R. Banastre restored the chancel of Passenham Church, Northamptonshire, and added fresh seats and screens. The Church of Leighton-Bromswould in Huntingdonshire was built for George Herbert in 1626; and when the spire and part of the tower of Higham Ferrers Church, in Northamptonshire, were blown down in 1631, they were rebuilt to the old design, and even, so far as was possible, with the old materials. The immense quantity of Jacobean woodwork, screens, pulpits, and seats, still existing in English county churches, show the renewed activity of the Church in the twenty years preceding the Civil War. In Northiam Church, Sussex, there is to this day a complete altar-piece, including the table, altar-rails, marble paving, even the faded green cloth cover with its silk fringe, unaltered since the date at which they were put up (about the year 1625). In St. John's Church at Leeds, we have a rare and very interesting example of an entirely new church. In 1632-3, the old parish church being too small for the congregation, John Harrison, a citizen of Leeds, built the Church of St. John's, and endowed it with £80 per annum and £10 for repairs. The church was consecrated by Archbishop Neill in 1634. In plan it consists of two aisles of the same size, treated throughout exactly alike, with a square tower at the west end of the north aisle. The aisle arcade has pointed arches, and both aisles have square-headed windows with cinquefoil lights. The two east windows have geometrical tracery of very fair

ST. JOHN'S CHURCH, LEEDS.

design, but rather wiry in execution. The parapets have battlements. With the exception of the semicircular arch to the porch, and the curious capitals to the pillars of the arcade, all the details of the masonry are late Gothic, with slight technical variations, which will be noticed in dealing with the Oxford seventeenth century Gothic. When, however, the carpenters, joiners, and carvers were turned into the church, Gothic detail was abandoned. The framing of the roof with its square plaster panels, the richly carved screen, running across the whole width of the church, with the two great semicircular arches and open strap-work spandrels, the details of the wainscot pews, the pulpit and the reading desk, are all of the ordinary Jacobean type, that is, based on German models, with variations according to the fancy of the workman. The probable explanation of the capitals, which, though Gothic in outline, are Renaissance in detail, is that a carver was set to work upon them at some little interval after they were built. It is clear from this church and from similar instances, such as Water-Eaton, Lytes-Cary, and Rycott, that the Gothic tradition was preserved in masonry long after it had died out in the other building trades. The same peculiarity is noticeable in the library of St. John's, Cambridge, built 1623-4, for Williams, Bishop of Lincoln. The windows, and particularly the great oriel at the end, have fair decorated tracery in the heads, and the buttresses have crocketted pinnacles, but all the details of the woodwork are ordinary Jacobean. The windows are the more remarkable, in that the wall to the court has two entablatures of ordinary Renaissance sections.

It is probable, from the heterogeneous character of the details, that no architect was employed to design this church at Leeds. John Harrison may have given general directions, but the building as a whole represents the unaided efforts of different craftsmen working together without the control of a single mind. The result is undoubtedly very picturesque, and the building is planned with excellent good sense in regard to the particular form of service contemplated. It has however the defect of its virtues. Though in the days when there was but one inevitable style, it was possible for workmen to produce homogeneous architecture without the control of an autocratic designer, this has not been possible since the Renaissance. In a less degree the men of the seventeenth century laboured under much the same disabilities as the modern architect. They had to select their manner of expression instead of having it ready to hand, and as much a matter of inheritance as their mother tongue. The consequence was that where

T

several men worked together, as it were all upon one plane, and yet independently, there was a certain confusion of speech and lack of cohesion, and such a result could not be avoided unless a single mind supplied the idea and controlled its execution down to the minutest details. A little later in the century, when the great school of the seventeenth century architects was in full swing, this happy-go-lucky system disappeared; and though with it much that was interesting was lost, the greater lucidity of idea which accompanied the change was a distinct gain on the hazy thought of the unassisted workman; a tradition of sane and reasonable architecture was established which lasted in this country down to the beginning of this century. It is on these grounds, and in view of the exceedingly complex conditions of modern architecture, that the idea of abolishing the architect and reverting to the combined work of independent craftsmen, seems to me to be little more than an archæological fad, the last piece of cant of the Gothic revival.

In 1628 Laud was translated to London, and in the same year the re-building of the Church of St. Catherine Cree was begun. It was consecrated by Laud in January, 1630, with an elaborate ceremonial which was misinterpreted at the time, and afterwards formed one of the grounds of his indictment.[1] The uncertainty of purpose noticed in St. John's Church, Leeds, is found in St. Catherine's in an aggravated form. The nave arcades consist of semicircular arches brought down on to Corinthian columns without an intervening entablature, and the details of the external cornice, and the two southern doorways, are more or less based on Renaissance models; but the roofs are groined with ribs of a rough Perpendicular section, the clerestory and side windows have cinquefoiled heads, and the east window has five lower lights cinquefoiled, with a Catherine-wheel rose in the upper half, and more or less orthodox cusping. As has been pointed out in the last chapter, there appears to be no foundation for the tradition that Inigo Jones designed this church, and it is unlikely that any architect pure and simple was employed. The church was probably designed as well as executed by masons who worked indifferently in either style. The Church of St. Paul's, Hammersmith, consecrated by Laud in 1631, and since destroyed to make way for the present church, showed a similar mixture of styles, and Laud's additions to St. John's, Oxford (1631-

---

[1] The charge against Laud of subverting the religion of the country, was partly based on this and similar ceremonials. No specific instance, however, is mentioned in the articles of impeachment exhibited by the Commons against him in 1640, or in the further articles of impeachment of 1643.

1635) show certain resemblances to St. Catherine Cree, in the heterogeneous details, and the arcades, which make it possible that he employed the same man in these two buildings. There is abundant evidence of Laud's activity in the city churches, most of which were destroyed in the Great Fire. Thus, in 1631, £2,400 was spent[1] in the repairs of St. Dunstan's in the East. In 1632-3 the roof of the nave of St. Olave's, Hart Street, was rebuilt on the old lines, and probably the clerestory windows. In 1633, St. Alban's, Wood Street, was rebuilt by Inigo Jones, apparently on the old design. Matthew Wren, no less zealous than Laud, in his desire to reform the service of the Church, completed the chapel and cloisters of Peterhouse, Cambridge, in 1632, as shown in Loggan's view before the alterations of 1709. The details of the cloisters somewhat resembled those of Laud's work at St. John's, except that the arches are four-centred, but the windows have late Perpendicular tracery, and the whole building is a curious mixture of Gothic intention and classical details ill-understood. George Thompson was the mason, but no name of any designer is given in the

NICHE AT W. END OF PETERHOUSE CHAPEL, CAMBRIDGE.

[1] Strype's "Survey."

account. Cosin, afterwards Bishop of Durham, who succeeded Wren, gave £390 towards the fittings, and introduced a crucifix on the high altar. Prynne says that he made a regulation that none of the fellows or scholars should turn their backs on the altar, either in entering or leaving the chapel; and it is evident that the interior was richly decorated, for Dowsing, the iconoclast, reported that, in 1643, he and others purified Peterhouse Chapel in his usual way. In his Diary (for December 21, 1643), Dowsing notes "we went to Peterhouse, 1643, December 21, with officers and souldiers and . . . . we pulled down 2 mighty great angells with wings, and divers other angells, and the 4 evangelists and Peter with his Keies over the chappel door, and about a hundred Cherubims and angells and divers superstitious letters in gold, and at the upper end of the chancel, these words were written as followeth : ' Hic locus est Domus Dei, nil aliud, et Porta cœli,' witness Will. Dowsing. Geo. Long." The glass of the east window was saved by being taken down and hidden away in boxes.

Abel's work at Abbey Dore Church (1634), which has been already described, is a good example of restoration as understood at the time. No attempt was made to replace the old work with copies, yet it is evident that Abel was conscious of its existence. The ceiling of the chancel, as rebuilt by him, is flat, carried by great oak rafters with carved brackets. These brackets spring from a slender shaft with an Ionic capital; but the proportions of this shaft are evidently based on the small engaged shafts of the original Early English work, and the shaft itself starts from the springing of the old groining. The effect is not very incongruous, and this method of dealing with old buildings has the advantage of preserving every fragment of the old work possible, and of avoiding the falsification of history, which has resulted from the church restorations carried out in England during the last fifty years. Abel had at least sufficient respect for the work of his forefathers to leave it alone, whereas the modern architect, with full ecclesiastical sanction and encouragement, has been in the habit of arbitrarily selecting one particular period in the history of the Church, and sweeping away all subsequent work to make room for his own inaccurate version of the style selected. The result, however gratifying to the architect and his client, is simply desperate for the historical student.

So again, where an addition was made to an existing church, no attempt was made to design the new work in laborious imitation of the old. The problem was met squarely and without affectation, and the new stalls, or pulpit, or panelling, were carried out according to the methods of woodwork prevalent at the time, with a richness and originality of which this generation can hardly form any conception, since most of our churches have been swept and garnished by eminent church

THE CHAPEL, LYTES-CARY.

restorers. At Cartmel Church, for instance, in 1640, George Preston, "out of his zeale to God, at his great charges, repaired this Church, being in greate decay, with a newe roof of tymber, and beautifyed it within very decently with fretted plaister work, and adorned the chancel with curiously carved wood-work, and placed therein a pair of organs of greate value." The screens have detached oak columns, carved with vines, and Corinthian capitals. In the cornice are the emblems of the Passion, with bunches of fruit interspersed. The naïveté of this work, and its entire freedom from self-consciousness, are a refreshing contrast to the archæological pedantry of modern restorations.

There is some uncertainty about the charming little domestic chapel of Lyte's-Cary in Somersetshire. This is of stone, with an open timbered roof, and excellent Perpendicular tracery to the windows. Round the building, immediately below the plate, runs a frieze of the shields and armorial bearings of various families. There are thirty-nine of these shields painted in red, blue, black, and yellow, but the chapel being in a ruinous state, the shields are nearly perished. There is no doubt that the roof, and wainscoting, and this decoration were put up by Thomas Lyte in 1631, and I incline to think that the whole chapel was added by him to the house in that year, as there is a straight joint at the west end, where the north and south walls abut against the house, and an incised tablet in the south side bears an inscription, "This chapel being founded by William Lyte . . . " and the date 1631; the rest is illegible.[1] The little church of Rycott, near Thame, is another remarkable instance of a private chapel. Whether built by the Berties or not, about 1620, it served as the private chapel to the great house of Rycott, now entirely destroyed. It consists of a single nave, covered by a pointed barrel roof of wood painted blue, the ribs painted red. The chancel is paved with black and white marble tiles, and at the footpace to the chancel are inclosed pews on either side. That on the north side is in two storeys, with an open arcade above panelling, and above is a gallery with open-work panels. The whole of this wood-work is picked out with gilt, the columns to the arcade painted black,

[1] Mr. Maxwell Lyte, in his account of the Lytes of Lytes-Cary, says "the existing chapel unquestionably dates from the middle of the 14th century," but he admits that "there is no direct evidence as to the foundation or endowments of the chapel." The only documentary evidence appears to be the inscription in the chapel and an entry in Thomas Lyte's common place-book. The inscription in 1889 was almost illegible, but Mr. Lyte gives it in full: "This chapell beinge founded by William Lyte. sergeant at law temp. Ed. 1 was in the vii. yere of K. Charles newely repayred by Thomas Lyte and Dame Constance Sydney his wyfe an°. do. 1631." The entry in Thomas Lyte's common place-book is as follows: "Ten foot and a halfe of glass sett up in the chapple windoe at Lytes Cary by Henry Lyte Esqr. a. d. 1567. whereby yt. appeareth that the chapple at Lytes Cary *was standinge in his tyme and by him lett downe.*" The last words seem to me conclusive evidence that Thomas Lyte rebuilt the chapel in 1631, and that it therefore dates not from the fourteenth, but the seventeenth century.

and arabesques in white paint fill the panels. The panelling by the stairs to this gallery was all gilt, except little oval portraits in the panels. The pew on the south side has an elaborate baldachino on Ionic columns. The windows have good Perpendicular tracery, and all the details of the stonework are Gothic, but I think it highly probable that the whole building was built by the Berties early in the seventeenth century.[1] Another well-known instance is the ruined chapel of Burford Priory in Oxfordshire, built after 1634 by Speaker Lenthall. The styles are mixed in this building with the most complete audacity. The chapel measures about 36 ft. by 12 ft., and appears to have been covered in with a stone segmental roof, the springing of the flat enriched ribs still remaining, though the roof itself has fallen in. A regular entablature with egg-and-tongue moulding runs round the interior, and the architrave is returned down the sides of the windows, the heads of which are filled in with tracery with no cusping. At the east end is a three-light window, with the Ten Commandments carved on stone tablets on either side. The adjacent north and south windows have wheel tracery. At the west end are remains of a wooden gallery on stone spiral-fluted columns; and on either side of the doorway two angels standing on pilaster balusters support a carving of the burning bush, with inscriptions "Exue calceos nam terra sancta est" and "quasi per ignes salvabimur." The building is in a most ruinous state, the gallery is half destroyed, the roof fallen in, and fragments of the stone carving and tracery lie scattered about among the nettles.

The Gothic tradition was tenaciously maintained at Oxford. When Sir Thomas Bodley built his schools he probably intended his tower to be a fine Renaissance composition, but the Gothic tradition creeps in at every point: in the groining of the gateway, the cusping to the windows, and the crockets to the pinnacles; and when a new college chapel was built, the Gothic method of fenestration was habitually followed. Wadham (1610-1613) is a characteristic instance. The windows to the choir and the east window have very fair Perpendicular tracery, but a curious variation is introduced into the windows of the ante-chapel: the tracery above the heads of the three lower lights has no cusping, but the oval in the centre has key-blocks, and the mouldings run out into scrolls. Jewit suggests that this was probably done in order to make the ante-chapel windows uniform with those of the hall; the remarkable thing is that the Perpendicular windows of the choir are actually the later of the

[1] This most interesting little building is in an out-of-the-way place, and was, when I examined it in 1890, in a very neglected and dilapidated state.

two. Mr. Jackson has proved from the building accounts of the college that the windows of the hall and ante-chapel were completed by William

THE CHAPEL, BRAZENOSE, OXFORD.

Arundel in 1611 to 1612, whereas John Spicer made the eleven windows of the choir in the spring and summer of 1612. Mr. Jackson remarks with justice: "John Spicer little thought what a pitfall he was digging for many an archæological reputation." At Jesus Chapel the east window (1636) has good geometrical tracery, but no subordination in the mouldings, and in the side window of the Chapel of St. Mary's Hall (1632-1644) the tracery starts from the mullions like cusping, and the fillets of the tracery do not meet. In Lincoln Chapel (1631) and Oriel (1637-1642) the fillet of the tracery has a hollow channel sunk on the face. The famous staircase to the hall at Christ Church (1640) was built by Dean Fell, " by the help of —— Smith, an artificer of London."[1] The fan tracery and the central shaft are so good that, except for a slight attenuation of detail, this might easily be mistaken for work a hundred and fifty years earlier. The most remarkable instance at Oxford is the latest. Brazenose Chapel was completed in 1666. The north window of the ante-chapel has flowing geometrical tracery, but is framed into an architrave with a broken pediment above, and the side windows of the chapel have pointed heads and geometrical tracery, but are flanked by pilasters with Corinthian capitals, supporting a regular entablature. Indeed, this Oxford seventeenth century Gothic is the most curious in England. It persistently peeps out through Renaissance ornaments and classic frontispieces—cusps and crockets mix indiscriminately with orders and entablatures. Oxford, in fact, remained essentially mediæval till the rude clash of the Civil War broke in upon her dreams.

A similar mixture of styles occurs in the Church of Berwick-on-Tweed, built by Colonel Fenwicke, the governor, 1648-1652. This church has a nave, and north and south aisles. The nave arcade has plain semicircular arches, brought down without any entablature on to the abaci of Tuscan columns; but the clerestory windows have three lights with cinquefoiled heads, the centre light stepped up above the two side-lights, as at St. Catherine Cree's. There is no tower, but two octagonal turrets with cupolas at the west end. In this case it almost seems as if the church was begun by a mason with classical tastes, and finished by one who preferred the Gothic. The latest example of a complete Gothic church is Charles Church at Plymouth, built in about 1657, though the upper part of the tower was rebuilt in 1708, and some atrocious woodwork was added at the end of the last century. With these exceptions, the church is entirely Gothic, and all its details were copied from those of St. Andrew's, Plymouth, which was completed in 1460. The nave and the north and south aisles have barrel roofs, divided into square

---

[1] Peshall's edition of "Wood."

panels by wooden ribs, with flat, square bosses at their intersection. The arches to the nave arcades are just pointed, and both the mouldings and the piers, which are very slender, are of ordinary Perpendicular section. The three east windows have elaborate geometrical tracery, which is much too crowded, and has the fault of having all the spaces of the tracery about equal in size. It is carried out, however, in the orthodox manner, with some attempt at subordination in the mouldings. Though the workmen evidently had difficulty in executing the details in granite with any precision, the general effect of the interior is good, and there is more of the feeling of late fifteenth century work in this church than in any other of so late a date.

The instances given above of the survival of Gothic could easily be added to. Bishop Hacket's work at Lichfield, for example, and Bishop Cosin's at Bishop-Auckland were inspired by the same motives and followed the same methods as the work undertaken by Laud and Matthew Wren, and the impulse lasted down almost to the end of the seventeenth century. The tower of Warborough Church near Shillingford bears the date 1666, but might easily be mistaken for work a hundred years earlier. It is short and square, with engaged octagonal buttresses at the angles, the walls are composed of coursed rubble, with bands of knapped flints at intervals, the parapet has battlements, and the west door and tower windows, flat four-centred heads. In every detail it exactly resembles an early sixteenth century tower, and it is very probable that, in some cases, work which has been assigned without hesitation to the fifteenth and sixteenth centuries was actually done at least one hundred years later. The latest examples of Gothic are said to be Welland Church, 1672, and the chancel and tower of Hanley Church, 1674, both in Worcestershire. Gothic details of a sort were of course used in the eighteenth century; these, however, were deliberate revivals and copies, and are entirely different in character from these last survivals of Gothic, the work of the country builder who, more or less, consciously adhered to the old tradition.

I have traced this curious chapter of architectural history, not so much on account of its artistic importance as on account of its intrinsic interest. Artistically, this late Gothic is inferior work, the detail mechanical, the execution ignorant and slovenly : it was the expression, not of men working freely in the full enjoyment of their traditional craft, but of workmen behind the time—of men brought up on a past tradition, who clung tenaciously to a half-forgotten art. On this ground alone it is profoundly interesting. It is clear indeed from this dying effort that

Gothic architecture was still most intimately associated with the religion of the English Church. The magnificent freedom of Renaissance art had no attraction for such men as Herbert and Crashaw, and so we find in this last flicker of mediæval art the fit architectural expression of that religious mysticism, which flamed out in dying brilliancy to resist the approach of Puritanism, and which, indeed, from one point of view, might itself be taken as the last serious effort of the mediæval world. But the energies of that world were now finally scattered. The conditions under which Gothic architecture had grown to its splendid maturity had long since ceased to exist, and could never be recalled. Some attempt was made in the last century, though, indeed, but half in earnest, to revive mediæval art, and in this present century the attempt has been made again with a devotion as intense as it was uncritical. It is, perhaps, not premature to say that this second endeavour is sharing the fate of the first. History follows its own irresistible course, and enthusiasm, however amiable, is fore-doomed to failure unless it can place itself within the lines of the inevitable development of facts.

CHAPTER VII.

SIR CHRISTOPHER WREN.

THE extreme gravity of the historical events which occurred in England between 1640 and 1660 threw architecture and the arts into the background, and it is owing to this apparent check that an undue distinction has been made between Wren and Inigo Jones. The stream of development was never in fact arrested. Webb, the pupil of Inigo Jones, was in full practice after the Restoration, and came into collision with Wren on the question of the Surveyorship. Captain Wynne, the pupil of Gerbier, did not complete Buckingham House till 1705, and the versatile Gerbier himself managed to get employment after 1660; but the most important evidence in regard to the continuity of the English Renaissance is to be found in the fact that, the more Wren advanced in mastery of his art, the more nearly he approached to the manner of Inigo Jones. The reason for the divergence of Wren's earlier work from the models left by his great predecessor is to be found not in any change of ideas, but in Wren's training, or rather, in the absence of it; for it was only by slow degrees and large experience of work that Wren attained to certainty of taste, and the full maturity of the accomplished manner of his later years.

Christopher Wren was born at East Knoyle in Wiltshire on October 20th, 1632. His father, the Rector of East Knoyle, and afterwards Dean of Windsor, was brother to Matthew Wren, Bishop of Ely, and was a man of some attainments as a herald, and possessed of some of that practical ingenuity which was perhaps the most striking characteristic of the genius of his son. As Dean of Windsor, he drew up an estimate amounting to £13,305 for a new building for the queen, which was never carried out, and it is evident that both Christopher (the elder) and Matthew Wren had some knowledge of building. Willis and Clarke suggest, on the strength of a passage in the "Parentalia," that Wren's father devised the arrangement of the Chapel of Peterhouse, Cambridge, with open cloisters on either side, which was built 1628-1632.

After four years at Westminster, under Dr. Busby, Christopher Wren entered at Wadham College, Oxford, as a Fellow Commoner in

1649, and very early gave evidence of his singular ability. He translated into Latin a mathematical treatise by W. Oughtred, who speaks of him as "a youth generally admired for his talents, who, when not yet sixteen years old, enriched astronomy, gnomics, statics, and mechanics, by brilliant inventions, and, in truth, is one from whom I can not vainly look for great things;" and throughout his career Wren showed an extraordinary capacity for assimilating knowledge, and reducing it to practical shape. His theoretical speculations were never of any very great value. In spite of his wide mathematical knowledge, Wren did not approach scientific problems from the point of view of a thinker such as Newton. His intellect was in this regard of a different and inferior calibre. Instead of seeking to establish any of those far-reaching principles which lay the ground-work for new departures in scientific discovery, Wren used his knowledge as a means of reducing to clear and logical shape the discoveries of others, and of extracting from those discoveries mechanical inventions which might be of immediate practical use. Such, for instance, were the weather-clock, and a pavement " harder, fairer, and cheaper than marble," or the piece of white marble, presented to Evelyn in 1654 by "that prodigious young scholar, Mr. Christopher Wren . . . . which he had stained with a lively red, very deepe, as beautiful as if it had been natural." Throughout his life Wren employed his very scanty leisure in these ingenious, if rather futile, inventions, which have long since ceased to be of the slightest importance. Wren's practical consciousness and extreme fertility of resource would, under modern conditions, have made him one of the most consummate engineers that have ever existed, but in this very comprehensiveness lay the single weakness of Wren as an artist. His interest in the various aspects of building was so evenly balanced, that he sometimes found himself unequal to the restraint of those costly sacrifices in art, without which the highest qualities of architecture are unattainable.

In 1653 Wren was elected to a fellowship at All Souls', and for the next few years was busy with the meetings at Wadham and Gresham College, which led to the foundation of the Royal Society. In 1657 he was appointed Professor of Astronomy at Gresham College, and when the charter of incorporation was granted to the Royal Society, in 1663, Wren drafted the preamble in a somewhat exuberant and involved style. In 1661 he was appointed Savilian Professor of Astronomy at Oxford, and in the following year he declined an offer from the king of a commission to survey the fortifications at Tangiers, and to superintend the building of the new works. This offer was due

THE ASHMOLEAN MUSEUM, OXFORD.

152 RENAISSANCE ARCHITECTURE IN ENGLAND

to the influence of Evelyn and Matthew Wren, whose steadfast loyalty had its reward; otherwise it is remarkable that John Webb should have been passed over, and such an offer have been made to a man whose reputation rested entirely on his scientific attainments: for Wren had as yet no training in architecture or practical acquaintance with building, and though in the end he more than justified the favour which led to his becoming an architect, his early works distinctly suffer from this absence of any sufficient training, and the fact that he was nearly thirty before he turned his attention to architecture.

In 1661 Wren was appointed assistant to Sir John Denham, the Surveyor-General of Works, from whom he can have learnt very little, and his first work was Pembroke Chapel at Cambridge for Matthew Wren (1663-4), a simple and well-proportioned design, though quite incongruous with the adjacent buildings; and in the same year he began the Sheldonian Theatre at Oxford, which was completed in 1668. Wren's knowledge of construction found its opportunity in the roof, which has a flat ceiling with a span of 68 feet;[1] but as yet he had not attained to the suavity of manner found in his later work. The inside is uninteresting, and the details of the exterior coarse and heavy. The Sheldonian compares very unfavourably with the Ashmolean (1677)[2] immediately to the west of it, on the whole the most charming example of work of this date in Oxford. This building is of considerable interest in regard to the development of English architecture, for with all the advance in scholarship shown in the design of the east elevation, there is a distinct reflection of the work of the Jacobean builders in the mullioned windows of the façade towards Broad Street.

---

[1] The roof was carried out by Richard Frogley, carpenter, and, considering the somewhat unscientific methods hitherto in use, is a skilful piece of construction. The scantlings of the timbers used are as follows: span, 68 ft.; height of queen posts, 8 ft.; tie-beam out of 21 in. by 20 in.; head, 18 in. by 12 in.; braces, 12 in. by 8 in. and 12 in. by 6 in.; principal rafters, 13 in. by 12 in.; queen posts, 12 in. by 9 in.; all the timbers are of pine except the queen posts, which are of oak. The principals are set 12 ft. centre to centre, and the iron straps at feet of queen posts and principal rafters are $3\frac{1}{2}$ in. by $\frac{1}{4}$ in. thick.

[2] The Ashmolean has always been attributed to Wren; on an old print, however, of the Ashmolean, by Burghers, reproduced in the Oxford almanack for 1895, the name of the architect is given as "T. Wood, architect"—an otherwise unknown man. It is possible that Wood's share in the architecture was confined to making the drawing of the building for the engraver. But the inscription on the print also says: "Sold, drawn, and engraved by Mr. Burghers," and if this is to be trusted, Wood, and not Wren, must be credited with the design of the Ashmolean, and Wood must rank with Bell of King's Lynn as one of those many able architects whom, it seems, the mere accident of history has consigned to oblivion.

Valentine, Photo.   *Face p. 152.*
TRINITY COLLEGE CHAPEL, OXFORD.

SIR CHRISTOPHER WREN 153

In 1665 Wren designed the inner court of Trinity College, Oxford,[1] and in the summer of this year started for Paris, where he stayed till the following Christmas, "Surveying the most esteemed fabrics in Paris and the country round" and making it his business "to pry into trades and arts." No better school of architecture was to be found in Europe at the time. The Louvre was then being built from the designs of Bernini, and Wren had introductions to the brilliant group of artists brought together by the intelligence of Colbert. That he made full use of his time is proved by his subsequent work. Wren never went to Italy, and this six months' stay in France was the only period of studentship that he ever went through. On his return to England, he was at once immersed in the business of a most laborious career which allowed him no leisure till he reached extreme old age, and his rapid advance in technical skill was gained by the experiments in actual building which his exceptional opportunities allowed him. In all the earlier work of Wren's middle period, the influence of the French decorators is very marked, but it gradually disappeared towards the end of the seventeenth century, and in his later work he shook off the exuberant ornament which disfigures some of his earlier designs.[2]

It is evident that Wren's connections, and his distinguished reputation as a scholar and mathematician, brought him quickly into prominence as an architect. As early as 1662 he was consulted on the repairs of Old St. Paul's.[3] Only part of the scheme proposed by Inigo Jones had been carried out, when the works were stopped by the Civil War; and the building was now in a very dangerous condition. The tower was unsafe, and the nave roof was thrusting out the walls. Wren proposed to build "a light thin shell of stone very geometrically made" as a roof, and to replace the tower with "a dome or rotunda, and upon the cupola for outward ornament, a lantern with a spring top to rise pro-

---

[1] His clients insisted on a quadrangle, though, as Wren pointed out, it was quite the wrong thing: "but," he added, "if any body will pay for a quadrangle, there is no dispute to be made; let them have a quadrangle, tho' a lame one, somewhat like a three-legged table"; apparently his astuteness gained the point, for the court is a three-sided one to this day.

[2] Wren, however, seems to have kept his head amid the splendours of the French Court. He wrote from Paris: "The women, as they make here the language and fashions, and meddle with Politics and Philosophy, so they sway also in architecture; works of Filgrand and little knacks are in great vogue: but building certainly ought to have the attribute of eternal, and therefore the only thing incapable of new fashions." "Parentalia," p. 261.

[3] Letter from T. Spratt to Christopher Wren, 1662.

x

portionately." It is evident that his secret intention must have been to gradually rebuild the cathedral on the lines begun by Inigo Jones, leaving certain portions of the old work inside. The question was raised in earnest in 1666, and Wren got out his designs. Four of the drawings, dated 1666 and signed, are preserved in the Library of All Souls', Oxford. The old choir was to remain, with the exception of the end bay westward ; and the outline of the steep lead roof of the nave was to be preserved, but pilaster buttresses with obelisks as terminals were to be added. Over the crossing was to be the new dome, consisting of an inner dome of masonry and an outer dome covered with lead with a lantern at the top surmounted by a huge open-work pineapple, 68 feet high, of monstrous and horrible design. The only attractive feature in this scheme was the double flight of eighteen semi-circular steps, leading from the crossing under the dome to the old choir. The fire of London, which began September 2nd, 1666, saved Wren from attempting to realize this impossible idea.

The Great Fire was Wren's opportunity. The city was "a ruinous heap ;" and Wren, who had succeeded Sir John Denham as Surveyor-General in 1668, had the field pretty well to himself. He at once drew up a masterly plan for laying out the city, which the king accepted ; but the necessity of immediate re-building, difficulties of compensation, and the want of money, prevented the scheme being carried out. The area covered extended from the Temple Gardens on the south, to the end of Fetter Lane on the north, and ran north-east by Hosier Lane, including Newgate, Aldersgate, and Cripplegate in the east. It stopped short of Broad Street and Leadenhall Street, but extended south-east in an irregular line to the east of Billingsgate, the Custom House occupying the extreme south-east corner. The three main features, going from west to east, were to be, (1) a circular space on the crown of Fleet Street Hill, about on the site of St. Dunstan's Church, from which eight streets radiated in straight lines, connected by cross streets laid out on an octagon plan in relation to the circular space ; (2) a triangular space, to include St. Paul's and Doctor's Commons, gradually widening out eastwards as it ascended Ludgate Hill ; (3) the Royal Exchange, on the old site, but placed in an open space, surrounded by the Post Office, the Excise Office, the Goldsmiths' Insurance Office, and the Mint. Wren intended this to be the centre of the City, and from it were to radiate ten streets each sixty feet wide. A broad quay was to run down the river bank, and, by means of straight streets, the Exchange would be seen from three separate points on the quay. Opposite the end of London

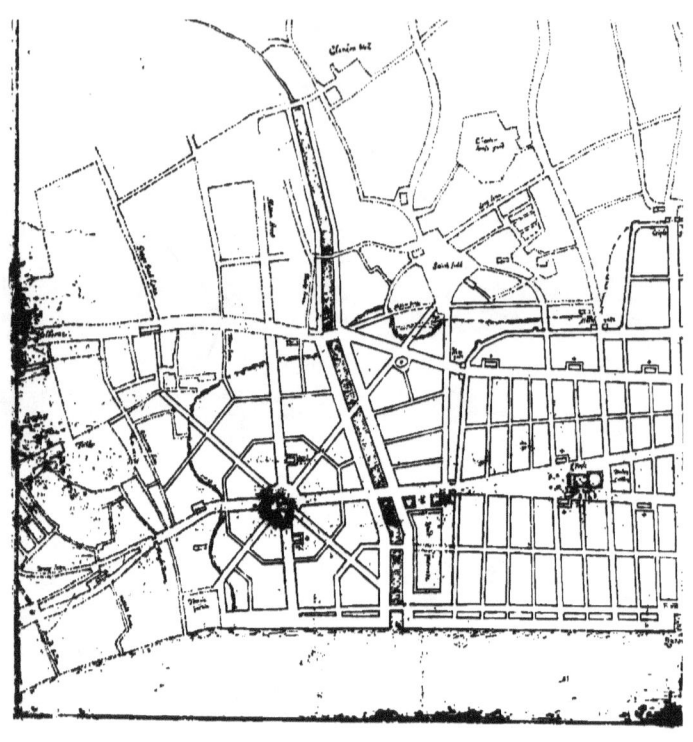

WREN'S PLAN FOR I
(All Souls Coll

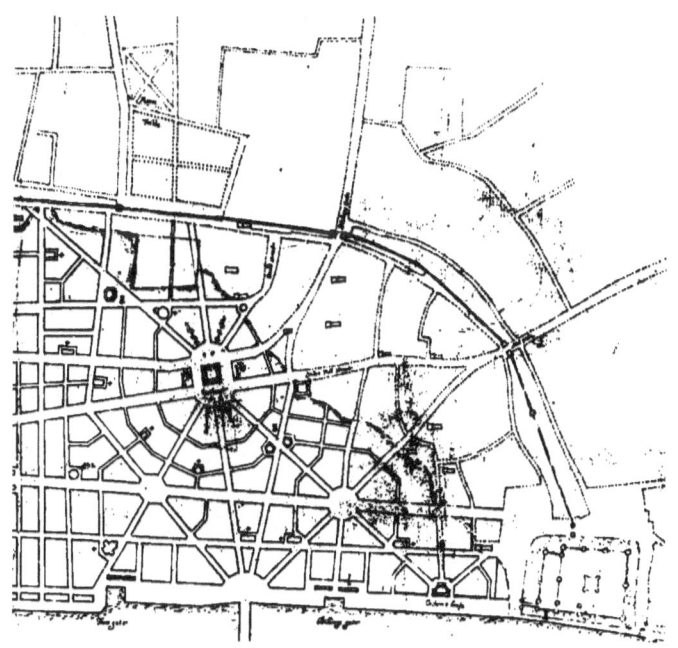

Bridge there was to be a large semicircular space, with arms radiating outwards to join the other streets. The scheme was indeed worthy of Wren's genius, and, had it been carried out, would have made the City of London one of the most beautiful in the world. Wren's fine intelligence grasped the full architectural possibilities of vistas of broad straight streets, linked together by groups of public buildings, the importance of a commanding site for these buildings, and the absolute necessity of a complete and consecutive scheme to the dignity of a great city, as opposed to a mere farrago of houses. Where any such scheme has been attempted in this century it has been spoilt by the poverty of average modern design. In London, the largest area of buildings in the world, the attempt has never been seriously made, and the various schemes that have been proposed from time to time have, in nearly every case, the defect of timidity. They lack comprehensiveness, the unflinching audacity of the autocrat, who might, for example, draw straight lines from St. Paul's to the British Museum, and from the British Museum to Somerset House. Wren saw at once that mere tinkering was worse than futile, and that it was a question of a large idea or nothing; unfortunately, his scheme was never even attempted.

Wren next turned his attention to the re-building of the City churches and St. Paul's. The two occupied him concurrently for the next thirty-eight years; but though the latter is far the more important work, it will be more convenient to deal with the churches first, as these, to some extent, represent Wren's tentative efforts, the mature results of which are to be found in the details of St. Paul's. In dealing with the City churches Wren had an exceedingly difficult problem. A great many of the sites were very irregular, the resources available were limited, and Wren had to adapt his buildings to severely Protestant requirements. Moreover, he had no precedents to refer to, from the conditions of the case. Wren, however, surmounted these difficulties with conspicuous success; and probably in none of his works is his extraordinary fertility of resource more evident than in his City churches. The problem before him was to provide the most practical and economical church possible for a Protestant congregation, and Wren had very clear ideas as to the proper way to set to work. In the report which he wrote as one of the Commissioners of Queen Anne's Act of 1708, for building fifty new churches, Wren says, " It would be vain to make a Parish Church larger than that all who are present can both hear and see. The Romanists, indeed, may build larger churches, it is enough if they hear the murmur of the mass and see the Elevation of the Host, but ours are to be fitted for auditories." This end Wren held steadily in view, and account of it must be taken in criticising his churches. The interiors are, with few exceptions, rather bald, and destitute of the mystery and play of light and shade to be found in the mediæval church; but Wren deliberately sacrificed these effects to practical considerations. He insisted that, if possible, everyone must both see and hear the preacher, and when that was provided for, he was less careful about those subtle qualities of architecture which appeal to emotions that lie less close to the surface. Wren was throughout his career thoroughly conscious of what he was doing, and though an architect of extraordinary capacity, he possessed little of the *abandon* of the purely artistic genius. On the other hand, the strong point about these churches is their extreme reasonableness, and their skilful adaptation of means to ends. Wren was essentially an architect, perhaps a little careless in detail, but most dexterous in emergency, and the ingenuity with which he met the difficulties of his sites has never been surpassed. To anyone but Wren, the site of the Church of St. Benet Fink[1] would have seemed almost hopeless. The external walls described a decagon, of an internal length of 63 ft. and width of 49 ft. Wren met the difficulty with an elliptical cupola in the centre, supported on six columns, with arched recesses from the columns to the outer walls, and the tower was attached to one of the shorter cants.

The remarkable variety of treatment shown in these churches makes them difficult to classify. Mr. Taylor has classified them by their towers or steeples, a method which has the merit of ·calling attention to their most attractive and successful feature. The tower, however, is not the church; and an examination of Wren's designs shows that he had three ways of covering in his churches. The sites with which he had to deal were usually irregular parallelograms, varying from 60 ft. by 30 ft. (St. Basil's, Gracechurch Street) to 114 ft. by 81 ft. (Christchurch, Newgate Street). The churches built on these sites had either (1) a single flat ceiling with a deep plaster cove; or, (2) domes with arched recesses, with or without detached columns; or, (3) naves covered with waggon ceilings, with flat or groined ceilings to the aisles. Under the first head will also have to be classified churches of the meeting-house type, but with a single aisle, such as St. Laurence Jewry. Mr. Loftie, in his admirable account, has pointed out how Wren

[1] Since destroyed. See "London Churches of the Seventeenth and Eighteenth Centuries," by George Birch, F.S.A. Batsford, 1896.

FONT, CHRISTCHURCH, NEWGATE STREET.

had recourse to all sorts of shifts in order "to work in every available morsel of space." He was not afraid of single aisles, or of interiors which were neither square nor parallel, as in the Church of All Hallows the Great; and whereas, in several modern London churches, architects working in the Gothic style have sacrificed parts of very costly sites in order to get their buildings symmetrical, Wren, who designed in a manner which is supposed to be rigid and unelastic, worked up to the very last inch of his site.[1] St. Benet's, Gracechurch Street (1685), and All Hallows, Lombard Street (1694), are good examples of the single-room type. Other instances are St. Mary Somerset, St. Nicholas Cole-Abbey, St. Michael's, Queenhithe, and St. Edmund's, Lombard Street. Of the second type of church the most familiar instance is St. Stephen's, Walbrook (1672-1679), a church which has been extravagantly praised, but which is undoubtedly one of the most original of all Wren's interiors. The plan consists of a parallelogram, 82 ft. 6 in. by 59 ft. 6 in.,[2] divided into five aisles of varying widths by rows of columns in six bays. The third and fourth columns from the east end in the centre aisle are omitted, leaving a square space which is covered in with a circular dome, springing from a heavy entablature on eight arches. The east bay of the centre aisle, and the two bays to the west, are groined, and the aisles have flat trabeated ceilings. The result is, that out of a rectangular room, Wren has got the effect of a church with a nave, aisles, and crossing. Mr. Fergusson has sought for the origin of this masterly conception in certain eastern domes. But Wren had certainly never seen such domes, even if he knew of their existence; and it is more probable that he arrived at his result by pure ingenuity and constructive skill. In fact, the fault of the design, apart from its details, is that it leaves the intellectual scaffolding too much in evidence. The re-entering angles of the square under the dome are rather bald and monotonous in treatment, and the suggestion of the constructive skeleton is unpleasant. Wren, with the instinct of an engineer rather than that of an artist, having broken the back of the difficulty, was a little careless about its ultimate form, for the details of St. Stephen's, Walbrook, are coarse and irrelevant. But taken as a whole, St. Stephen's is a most

---

[1] Mr. Birch ("London Churches," 1896, page 2) points out that in most cases the churches were built on the old sites, and often actually on the old foundations.

[2] The general dimensions given in Godwin and Britton's "Churches of London" are: length, 82 ft. 6 in., width, 59 ft. 6 in., height to ceiling of aisles, 36 ft., diameter of dome, 45 ft., height to top of dome, 63 ft. The dome is constructed of wood. Mr. Birch gives the date 1676-78.

INTERIOR OF ST. STEPHEN'S, WALBROOK.

impressive interior. It is the more interesting in that it is one of Wren's earlier works, and that in this church he made his first venture in the treatment of domes, one of the noblest expressions of architecture, and one in which he was probably more successful than any architect before or since.

Wren used cupolas at St. Antholin's, St. Mary Abchurch, St. Benet Fink, and St. Swithin's, Cannon Street, and employed a charming variation in St. Mildred's, Bread Street. The plan is a parallelogram, 62 ft. by 36 ft. Wren divided this into three parts, the centre covered by a dome the full width of the building, and the two end spaces by bold semicircular arches. His usual treatment of such a space was to form a bold cove cornice with a flat ceiling. It is probable that the success of St. Stephen's, Walbrook, tempted him to this fresh experiment at St. Mildred's. St. Stephen's was building from 1672-1679; and St. Mildred's, Bread Street, was built between 1677 and 1683.

For larger sites Wren generally adopted the ordinary nave and aisle treatment, usually with galleries round the west, north, and south sides. On the whole the finest examples of this class are St. Bride's, Fleet Street, and Christ Church, Newgate Street; and Wren's versatility is clearly shown in these two interiors. St. Bride's is as light and cheerful as Christ Church is austere and almost forbidding. Both churches have galleries, but the treatment is more satisfactory in Christ Church than in St. Bride's. In the latter the columns are coupled, and small pilasters at the side of the columns carry the gallery front, with the unhappy result that the columns are divided half way up by the gallery front. At Christ Church the columns carrying the entablature, from which springs the waggon ceiling, stand on a lofty pedestal reaching up to the soffit of the gallery. The effect is to increase the apparent stability of the columns, and this impression is further heightened by the continuous entablature which they carry, instead of the detached fragments of an entablature used at St. Bride's. In St. Clement Danes (1684) solid rectangular piers support the gallery, the front of which is returned above these piers, and the Corinthian columns supporting the arcade start clear above the gallery front. The idea which Wren had in view in Christ Church is still further developed in the Church of St. Andrew by the Wardrobe. Wren was evidently striving to bind the gallery and the piers supporting the nave roof into a homogeneous composition. He failed to do so in St. Bride's (1680), and St. James's, Westminster (1683), was partially successful in Christ Church (1687), and finally realized his idea in St. Andrew by the

Wardrobe (1692). In this church he again used the high pedestals up to the gallery, but instead of columns he used square panelled pillars, and dispensed with an entablature altogether. This interior is, notwithstanding, one of the least attractive of Wren's designs. A fault almost inevitable in Wren's treatment of his waggon ceilings is conspicuous in the ceiling of St. Andrew's. Wren introduced in each bay large circular wreaths of flowers on the arched soffit of the ceiling, and the conflict of the circle on plan, with the curve in section, is exceedingly unpleasant. The same fault occurs in the ceiling of St. Peter's Cornhill. St. Andrew's Holborn, St. Magnus, St. James's Westminster, St. Nicholas Cornhill, St. Mary Aldermary, St. Mary-le-Bow, are the most important examples of the waggon roof and side aisle type; but on the whole the interior of Christ Church, Newgate Street, is the strongest and most impressive of any of the churches of this class.

Though some of his interiors are attractive, and nearly all of them eminently reasonable, Wren's design is seen to greater advantage in the outside than in the inside of his churches. He selected the position of his towers and determined their general outline with fine judgment. He foresaw that in course of time most of his churches would be hidden away by adjacent buildings, and he accordingly concentrated his ornament on his steeples and the upper part of his towers. Here again Wren's fertility of invention is astonishing. With obvious ease, and without affectation, he varied his design for each fresh steeple, only adhering to two fundamental principles: (1) that the tower should, if possible, stand clear of the building, so that nothing should be lost of the full effect of its height and proportions; and (2) in view of the adjacent buildings, and also to emphasize the effect of the richer work above, he kept his lower storeys simple and almost entirely free from ornament. The tower and steeple of St. Mary-le-Bow, Cheapside, is an almost perfect example. Wren proposed to erect an arcade to the east of the tower, which would have shown up the rest of the church, and separated the tower from the adjacent houses. This was never carried out, but Godwin and Britton say it is shown in engravings from a drawing by Hawksmoor. The tower and steeple of St. Mary-le-Bow are peculiarly fine in the nice determination of the quantities of ornament, and the curious finials which surmount the pilasters at the angles of the tower are, for their purpose, an inspiration of genius. They are just sufficiently weighty in mass and fanciful in form to effect the transition from the square tower to the circular stylobate which begins the steeple, and are happier than the urns which have to answer the purpose at St. Bride's, Fleet Street. In both these steeples Wren depended largely on the repetition of forms, adjusting their dimensions with an extremely delicate proportion. St. Mary-le-Bow is less monotonous in outline than St. Bride's, but it has the advantage of site; and at any point from which the tower and steeple of St. Bride's can be seen as a whole, the repetition of, one might almost say the insistence upon the dark spaces of the arched openings of the steeple, are entirely justified. St. Bride's is less picturesque than St. Mary-le-Bow, but it is the stronger design of the two, and in its stern simplicity shows a finer quality of imagination than is generally found in Wren, whose work, though always graceful and ingenious, is not always entirely masculine.

St. Mary-le-Bow was completed in 1680, whereas the steeple of St. Bride's was not built till 1701-2; and this bears out a remark made earlier in the chapter, that, as Wren advanced in experience and mastery of his art, he gradually shook off the insincere and artificial manner which he learnt in France, and returned to the purer models of Palladianism, and the strenuous architecture of Inigo Jones. The latter might have designed St. Bride's, whereas in St. Mary-le-Bow there is just the faintest reminiscence of the work of the Jacobean architects.[1] In spite of certain details which are open to criticism, these two steeples, and the exquisitely simple and perfect steeple of St. Margaret Pattens, are of their kind the most perfect specimens of Renaissance architecture in England. Scarcely less beautiful is the tower and steeple of St. Magnus, London Bridge, built in 1705, the upper part of which seems to be borrowed from the lantern and cupolas designed by Inigo Jones for Whitehall. The tower of Christ Church, Newgate Street, completed in 1704, is less happy, the parts do not grow out of each other, and the architect must have been hard put to it when he had to complete his steeple with a baluster.

Of the smaller steeples, that of St. Martin's, Ludgate Hill, is one of the most beautiful. Though his scheme for the re-building of London was not realized, Wren never lost sight of his great conception of the city as a whole, and kept in full consciousness the relations of his buildings to each other. Nowhere is this more evident than in the grouping of St. Martin's steeple with St. Paul's. Its tall slender outline, poised in the middle distance from the foot of Ludgate Hill, at once throws back the tremendous mass of St. Paul's, and at the same

[1] The height of the steeple of St. Mary-le-Bow is 225 ft., that of St. Bride's as left by Wren was 234 ft. high, but in 1764 the spire was injured by lightning, and Sir William Staines, who repaired it, for some unknown reason, lowered it 8 ft.

ST. BRIDE'S.

time calls attention to its magnificent silhouette. The steeple of St. Martin's is covered with lead, a material for which Wren had a special liking, on account of its durability, and because it was produced in this country. No English architect ever more thoroughly understood his materials, in regard not only to their permanence, but also to their possibilities of colour and their decorative qualities. The contrast of lead with the silvery white of Portland stone is the most beautiful colour effect to be found in any building in London, and Wren, by preference, always employed these materials, or, if economy was necessary, he reserved his Portland stone for quoins and dressings, and used for his walls the fine old London brick, or red gauged brick work of most excellent quality.

For reasons which he has not explained, Wren occasionally designed his towers in what he supposed to be the Gothic style, even when he designed the rest of the church in his habitual manner. St. Dunstan in the East (1698), St. Mary's Aldermary (1711), and St. Michael's, Cornhill (1721), are well-known examples. Whether Wren made these designs under pressure, or merely as academical exercises for the entertainment of his friends, is unknown, but it is very evident that he had not the least sympathy with Gothic architecture, or taken any trouble to master its most rudimentary features. His great architectural capacity saved him from gross faults of outline and proportion, and the lantern of St. Dunstan's is a skilful piece of construction, but the details are preposterous. They are obviously insincere, and that Wren could have tolerated such work shows either that his taste must have been uncertain, or his artistic conscience somewhat lax. His addition to the gateway of Christchurch, Oxford, is perhaps the most successful instance of his Gothic. But the coarseness of its detail is out of scale with the delicate sixteenth century work below, and here, as at Westminster Abbey, Wren seems to have paid the very scantiest attention to the nature of the older work with which he had to deal.

Meanwhile Wren had devoted his best energies to the new Cathedral of St. Paul's. The first idea had been to patch up the ruins left by the Fire, and some work was actually begun at the west end, but as Wren foretold, it was lost labour, for in 1668 the work fell down about the workmen's ears,[1] and Wren was summoned in haste to advise

[1] Sancroft, in his letter to Wren (quoted in Miss Phillimore's "Life of Wren," p. 166), attributed this to Inigo Jones's mistake in not bonding in his new work to the old. It is known, however, that the old fabric had been thoroughly shaken by previous fires, and, as Wren pointed out, the apparently massive piers were merely cases of ashlar filled in with

ST. BENET'S, UPPER THAMES STREET,

166 RENAISSANCE ARCHITECTURE IN ENGLAND

the Commissioners. He was at once instructed to clear the site of the ruins, a difficult task which he carried out with his usual address, and to prepare designs for an entirely new cathedral. Wren prepared several designs, only three of which, however, are of historical importance. The first is the famous design on which Wren had set his heart, but which was rejected owing to the obstinacy of the Duke of York, and the timidity of the clergy, who were aghast at the novelty of its plan. The second is the design which was declared in Charles's warrant to be "very artificiall, proper, and useful;" the third, the design actually executed. The plan, elevation, and section of the rejected design are preserved in All Souls' Library, and the model which Wren had made of it is now in the South Kensington Museum. The plan roughly speaking, consisted of a square, 300 ft. by 300 ft., with the four angles cut off on a quadrant described from the four points of the square. Over the central space there was to be a dome of 120 ft. diameter, and 180 ft. high from the floor, with four smaller domes at the north-east, south-east, north-west, and south-west angles of 45 ft. diameter. The north, south, and west arms of the cross were to be square in plan, and the east arm, forming the choir, was circular in plan, but the east and west ends of the circle were to be cut off, and the choir stalls were ranged on the north and south sides on the segment of a circle. A screen with a flight of five steps separated this choir from the space under the dome.[1] An outer and inner dome over the centre is shown in the drawing, both constructed in masonry, and the whole building was to stand on a podium or platform raised some 10 feet high above the ground level, with entrances on the north, south, and west sides approached by flights of sixteen steps. The nave was carried westward by an extension[2] with a secondary dome, which was to have a narthex and portico at the west end with detached colonnade. Instead of the double order of the design executed, the exterior consisted of a single rubble work. Wren's own words in his report to the Commissioners are: "The portico is nearly deprived of that excellent beauty and strength which time alone and weather could have no more overthrown than the natural rocks; so great and good were the materials, and so skilfully were they laid together after a true Roman manner."

[1] I have drawn up this description from the drawing in All Souls' Library, and it will be found to vary in detail from the accounts of Ferguson, Loftie, and Miss Phillimore.

[2] This extension is not shown in the plan reproduced from the All Souls' Collection, in which all four façades have the same treatment. It is shown, however, in another of Wren's studies for this design, and in a print by B. Cole, a reproduction of which will be found in Longman's "Three Cathedrals dedicated to St. Paul," pp. 110-111, the best authority on all the details of Wren's designs for St. Paul's. Very full illustrations will be found in Mr. Birch's "London Churches."

From Birch's "City Churches."

ST. PAUL'S CATHEDRAL.

order on a lofty stylobate, with an attic storey over, surmounted by a balustrade. The design was in many ways an exceedingly fine one, but the plan would have been ill-suited for service, as from more than half the points of view the high altar would have been invisible, and it is probable that, seen from outside, the great central dome would have looked overpowering. Wren's idea, in the quadrant walls uniting the points of the cross, may have been to free the dome; but it is probable that he would have overreached himself in this; anyhow, in the design actually executed he did the exact opposite, and instead of a hollow recess, put square projections at the angles with most satisfactory results.

The design accepted by the warrant of the 14th of May, 1675, was very inferior to this.[1] In its general plan it was not so very unlike the plan actually executed, though there are many variations in detail; but its main feature was a most grotesque design for the central dome. This was to consist of a lower dome, of 112 feet diameter, of masonry, partly covered with a lead roof, but instead of forming a complete dome, this was stopped about half way up by a drum of 56 feet diameter, covered in with a semicircular dome, above which rose the false outer dome terminating in a steeple in six stages, like St. Bride's. The height to the crown of the upper internal dome was to have been 215 feet, and to the top of the cross 390 feet. This extraordinary freak has been a stumbling-block to all Wren's admirers. Miss Phillimore explains it by worry and overwork. Mr. Loftie maintains that it was a mere hoax to pacify the Court, and that Wren reserved to himself the design which he meant to carry out. There are, however, considerations which make this improbable: (1) In the first place, Wren was a gentle, amiable man, quite devoid of the grim humour, the *terribilita* necessary to carry off this ferocious practical joke; (2) and in the second place, his enemies on the commission thirty years later would certainly have brought this up against him, if Wren's attitude throughout had not been *bona-fide*. It must be remembered that at the time this design was made Wren was still young as an architect, and by no means sure of himself. He advanced *per saltum* through the experience of actual practice, and his increasing knowledge led him to reject this design as

---

[1] The five drawings which accompanied the warrant are preserved in the All Souls' Library, and the description in the text is based on these drawings. Mr. Longman, in his "Three Cathedrals, etc." refers to the rejected design of 1673 as the warrant design. It seems, however, clearer to refer to the design of 1675, which was finally sanctioned, as "the warrant design," and to the rejected design as "the model design."

the work went on; but he probably designed it in all good faith in the first instance, and that he did so may be taken as further evidence that the faults and inferior technique of Wren's earlier work were the result of inadequate training. It was not, in fact, till middle age that Wren shook off this amateurishness, and, in point of fact, there is little to choose between this design and the pineapple scheme which Wren suggested immediately before the Fire. In the warrant of 1675 Wren was authorized to make some variations, rather ornamental than essential, "as from time to time he should see proper." The variations actually made are so essential that it is almost impossible that Wren could have slipped them in without obtaining the consent of the commissioners.[1] He entirely abandoned his nightmare conception of two domes and a telescope steeple, and made a fresh design (the one actually executed), of which the most conspicuous characteristic is its magnificent sanity. In this, his final design, Wren avoided that excessive multiplication of parts which had been the weak point in all his previous attempts.

In regard to the ground plan, Wren adhered to the general conception of the warrant plan (1675), consisting of choir and aisles, transepts and nave with aisles, with a dome over the crossing, which, in its general arrangement, was based on Gothic precedent. The chief variations which he introduced as the work went on were: (1) an entirely different dome over the crossing; (2) the circular recesses to the north and south windows of the choir aisles; (3) the north and south transepts were contracted by one bay, and a circular peri-style added on north and south fronts; (4) the nave was considerably altered. In the 1675 plan the nave consisted of five bays, with a narrower bay at the west end. In the actual plan, going west from the crossing, there are three oblong bays, then a wider bay, covered in with a circular dome, with oblong chapels[2] on either side, and projecting beyond the north and south aisles. Beyond these chapels are the two west towers with the

[1] It is not known how Wren got round the authorities. Mr. Birch quotes an exceedingly significant note from the "Parentalia," p. 283: "From that time the surveyor (Wren) resolved to make no more models, or publicly expose his drawings, which, as he had found by experience, did but lose time, and subjected his business many times to incompetent judges." Notwithstanding, versions of his designs, probably pirated, appeared from time to time. In the volumes of Wren's drawings, now in the Vestry of St. Paul's, there are various engravings of the building which appeared during the progress of the works, probably without Wren's authority. It is evident, from the number of these prints, that the public took the keenest interest in the building of the great cathedral, and further, that from first to last the design was constantly being modified.

[2] These chapels were insisted on by the Duke of York, in spite of Wren's protests that they were most injurious to his design.

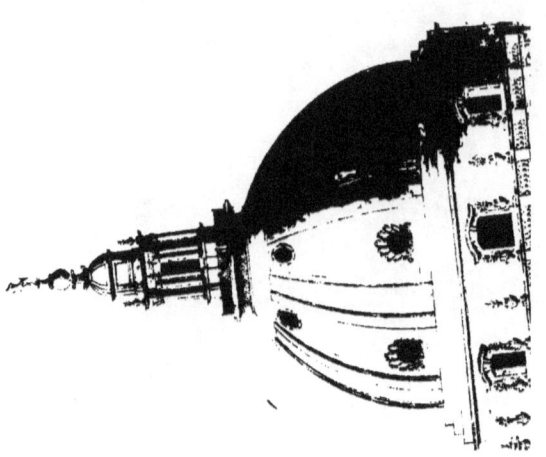

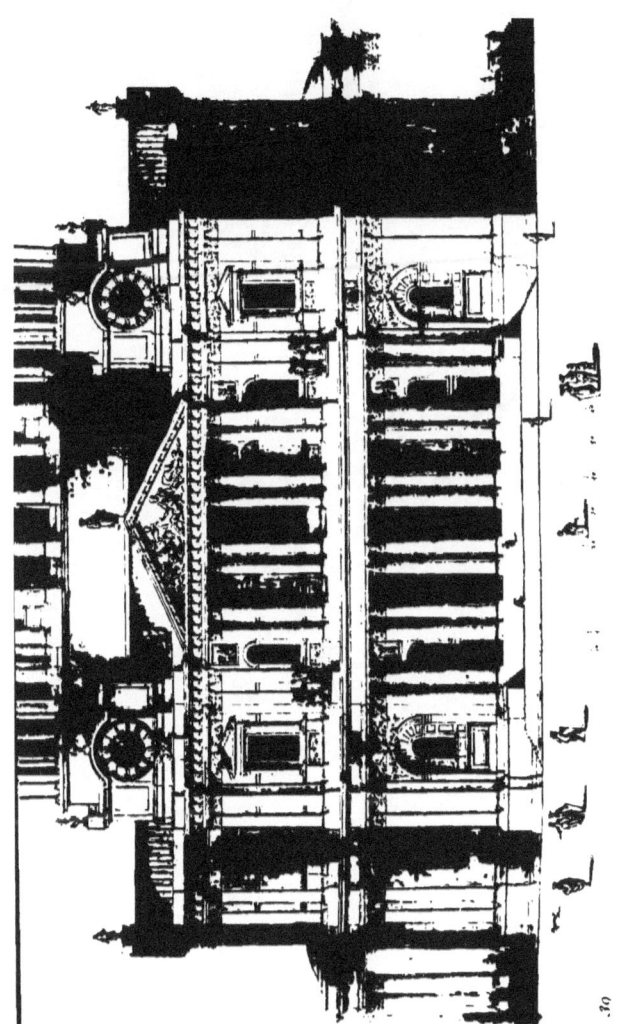

ST. PAUL'S, WEST ELEVATION
THE DOME AND TWO CLOCK TOWERS ALTERED IN EXECUTION
(All Souls College Collection)

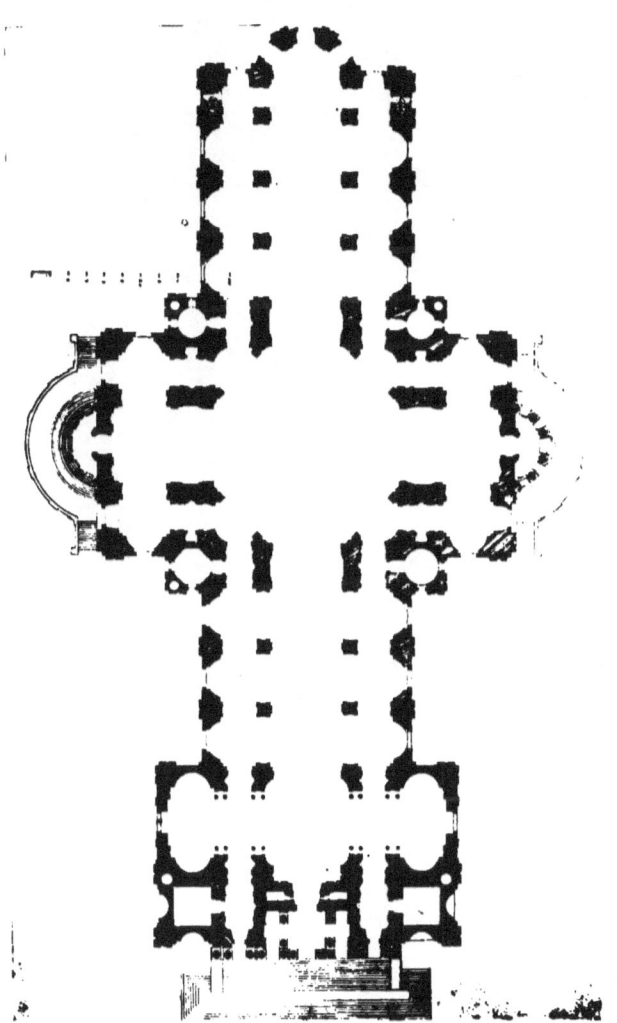

PLAN OF ST. PAUL'S, NEARLY AS EXECUTED
(*All Souls College Collection*)

entrance ways to the aisles, and a recess behind the three centre bays of the great west portico. (5) In the warrant design the north and south walls of the nave aisles terminated in a parapet course, showing the upper walls of the nave behind them. In the actual building the north and south walls of the aisles were carried up the full height, concealing the external upper walls of nave, and a double order was adopted, because Wren found himself unable to get stones of sufficient size for the diameter (more than 4 ft.) of the columns of a single order. Among other variations in detail, it is to be noted that, in execution, Wren largely increased the area of the detached piers under the central dome, beyond what was shown in the warrant plan. He was evidently anxious about the tremendous weight and thrust of his dome, and as an additional precaution he built round the base of the inner brick cone which he constructed to carry the Portland stone lantern a course of large Portland stones, in which was imbedded a massive iron chain.[1]

St. Paul's as actually executed was, in fact, the result of many experiments. The one fundamental idea with which Wren started was the great central dome, and from the very first, as early as 1666, Wren hit on the happy constructional expedient of an outer and inner dome, the only possible solution to the problem of making a dome beautiful both from within and without. Starting with this, and restrained at once by his own practical sense and the incessant limitations imposed on him by the commissioners, Wren gradually worked out the present superb design; and it is interesting to notice how again and again he went back on his own ideas. The second internal dome at the west end is a reminiscence of the west extension of the nave of his rejected plan. So, again, there is a drawing at All Souls' (No. 39, vol. ii.) showing the treatment of the dome. In this drawing only eight lights are shown in the drum, and the dome is divided by eight external ribs, with small lucarnes in each bay of the dome. In the dome as executed, all the windows are kept below the springing, and there are no lucarnes to intercept the grand outline of the dome In spite of Wren's own predilections for his rejected design, one cannot escape the impression that the design actually executed is far better than any of those shown in his previous drawings. Wren, like all great architects, had an extraordinary aptitude for bringing his work along in the actual process of building. He was a poor draughtsman, but he was the last man in the world to be deceived by his own drawings, and there can be no doubt that the superiority of the actual building to any of the designs on paper was

[1] See "Parentalia," p. 292.

due to Wren's constant care and minute supervision of detail. Leaving St. Peter's out of account, as differing both in scale and intention, the result is unquestionably the finest church in Europe produced by any architect of the Renaissance. Various amateur criticisms have been made on St. Paul's, more particularly on the internal and external domes, and on the screen walls of the north and south aisles. In regard to the first, as has been mentioned already, there is absolutely no other way of forming a dome which shall be satisfactory both inside and outside. If the outer dome were taken, its effect from inside would be that of a chimney, and if the inside dome were taken, its external outline would be little more than a hump over the centre of the building. The brick cone which supports the lantern and cupola is an extremely skilful expedient, and an architect is not bound to show every detail of his construction, however ugly it may be. The ultimate justification of architecture is that it should be stable and beautiful. It is in the architect's discretion to choose his means of impressing the imagination, and, provided he attains his result, he is not to be bound by any pedantic and irrelevant criticism as to his means—criticism, moreover, which assumes an intention which never existed in the architect's mind. As to the second objection, that to the screen walls, Mr. Loftie suggests that, for all his critics know, Wren may have considered the additional weight of these walls necessary as a counterpoise to the transverse thrust.

The first stone of St. Paul's was laid in 1675 by Henchman, Bishop of London, who died the same year. The Strongs, father and son, were the chief masons, Richard Jennings the chief carpenter, the wood-carving was by Grinling Gibbons and his assistants, and Caius Cibber and Thomas Bird did the external figure carving. The last stone to the top of the lantern was laid by Wren's son in 1710. Godwin and Britton state that the total cost was £747,954 2s. 9d.[1] This probably does not include the cost of Thornhill's painting, which was paid for at the cost of 40s. a square yard.[2] In the exquisite ironwork

[1] Mr. Longman, however, says that up to September, 1700, a total sum of £1,167,474 17s. 11d. had been received, the whole of which had been expended except £49,384 0s. 3d. remaining in hand. Of this balance in hand £11,000 was spent up to 1723.

[2] In vol. iv., p. 98, of the All Souls' Collection, there is a drawing showing Wren's plan of the pavement to the apse and part of the choir, a side elevation of the altar-piece, and part elevation of the rails which Wren intended to run across the chord of the apse : "The Rayle of wainscot with brass ornament and ballaster of hard wood, or marbel with open carved pannell, or pannells of brass and rail and pillaster of Timber." Whatever the

SECTION OF WREN'S REJECTED DESIGN FOR ST. PAUL'S
(*All Souls College Collection*)

WREN'S REJECTED DESIGN FOR ST. PAUL'S
(*All Souls College Collection*)

THE WARRANT DESIGN FOR ST. PAUL'S
(All Souls College Collection)

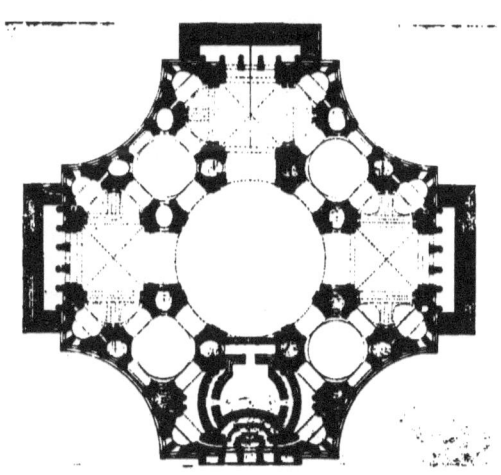

PLAN OF WREN'S REJECTED DESIGN FOR ST. PAUL'S
(All Souls College Collection)

FONT, ST. STEPHEN'S, WALBROOK.

of the screens Wren employed Tijou, a French smith of unsurpassed ability, who designed the beautiful gates of Hampton Court, since removed to South Kensington.[1]

Wren's career was one of incessant labour. Besides St. Paul's, and the fifty-three City churches built between 1670 and 1711, Wren designed three palaces, two hospitals, and a vast quantity of less important work, and in his capacity of Surveyor-General had to deal with constantly recurring questions of alignment of sites, and compensations, and compliance with such building regulations as were then in force. Miss Phillimore and Elmes assign to him the design of some thirty-seven of the City halls built between 1666 and about 1700. There is no mention of these in the list of Wren's works, drawn up by his son and collated by Wren in 1720, though the City churches are mentioned generally; and it is probable that several of these halls were designed by Mills, the City Surveyor, and by Edward Jarman (who also designed the new Exchange), though the designs were doubtless submitted to Wren for his approval. In 1671 Wren designed the Monument, by no means a masterpiece; and Temple Bar,[2] a graceful design, though a little wanting in weight. From 1674-1684 he was engaged in rebuilding the greater part of the Temple. The work is quite plain, only enriched with quoins and well-proportioned cornices, and a few charming doorways; and Wren reserved his ornament for the chief entrance in Fleet Street, completed in 1684, of Portland stone and gauged brick. The design consists of a single order on a high stylobate with an entablature and pediment, and suggests generally Inigo Jones's houses in Lincoln's Inn Fields. Its fine proportion and colour make this design one of the most beautiful instances of Wren's domestic work in London. The entrance to Christ's Hospital, built in 1682, is another good example of his treatment of gauged brick.

In 1678 Wren prepared designs for a mausoleum to Charles I. The drawings,[3] now at All Souls', show a dome of 60 feet diameter, with a total height of 90 feet from the floor, within which was to stand a large allegorical group of Charles I., and other figures in bronze and

merits of the modern reredos, it is something very different from what Wren conceived to be appropriate.

[1] Tijou, who was father-in-law to Laguerre, published in 1693 a "Nouveau Livre de desseins, inventés et dessinés par Jean Tijou," in French and English. He made the gates on the north side of the Long Walk at Hampton Court. In making these gates (which are now at South Kensington) Tijou was helped by Huntingdon Shaw. (See chapter xv.)

[2] Since destroyed and re-erected as the entrance to Theobald's Park.

[3] They are numbered 89-95, vol. ii., in the All Souls' Collection.

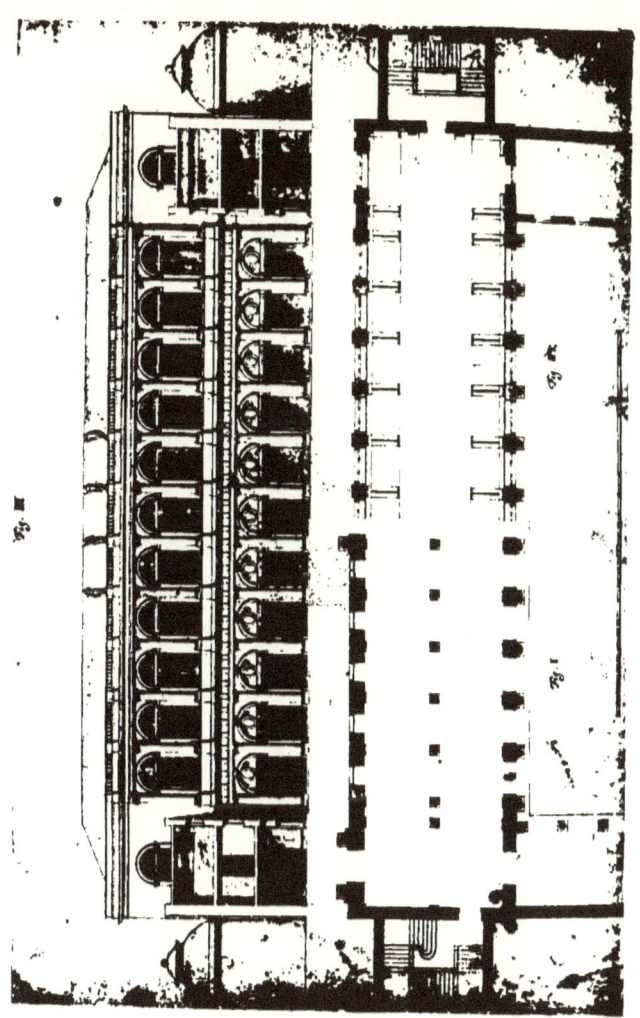

marble. The top was to be surmounted by a bronze figure, 10 feet high, which Wren estimated at £1,000. He intended to ornament the interior with bronze, marble and mosaics, and to inlay the pilasters with "incrustations with various marbles," and estimated the total cost at £43,663 2s. 0d. Seventy thousand pounds was voted by Parliament for its execution, but this money was taken by the king for his private purposes, and the scheme was quietly dropped. In the same year Wren designed the Library of Trinity College, Cambridge, and in 1682, the Library of Queen's College, Oxford, a reminiscence of the Trinity Library, but on a smaller scale. Robert Grumbold, who rebuilt the fountain in 1715-1716, and was himself an architect of much capacity, was master mason for the Library at Trinity, Cambridge. The "classes," or bookcases, were executed by Cornelius Austin, of London, from Wren's designs. The iron gates in the cloisters and stair-rails were made by " Mr. Partridge, the London smith," for £400 ; the carving in limewood was, as usual, by Grinling Gibbons, and the stone-carving by Cibber and his men.

Wren was evidently very much taken with the idea of square, octagon, or circular buildings, covered in with domes. His first design for the Library of Trinity, Cambridge, consisted of a circular building of 65 ft. diameter, and 90 ft. high[1] from the floor to the crown of the dome, pretty nearly the dimensions of the mausoleum design. This design was rejected in favour of the design actually executed, which consists of a magnificent room, 150 ft. long by 38 ft. wide inside, with cloisters underneath. In order to bring the floor of his library on to the same level as the adjacent floors, and to get his fittings below the sills of the windows, Wren had to fill up the tympana of the arches to the cloisters with solid stonework, an expedient to which he also had recourse with less success in the Courtyard of Hampton Court.[2] Wren, in his report on Trinity Library, says he had "seen the effect abroad in good buildings," and liked it. He also says, " I chose a double order rather than a single, because a single order must either have been mutilated in its members or have been very expensive, and would have made the solids too grosse for the openings;"—considerations which never seem to have entered the heads of Vanbrugh and Hawksmoor.

[1] These dimensions are given by Willis and Clarke. The original drawing, however, in All Souls' Library scales 79 ft. internal diameter, and 97 ft. from floor to the top of the lantern.
[2] See *ante*, p. 118.

174 RENAISSANCE ARCHITECTURE IN ENGLAND

Wren's next important building was the Royal Palace at Winchester, begun in 1683, since turned into barracks, and so altered as to convey little idea of Wren's original intention; and to this date belong the episcopal palace of Wolvesey at Winchester, rebuilt by

CHAPEL TO BISHOP'S PALACE, WOLVESEY, WINCHESTER.

Morley in 1684, and the schoolroom at the College, 1684-1687. The Royal Palace at Winchester was intended to rival Versailles, but the king's death suspended the works, and the scheme was never completed, only the central part and wings were built. The grand staircase was to have had marble columns sent over from Italy by the Grand Duke of Tuscany. This, however, was not carried out, and the columns were

NEVILLE'S COURT AND THE LIBRARY, TRINITY COLLEGE, CAMBRIDGE.

HAMPTON COURT, NORTH-EAST CORNER.

afterwards given by George I. to the Duke of Bolton, who used them at Hackwood. The point of interest in Wren's design is the large scope of his conception. Wren had intended to carry a broad street in a direct line from the east front of the palace to the west front of the cathedral; he would thus have brought the two great buildings of the city into direct relation, and made one of those superb vistas such as he had proposed in vain for the re-building of London, and afterwards suggested at Hampton Court.

The special strength of Wren's genius lay in this largeness of idea, in this power of conceiving a great architectural scheme as a whole, of grasping it in complete perspective, and keeping his purpose proof against all the temptations of unnecessary detail. Wren was a true child of the Renaissance in this, fairly claiming kinship with Bramante and Michael Angelo, with the French architects of Louis Quatorze, and with his great forerunner, Inigo Jones. The inevitable result of the Renaissance has been that the individual ideal has taken the place of the collectivist. Whereas generations of mediæval craftsmen could go on building a great cathedral without material check or abrupt transition, since the days of the Renaissance a great work has had to be the conception of a single mind, clearly foreseen from the first, and dependent for its full realization on the permanence of its initial impulse. In this regard Wren was a master among architects. The details of his work, his actual methods of expression, are sometimes open to criticism, but for range of idea, and comprehensiveness of view, he stands unrivalled. In the vestry of St. Paul's there is a design by Wren showing his idea for the right sitting of his building. He proposed to surmount it by an arcade, leaving a free space round the cathedral, wider at the east end and drawing in towards Ludgate Hill; at some distance from the west end, but on its axis line, was to be a baptistery. This design was never carried further. So again at Hampton Court, Wren's addition, noble as it is, was only a fragment of his complete design. Besides the court actually built at the south-east corner, Wren proposed and designed a magnificent forecourt, 300 ft. long and 230 ft. wide, on the north side of Hampton Court. The great hall was to be the centre, with a double flight of stairs to the entrance. The east and west sides of the court were to consist of buildings with an open colonnade to the court. From the entrance to the forecourt a straight road was to be drawn across the moat and through the wilderness, connecting the forecourt with the great Chestnut Avenue of Bushey Park, which was to be a mile long and 60 yards wide. The avenue, which was planted about 1700, was the only

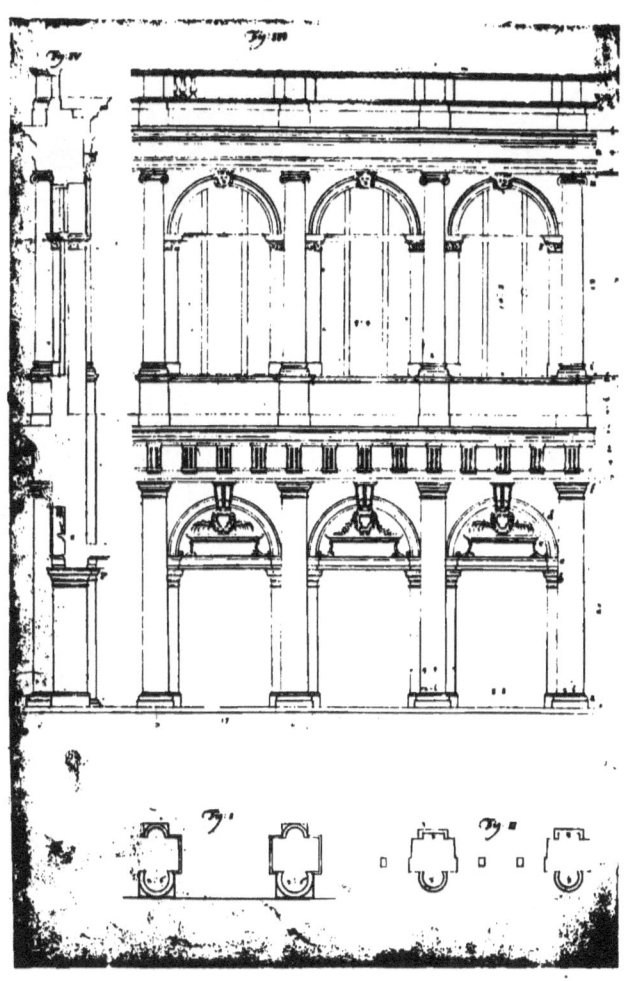

DETAIL OF TRINITY COLLEGE LIBRARY, CAMBRIDGE
(*All Souls College Collection*)

DETAIL OF GATES, EAST FRONT OF HAMPTON COURT.

part of this gigantic scheme which was ever attempted, and this was carried out not from Wren's, but from Talman's designs.

Wren's original plan, dated 1699, is preserved in the Office of Works, and there is also a drawing in the All Souls' Collection, vol. iv., showing the avenue coming straight up to the hall. The whole conception was most masterly; it would have given the palace a satisfactory approach, and brought the new buildings into compact relation with the rest of the palace. Defoe says[1] that William had intended to have rebuilt the whole palace, but his death put a stop to the works. It does not appear that Wren said a word in defence of the charming old buildings of Henry VIII. These were destroyed without remorse, and the old gardens, with one small exception, entirely re-modelled. The mount in the Privy Garden, which contained 10,000 cubic yards of earth, was levelled to the ground, and the old water gallery destroyed, because they obstructed the view from the new state rooms. Wren, indeed, had a heavy hand on an old building. Though he dealt tenderly with the spire of Salisbury, he showed a ruthless disregard for the west front of Chichester, for he proposed to remove the ruins of the north-west tower, to pull down the south-west tower, "for symmetry," to shorten the nave by one bay, and to substitute a new west end of his own design, proposals which were not carried out.

Wren's work at Hampton Court was begun in 1689, and the decorations were not completed in 1700. He again employed Gibbons and Cibber for the carving, and Tijou for the smith's work. The building is of red brick and Portland stone, simple in composition and beautiful in colour. In spite of the jealousy of Talman, and the extreme obstinacy of William, Wren was completely successful with his design, except in one or two points of detail, such as the segmental arches in the tympana of the arches to the cloister arcade, and even here it is stated in the "Parentalia" that this was done by his majesty's express order. About the same time Wren made considerable additions and alterations to Kensington Palace, including probably the orangery. The building is very plain, but characterized by the solidity of taste and entire reasonableness which marks all Wren's later work. Chelsea Hospital, 1682-1692, is another fine example: in spite of a certain lankiness in the cupola, the building is dignified and impressive. Its freedom from pretentiousness, and the restful feeling which pervades the whole design, should have made this building the model for future

[1] "Tour through Great Britain," quoted by Mr. Law.

THE ENTRANCE, KENSINGTON PALACE.

180 RENAISSANCE ARCHITECTURE IN ENGLAND

hospitals and asylums. Unfortunately, other precedents have been followed, and modern buildings of this kind, though often admirably arranged, have been built with an anxiety for picturesqueness and ornament which shows a total disregard for the architectural conditions of the case.

. Wren's masterpiece, however, in public buildings, is undoubtedly Greenwich Hospital. When Wren began this work there were two buildings on the spot: (1) the house facing the park, designed by Inigo Jones for Henrietta Maria, and built under his superintendence with the assistance of John Webb; and (2) the unfinished palace, begun by John Webb, from designs by Inigo Jones, for Charles II. This building forms the left hand, or western block,[1] facing the river; it was already partially completed, and Mr. Loftie thinks that Wren only added the attic storey. His work, however, must have been begun below the entablature, as the date on the frieze is Carolus II., Rex. a. reg. xvi. (1676). Wren's ultimate object was to include both the existing buildings as part of his general scheme; he made the Queen's Palace of Inigo Jones the centre at the extreme end on the landward side, and starting from this point he designed two courts with colonnades facing each other, and running northwards towards the river till they joined the great court, the west side of which was already occupied by King Charles's block. The junction with the great court is marked by two beautiful domes, surmounting the entrances to the chapel on the east side and the hall on the west. The court to the south of the hall and west of the colonnade is called King William's block, the court to the south of chapel and east of colonnade Queen Mary's block, and the block begun by Wren on the river front, ranging with King Charles's block, is called Queen Anne's block.

Wren thus brought his buildings up to Charles II.'s palace, which was already *in situ* facing the river on the west or upper side, going up stream. Opposite this palace he now built another block, in exact imitation of the original design of Inigo Jones, which was completed in 1715, and named after Queen Anne. In this masterly manner he succeeded in working in the old buildings, and in planning at the same time the noblest palace in England.[2] Along the east and west fronts of King

---

[1] Dallaway, quoting Lysons, says that Webb's building is that on the east side of the court; this part, however, was carried out under Wren, following the design of Inigo Jones.

[2] It is significant of the extreme malice and untrustworthiness of Colin Campbell that, when describing the plates of Greenwich Hospital in his "Vitruvius Britannicus," he men-

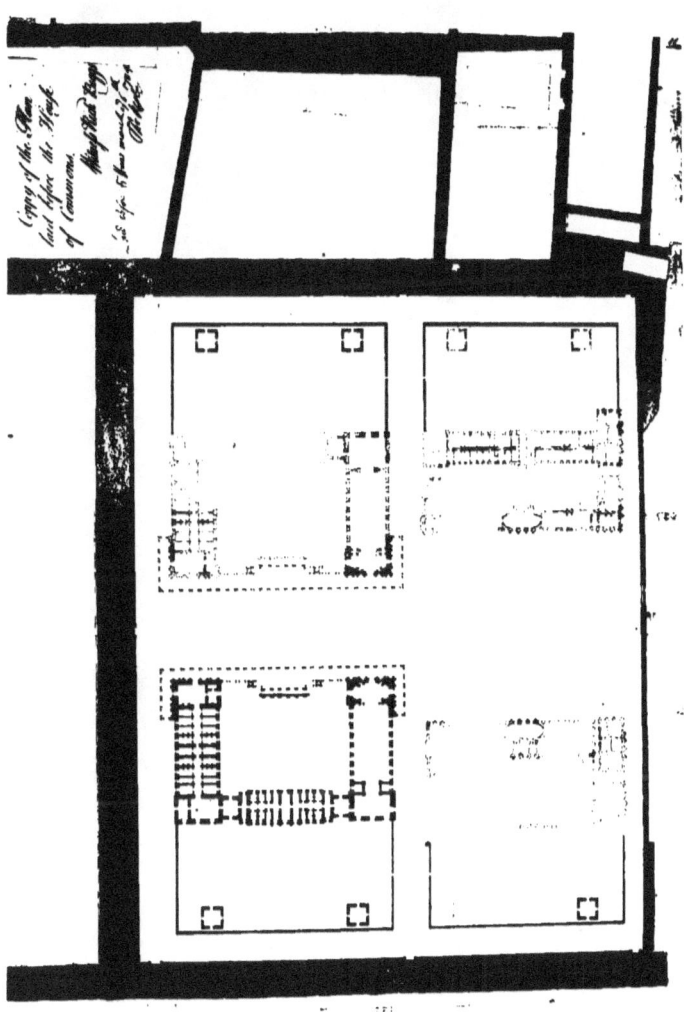

SIR CHRISTOPHER WREN

William and Queen Mary's blocks, and facing each other on either side of the space leading up to the Queen's House, Wren built a colonnade of pairs of Tuscan columns on detached blocks, supporting an entablature and balustrade; at the north or river ends of these blocks come the domes. The drums of the domes start from square pedestals with canted angles. These angles are filled up with bold projecting buttresses, faced with columns of the Composite order. The entablature is returned round these buttresses, and above is a short, circular attic, from which springs the lead-covered dome, with an open lantern at the top. Seen from close at hand, the domes are disappointing, and the outline is a little too precipitous; but at any distance, the grouping of these domes with the general composition is superb.

Thus the general design and arrangement of the building was due to the genius of Wren. He was, however, ultimately superseded by Vanbrugh and others, and it is not always easy to disentangle the additions by other hands. In 1696 the river side of the north-west, or King Charles's block, was already completed, with probably part of the remaining three sides to this block. Wren's work consisted of the river front of the north-east or Queen Anne's block, the north and south sides of King William and Queen Mary's blocks, including the hall and chapel, the return angles of the west side of King William's Court (date on rainwater heads, 1706), the colonnades, and the two domes. In this work he was assisted by Hawksmoor, who was appointed clerk of the works in 1698 and deputy-surveyor in 1705, and who seems to have been allowed to design part of the work himself, such as the east front of Queen Anne's block, and probably the interior of this court as well. The point of junction between Wren's work and Hawksmoor's can be seen in the re-entering angle on the east side. It is also probable that Hawksmoor is responsible for the sides of the colonnades facing the courts with square rusticated piers, the great flat pediments over the five centre bays, and the bell turrets, which are hardly in Wren's manner. Wren was superseded as surveyor in 1716 by Vanbrugh, who added the west front of King William's block and the projecting centre bay on the east side (the side to the court). On Vanbrugh's death, in 1726, Campbell was appointed surveyor, and to Campbell is probably due the south sides of King Charles and Queen Anne's blocks, the Venetian windows to these façades, and the exaggerated severity of the wide, bare wall spaces, introducing an element quite foreign to Wren's design.

tions Inigo Jones, Mr. Webb, and Mr. Thornhill who did the ceiling in the hall, but never makes the slightest reference to Sir Christopher Wren.

In 1729 Campbell was superseded by Ripley, to whom may be attributed the extremely ugly west front of Queen Mary's block. It partly recalls the baldness of the worst parts of the Horse Guards': and Ripley was on familiar terms with Kent. Ripley prepared a report on the state of the building up to date, with plans and estimates for its completion, from which it appears that up to September, 1727, £210,761 13s., and a further sum of £41,864 13s. had been expended on the building, and the estimate for completion was £131,750. On March 6th, 1734, a plan was laid before the House of Commons, showing the building complete, but with Queen Mary's court not yet built. Ripley's estimate for this was £80,444 16s., and he appears to have carried out the work soon afterwards.[1] Finally, in 1814, the west front of King Charles's block was completed for George III. by Stuart, who, in re-building the chapel, introduced his own exceedingly barren ideas of design into the interior.

In the collection in All Souls' Library there are several plans for large houses, including a large sketch design for a house for the Duke of Norfolk, on the site of old Arundel House in the Strand, which was destroyed in 1678. This plan, which was never carried out, consists of a quadrangle about 90 feet square inside, surrounded by buildings, with four square pavilions at the angles projecting beyond the façade. A forecourt with stables to the right and left led to the main entrance. Marlborough House, built for the Duke of Marlborough in 1709, since altered by the addition of a storey, is a well-known instance of Wren's domestic work. The elevation is plain, and probably was inspired by the elevation of old Montague House, built by Pouget, a French architect, in 1678, which it follows rather closely from the ground line up to the cornice. The chapel, in its extreme simplicity and fine pro-

[1] These drawings are in the Soane Museum. This collection contains about forty-nine original drawings of Greenwich Hospital of very great interest. The two elevations reproduced in the text are not signed, but I think it very probable that they are the original designs made by Inigo Jones for King Charles's palace at Greenwich, the design which was actually executed in the river front. It is evident from certain drawings in this collection that when Wren was called in he prepared an alternative scheme. Drawings 4 and 5 in the folio of designs by Jones, Wren, and others, show a large building with a portico in three bays, and a dome over, and flanked by quadrant colonnades occupying the open space between the existing hall and chapel, and it would appear from this that Wren's first idea was to ignore the Queen's Palace by Inigo Jones, and to terminate the great front river court at a line drawn east and west through the present hall and chapel. This idea must have been abandoned in favour of the larger scheme actually executed. It is probable that the design of a series of six detached blocks or pavilions shown in drawing No. 12 belongs to this rejected scheme. It anticipates in a remarkable manner the general idea of St. Thomas's Hospital.

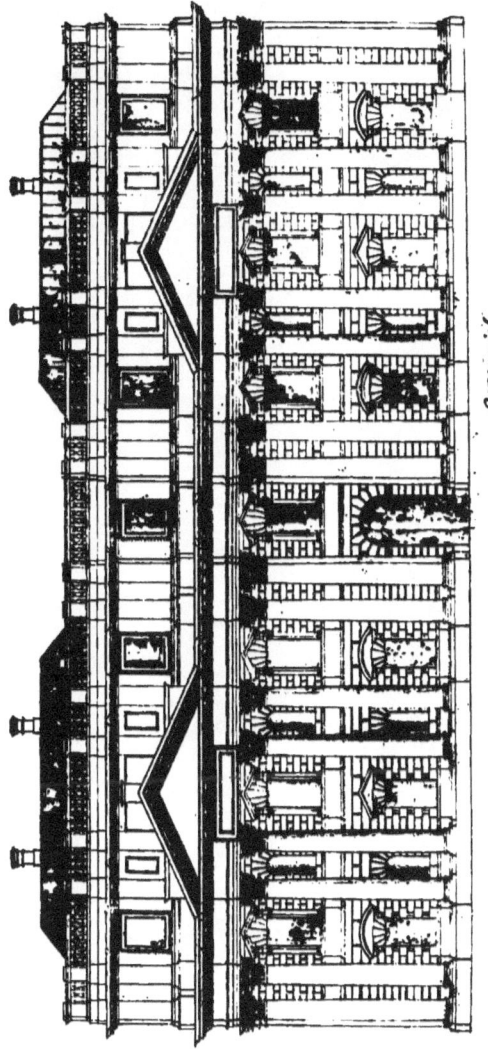

Greenwich.

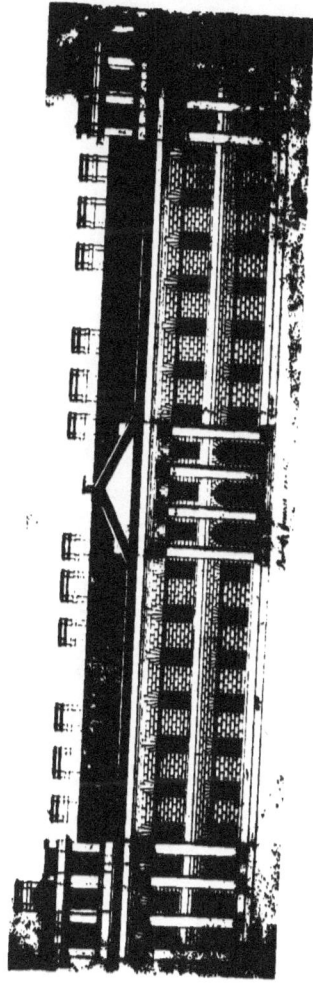

AN ELEVATION OF GREENWICH HOSPITAL.

(Swan Collection)

GROOMBRIDGE IN KENT.

184 RENAISSANCE ARCHITECTURE IN ENGLAND

portion, suggests the best work of Inigo Jones. The collection also contains the plans of some new barracks for Hyde Park, of a total area of 1,590 ft. by 430 ft., which were never carried out. Of Wren's smaller buildings, Morden College, Blackheath, 1694, probably Groombridge in Kent, and the house in West Street, Chichester, are good examples. It is not known that Wren had anything to do with Emmanuel Hospital, or the Trinity Almshouses, and it is not necessary to assign directly to his design all the charming brick and stone houses built between the Restoration and 1700; such, for instance, as the beautiful interior of the

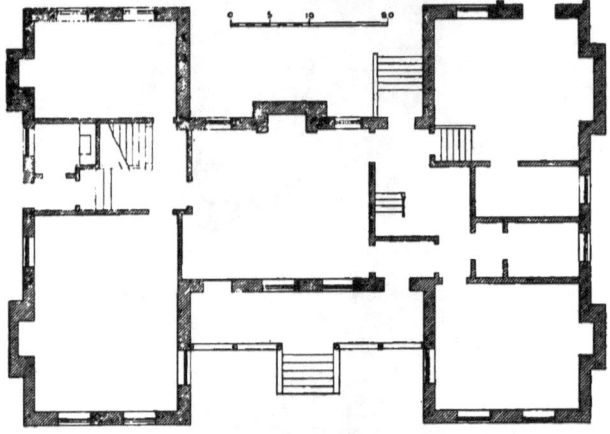

PLAN OF GROOMBRIDGE PLACE, KENT.

house at Eltham, now used as a club-house by the Eltham Golf Club, or the dainty little school-house in the Close at Salisbury. On the other hand, it would be idle to attribute buildings at once so simple, lovable, and dignified; to academical designers such as Talman or Hawksmoor, and if not by Wren, they were certainly inspired by his work.

The end of Wren's splendid career was clouded by the intrigues and jealousy of inferior men. George I., from whom he had hoped much, turned out to be stupid and unintelligent, and the German *clique* at Court had no sympathy with the man who, alone among his contemporaries, adequately represented the noblest tradition of English art. In 1717 the Commissioners for St. Paul's insisted on the balustrade

Wm. Spooner & Co., Photo. *Face p. 184.*

HAMPTON COURT.

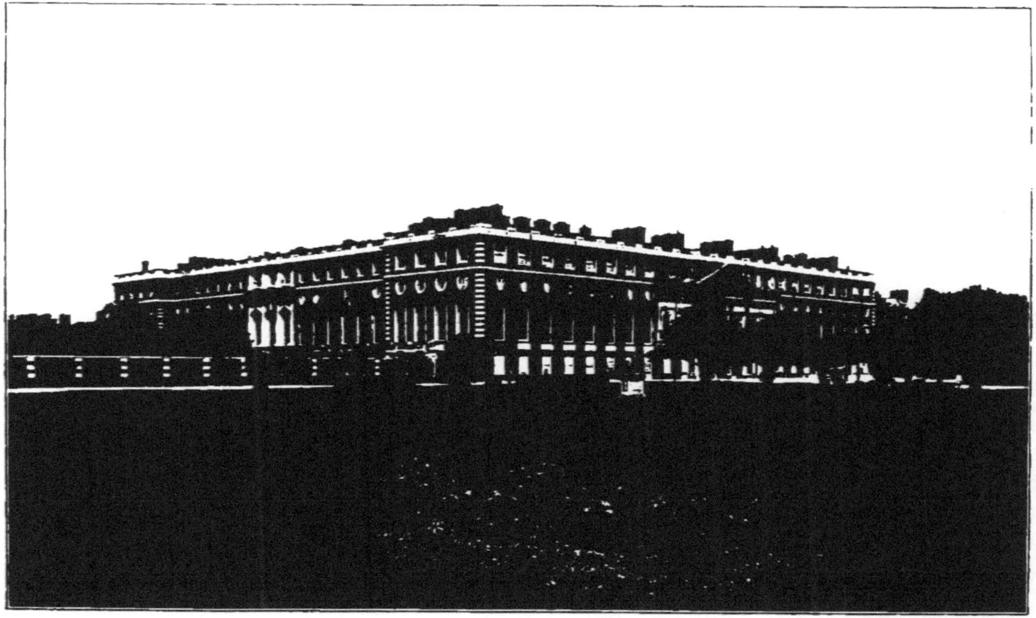

above the entablature, in spite of Wren's protest, and in 1718 a complaint of mismanagement was preferred against him by Colin Campbell and a person named Benson, and Wren was dismissed from the post of surveyor-general, which he had held for fifty years, in favour of Benson's brother, an entirely incompetent and unscrupulous adventurer.[1] The complaint was sent by the Lords of the Treasury to Wren to report upon. He replied that the charges were groundless, and that as he was only one member of the board, he referred them for fuller explanations to the other members. Wren's closing words are pathetic : "As I am dismissed, having worn out by God's mercy a long life in the Royal service, and having made some figure in the world, I hope it will be allowed me to die in peace." He spent the few remaining years of his life in quiet at his house near Hampton Court, and died on February 25th, 1723.

By unwearied labour and indomitable effort after a high ideal, Wren had grown to be an artist of first-rate genius, superior in skill and imagination to any architect of his time in Europe. He began almost as an amateur, rich in friends and opportunity, and buoyed up by the confidence of his brilliant career at Oxford and his own extraordinary inventiveness. As yet he was ignorant of the technique of his art, and the results were seen in artistic fiascoes, such as the Sheldonian. But Wren was a man who picked up knowledge on every hand, and he was rarely fortunate in his school, for he was allowed to learn his art on the scaffolding of his own buildings, and so gained a practical mastery of planning and construction never since equalled. Moreover, Wren's own instincts led him this way. From the very first he was an inventor—keen, alert, and quick to make immediate use of actual observation and discovery; he had none of the dreamer's disease of inactivity; he seems indeed to have possessed a fertility of invention which sometimes tempted him to turn out work before it was mature, and to shirk the labour of fastidious finish inevitable to the scholar and the artist. For in fact Wren's taste was always a little uncertain. The fine design of St. Stephen's, Walbrook, for instance, is seriously impaired by its ornament. Nor, again, is it easy to understand how a man of concentrated purpose and refined

[1] Benson was dismissed from his post in the following year for a dishonest report on the state of the buildings of the House of Lords. A house which he designed for himself in Wiltshire is given in "Vitruvius Britannicus," vol. i. In spite of Campbell's fulsome compliments, the house is at best a bad adaptation of other people's ideas, and one of the worst planned houses in the whole series.

taste could have allowed himself such experiments as Wren indulged in at St. Michael's, Cornhill, and his other designs in Gothic;—not, of course, that Gothic architecture is anything but beautiful, but the fact that Wren should have deliberately designed in a style of which he knew nothing except that he disliked it, tends to show that in his earlier practice Wren's artistic convictions were at least indefinite. His taste, however, acquired a firmer fibre as he gained in experience; and the distance that separates his noblest works, such as St. Paul's and Greenwich, from his early designs, is one of the most remarkable features of his development. His strong practical sense saved him from the absurdities of his successors. He might occasionally make slips of grammar, but would never have been guilty of such pretentious pedantry as Colin Campbell, who, as a commendation to a church of his own designing, advises his subscribers that "the aspect of this Church is Prostyle, Hexastyle, Eustyle, which by Vitruvius, Palladio, and the general consent of the most judicious architects, both ancient and modern, is esteemed the most beautiful and useful disposition."[1] Wren's work in its main features was eminently sane and reasonable, and this not from lack of ideas, but from a clear insight into the limits and intention of architecture. Where he had the opportunity Wren designed with a largeness of conception rare among English architects. His great schemes for Winchester and Hampton Court, and his magnificent achievements at Greenwich, are at the highest level of architecture ever attained in this country. His earlier work was influenced in detail by French contemporary architecture, yet Wren maintained his individuality throughout, and one finds in his later manner a singularly direct and unaffected method of expression, free from pedantry and foolishness, and, above all, eminently English in its sober power. The men who succeeded him were undoubtedly able, but they lacked the warm humanity of Wren. Their work was not spontaneous, and their inferiority appears in their conscious effort after academical correctness and their attempts to systematize architecture into a mere grammar of ornament. They sheltered their weakness under the genius of Inigo Jones, but in spite of their laborious imitation, Wren was the true successor of that great architect in all that makes architecture vital, in all the qualities that gave to the English Renaissance its sterling masculine character.

[1] On examining the drawings it appears that Campbell proposed to light this church, measuring 74 by 54 by 54 ft. high, with a single Venetian window at one end, placed below the springing of the vaulted ceiling.

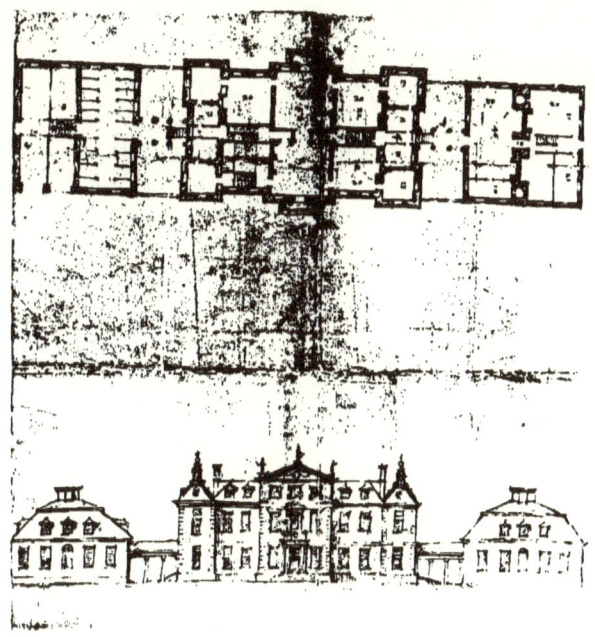

PLAN AND ELEVATION. WREN'S DRAWINGS
(*All Souls College Collection*)

DESIGN FOR A MONUMENT BY WREN, PROBABLY DRAWN BY
GRINLING GIBBONS
(All Souls College Collection)

www.ingramcontent.com/pod-product-compliance
Lightning Source LLC
Chambersburg PA
CBHW030744230426
43667CB00007B/834